THE ENGAGED UNIVERSITY

This timely volume offers three special contributions to the literature on higher education policy and practice: an historical overview of university foundation, together with a survey of how these "founding" intentions have fared in different systems of higher education; a contemporary account of the policies and practices of twenty universities from sixteen countries making civic and community engagement a strategic priority; and an overview of generic issues which emerge for the "engaged university."

David Watson is Principal of Green Templeton College, University of Oxford.

Robert M. Hollister is Dean, and Pierre and Pamela Omidyar Professor of Citizenship and Public Service, in the Jonathan M. Tisch College of Citizenship and Public Service at Tufts University.

Susan E. Stroud is Executive Director, Innovations in Civic Participation.

Elizabeth Babcock is Talloires Network Coordinator, Innovations in Civic Participation.

International Studies in Higher Education
Series Editors:
David Palfreyman, OxCHEPS
Ted Tapper, OxCHEPS
Scott Thomas, Clarement Graduate University

The central purpose of this series of a projected dozen volumes is to see how different national and regional systems of higher education are responding to widely shared pressures for change. The most significant of these are: rapid expansion; reducing public funding; the increasing influence of market and global forces; and the widespread political desire to integrate higher education more closely into the wider needs of society and, more especially, the demands of the economic structure. The series will commence with an international overview of structural change in systems of higher education. It will then proceed to examine on a global front the change process in terms of topics that are both traditional (for example, institutional management and system governance) and emerging (for example, the growing influence of international organizations and the blending of academic and professional roles). At its conclusion the series will have presented, through an international perspective, both a composite overview of contemporary systems of higher education, along with the competing interpretations of the process of change.

Published titles:

Structuring Mass Higher Education
The Role of Elite Institutions
Edited by David Palfreyman and Ted Tapper

International Perspectives on the Governance of Higher Education
Steering, Policy Processes, and Outcomes
Edited by Jeroen Huisman

International Organizations and Higher Education Policy
Thinking Globally, Acting Locally?
Edited by Roberta Malee Bassett and Alma Maldonado

Academic and Professional Identities in Higher Education
The Challenges of a Diversifying Workforce
Edited by Celia Whitchurch and George Gordon

THE ENGAGED UNIVERSITY

International Perspectives on Civic Engagement

*David Watson, Robert M. Hollister,
Susan E. Stroud, and Elizabeth Babcock*

Routledge
Taylor & Francis Group
NEW YORK AND LONDON

First published 2011
by Routledge
711 Third Avenue, New York, NY 10017

Simultaneously published in the UK
by Routledge
2 Park Square, Milton Park, Abingdon, Oxon OX14 4RN

Routledge is an imprint of the Taylor & Francis Group, an informa business

The right of David Watson, Robert M. Hollister, Susan E. Stroud, and
Elizabeth Babcock to be identified as the authors of this work has been
asserted by them in accordance with sections 77 and 78 of the Copyright,
Designs and Patents Act 1988.

Typeset in Bembo by Swales & Willis Ltd, Exeter, Devon

Library of Congress Cataloging-in-Publication Data
The engaged university : international perspectives on civic engagement / David
Watson . . . [et al.].
p. cm. — (International studies in higher education)
Includes bibliographical references and index.
1. Community and college—Cross-cultural studies. 2. Higher education and
state—Cross-cultural studies. 3. Education, Higher—Social aspects—Cross-
cultural studies. 4. Education and globalization—Cross-cultural studies.
I. Watson, David, 1949– II. Title. III. Series.
LC237.E54 2011
378.1'03—dc22
2010045364

ISBN13: 978–0–415–87465–6 (hbk)
ISBN13: 978–0–203–81876–3 (ebk)

CONTENTS

TABLES

ABBREVIATIONS

AACU:	Association of American Colleges and Universities
AAU:	Association of African Universities
ABC:	Australian Broadcasting Corporation
ACE:	American Council of Education
ACP:	Active Community Program
ACU:	Association of Commonwealth Universities
ACU Extension Network:	Association of Commonwealth Universities Extension Network
AIDS:	Acquired immune deficiency syndrome
AIESEC:	Association Internationale des Étudiants en Sciences Économiques et Commerciales (International Association of Students in Economics and Business Management)
AK:	Aga Khan
AKDN:	Aga Khan Development Network
AKU:	Aga Khan University
AMEP:	Adult Migrant English Program
AMSA:	Ahfad Medical Students Association
ANUIES:	Asociación Nacional de Universidades e Institutiones de Educacion Superior (National Association of Universities and Higher Education Institutions)
APEL:	Accreditation of Prior Experiential Learning
AQU:	Al-Quds University
ASCUN:	The Association of Colombian Universities
AUCEA:	Australian Universities Community Engagement Alliance
AUQA:	Australian Universities Quality Agency
Aus$:	Australian dollars

AusAID:	Australian aid agency
AUSJAL:	La Asociación de Universidades Confiadas a la Compañía de Jesús en América Latina (The Association of Universities Committed to the Company of Jesus in Latin America)
AUW:	Ahfad University for Women
B. Tech:	Bachelor of Technology
BBC:	British Broadcasting Corporation
BRIC:	Brazil, Russia, India, and China
BS:	Bachelor of Science
CACSL:	Canadian Alliance for Community Service-Learning
CATS:	Credit Accumulation and Transfer
CBL:	Community-Based Learning
CBO:	Community-Based Organization
CCC:	Champagnat Community College
CDESR:	Steering Committee for Higher Education and Research
CDU:	Charles Darwin University
CEBEM:	Centro Boliviano de Estudios Multidisciplinarios International
CEDECOM:	Centros de Desarrollo Comunal
CEO:	Chief Executive Officer
CGI:	Clinton Global Initiative
CHE:	Council for Higher Education
CHED:	Commission on Higher Education (Philippines)
CIDA:	Canadian International Development Agency
CIE:	Centro de Initiatives Emprendedoras
CIRCLE:	The Center for Information and Research on Civic Learning and Engagement
CLAYSS:	El Centro Latinoamericano de Aprendizaje y Servicio Solidario (Latin American Center for Service-Learning)
COPIA:	Code of Practice for Institutional Audit
CPA:	Certified Practicing Accountants
CPUT:	Cape Peninsula University of Technology
CSHE:	University of Melbourne's Centre for the Study of Higher Education
CSIRO:	Commonwealth Scientific and Research Organization
CSL:	Community-Service-Learning
CUC:	Council of University Chairs
DAI:	Degree Awarding Institute
DET:	Department of Education and Training
DFID:	UK Department for International Development
DHF:	Northern Territory Department for Health and Families
DRC:	Development Research Centre
DSTO:	Defense, Science and Technology Organization

DVC:	Deputy Vice-Chancellor
EABER:	East Asian Bureau of Economic Research (footnote)
ELQ:	Equivalent or Lower Qualification
EU:	European Union
EUA:	European University Association
GDP:	gross domestic product
GER:	Gross Enrollment Ratio
GNU:	Government of National Unity
GP:	General Practitioner
GTZ:	Gesellschaft fuer Technische Zusammenarbeit (Society for Technical Cooperation)
GUNI:	Global University Network for Innovation
GWS:	Greater Western Sydney
HE:	Higher Education
HEAT:	Health Education and Training
HEC:	Higher Education Commission
HEFCE:	Higher Education Funding Council for England
HEI:	Higher Education Institution
HEP:	Higher Education Provider
HEQC:	Higher Education Quality Commission
HIV:	Human immunodeficiency virus
IAU:	International Association of Universities
ICT:	Information and Communication Technology
IED:	Institute for Educational Development
IOC:	International Outreach Coalition
IT:	Information Technology
ITESM:	Instituto Tecnológico y de Estudios Superiores de Monterrey (The Monterrey Institute of Technology and Higher Studies) [or] Tecnológico de Monterrey
JEM:	Justice and Equality Movement
KPI:	Key Performance Indicators
KT:	Knowledge Transfer
LIVE:	The Leadership, Involvement and Volunteer Experience Unit
LJM:	Liberation and Justice Movement
LUCs:	Local Universities and Colleges
MA:	Master of Arts
MALU:	Mobile Adult Learning Unit
MEd:	Master of Education
MENA:	Middle East and North Africa
MERCY:	Malaysian Medical Relief Society
MIT:	Massachusetts Institute of Technology
MOHE:	Ministry of Higher Education

MP:	Member of Parliament
MS:	Master of Science
NAB:	National Advisory Body for Public Sector Higher Education
NCCPE:	The National Coordinating Centre for Public Engagement in Higher Education
NDMU:	Notre Dame of Marbel University
NESTA:	UK's National Endowment for Science Technology and the Arts
NGO:	Non-governmental organization
NRETAS:	Department of Natural Resources, Environment the Arts and Sport
NSS:	National Student Survey
NSS:	National Service Scheme
NSTP:	National Service Training Program
NT:	Northern Territory
NTG:	Northern Territory Government
OBU:	Open Broadcasting Unit
ODL:	Open and distance learning
OECD:	Organization for Economic Cooperation and Development
OPT:	Occupied Palestinian Territories
OU:	Open University
PADEL:	Local Development Assistance Program
PBC:	Planning and Budget Committee
PhD:	Doctor of Philosophy
PLO:	Palestine Liberation Organization
PMBSU:	Petro Mohyla Black Sea State University
PNA:	Palestinian National Authority
PPP:	Purchasing Power Parity
PSU:	Portland State University
PVC:	Pro Vice-Chancellor
QA:	Quality Assurance (used as adjective)
QAA:	Quality Assurance Agency
QEC:	Quality Enhancement Cell
QMUL:	Queen Mary University of London
RAE:	Research Assessment Exercise
RDA:	Regional Development Agencies
REDIVU:	Ibero-American University Volunteer Network for Social Inclusion
REED:	Rural Extension Education and Development
REF:	Research Excellence Framework
RN:	Registered Nurse
RSA:	[Republic of] South Africa
RTO:	Registered Training Organization

SADC:	Southern African Development Community
SAHECEF:	South African Higher Education Community Engagement Forum
SALP:	Student Ambassador Leadership Program
SARUA:	Southern African Regional Universities Association
SIFE:	Students in Free Enterprise
SME:	Small or Medium Enterprise
SNDT:	Shreemati Nathibai Damodar Thackersey
STEM:	Science, Technology, Engineering and Mathematics
SUCs:	State Universities and Colleges
TAFE:	Technical and Further Education Colleges
TESSA:	Teacher Education in Sub-Saharan Africa
TICE:	Tracking and Integrating Community Engagement
TRaCK:	Tropical Rivers and Coastal Knowledge
TRUCEN:	The Research University Civic Engagement Network
UCMK:	University Centre Milton Keynes
UDSM:	University of Dar es Salaam
UGC:	University Grants Commission
UH:	University Hospital
UK:	United Kingdom
UKM:	Universiti Kebangsaan Malaysia
UN:	United Nations
UN HDR:	United Nations Human Development Report
UNAM:	National Autonomous University of Mexico
UNESCO:	United Nations Educational, Scientific and Cultural Organization
UNFPA:	United Nations Population Fund
UNICEF:	United Nations Children's Fund
UNIMET:	Universidad Metropolitana en Caracas
UNRWA:	United Nations Relief and Works Agency
USAID:	United States Agency for International Development
USS:	Universidad Señor de Sipán
UUK:	Universities of the United Kingdom
UWS:	University of Western Sydney
VC:	Vice-Chancellor
VET:	Vocational Education and Training
VicHealth:	Victorian Health Promotion Foundation
WEI:	World Education Indicators
WHO:	World Health Organization
WIL:	Work Integrated Learning
WP:	Widening Participation
YASS:	Young Associate Students in Schools
YES:	Youth Engaging Society

CONTRIBUTORS

Elizabeth Babcock is the Coordinator of the Talloires Network. She directs the outreach, information-sharing and strategic planning for member universities and the governing body of the network. Previously, she was the Director of the Civic Knowledge Project at the University of Chicago, working to increase quality educational and cultural programming and knowledge exchange between the university and its neighboring communities. In this position, she worked on an asset mapping project of community cultural organizations funded by the MacArthur Foundation, leading to the creation of a new university-based support network for these organizations. Elizabeth holds an MA in Latin American Studies from the University of Chicago and a BA in Anthropology from the University of Florida. She co-authored a 2010 publication entitled *Finding Their Voice: Engaging Adolescents in Meaningful Participation Strategies* for the UNICEF office in Latin America and the Caribbean.

Robert M. Hollister is founding Dean of the Jonathan M. Tisch College of Citizenship and Public Service and the Pierre and Pamela Omidyar Professor of Citizenship and Public Service at Tufts University. He received a BA in Sociology from Antioch College, an MCP (Master's in City Planning) from Harvard University, and a PhD in Urban Studies and Planning from MIT.

A pioneer in the engaged university movement, Dean Hollister has led the creation and growth of Tisch College, a uniquely comprehensive university-wide initiative to prepare students in all fields for lifetimes of active citizenship—to educate citizen engineers and citizen physicians, citizen humanists and citizen businesspeople. In 2005, Dean Hollister co-founded the Talloires Network, a global coalition that has grown to number 180 universities in 59 countries working together to strengthen their civic engagement missions.

Also in 2005, in partnership with Campus Compact, he initiated The Research University Civic Engagement Network, an alliance of 40 major US research universities.

Dean Hollister was an Assistant Professor and Associate Professor in the MIT Department of Urban Studies and Planning from 1971 to 1980. He moved to Tufts in 1980 to serve as founding chair of the Department of Urban and Environmental Policy and Planning, a distinctive graduate program for educating practical visionaries. He went on to become director of the Lincoln Filene Center for Citizenship and Public Affairs from 1991 to 1996. He subsequently served as dean of the Graduate School of Arts and Sciences from 1996 to 2001, where he increased student diversity and strengthened ties between undergraduate and graduate education.

A specialist in the leadership and management of non-profit organizations and in citizen participation in public affairs, Dean Hollister is co-author of *Development Politics*, and co-editor and contributing author of *Governing, Leading and Managing Nonprofit Organizations*; *Cities of the Mind*; *Neighborhood Policy and Planning*, and *Neighborhood Health Centers*.

Susan E. Stroud is the founder and Executive Director of *Innovations in Civic Participation* (ICP, www.icicp.org), a non-profit organization in Washington, DC that supports the development of innovative, high-quality youth civic engagement policies and programs in the United States and in other countries. ICP serves as the Secretariat of the International Association for National Youth Service (IANYSO), a global network of policymakers and practitioners with an interest in youth civic engagement. In 2005, Ms Stroud co-founded the Talloires Network, a global coalition has grown to number 180 universities in 59 countries working together to strengthen their civic engagement Missions. Ms Stroud founded ICP in 2001 with support from the Ford Foundation.

Prior to 2001, she served as the senior advisor to the director of the White House Office of National Service. She played a key role in drafting the *National and Community Trust Act of 1993*, which created the AmeriCorps program and the Corporation for National and Community Service. Ms Stroud was the first director of Learn and Serve America, a $43 million annual grants program that supports young people's civic engagement through schools, universities, and community organizations.

From 1998 to 2001, Ms Stroud worked at the Ford Foundation on a special initiative to support the development of youth civic engagement policies and programs in South Africa, Mexico, Russia, and other countries.

Prior to moving to Washington, DC in 1993, she was Assistant to the President at Brown University and the founding Director of both the Howard R. Swearer Center for Public Service and *Campus Compact*, a national coalition of over 1,500 university and college presidents committed to civic engagement and service-learning.

David Watson is an historian and Principal of Green Templeton College, Oxford. He was Professor of Higher Education Management at the Institute of Education, University of London, from 2005 to 2010, and Vice-Chancellor of the University of Brighton between 1990 and 2005. His most recent books are *Managing Civic and Community Engagement* (2007), *The Dearing Report: Ten Years on* (2007), and *The Question of Morale: Managing Happiness and Unhappiness in University Life* (2009).

He has contributed widely to developments in UK higher education, including as a member of the Council for National Academic Awards (1977–1993), the Polytechnics and Colleges Funding Council (1988–1992), and the Higher Education Funding Council for England (1992–1996). He was a member of the Paul Hamlyn Foundation's National Commission on Education (1992–1993), and the National Committee of Inquiry into Higher Education chaired by Sir Ron Dearing (1996–1997). David Watson was the elected chair of the Universities Association for Continuing Education between 1994 and 1998, and chaired the Longer Term Strategy Group of Universities UK between 1999 and 2005. He is President of the Society for Research into Higher Education, a Trustee of the Nuffield Foundation, a Companion of the Institute of Management, and a National Teaching Fellow (2008). He chaired the national *Inquiry into the Future for Lifelong Learning*, and co-authored its report *Learning Through Life* (2009). David Watson was knighted in 1998 for services to higher education. In 2009, he received the *Times Higher Education* Lifetime Achievement Award.

SERIES EDITORS' INTRODUCTION

International Studies in Higher Education

This Series is constructed around the premise that higher education systems are experiencing common pressures for fundamental change, reinforced by differing national and regional circumstances that also impact upon established institutional structures and procedures. There are four major dynamics for change that are of international significance:

1. Mass higher education is a universal phenomenon.
2. National systems find themselves located in an increasingly global marketplace that has particular significance for their more prestigious institutions.
3. Higher education institutions have acquired (or been obliged to acquire) a wider range of obligations, often under pressure from governments prepared to use state power to secure their policy goals.
4. The balance between the public and private financing of higher education has shifted—markedly in some cases—in favor of the latter.

Although higher education systems in all regions and nation states face their own particular pressures for change, these are especially severe in some cases: the collapse of the established economic and political structures of the former Soviet Union along with Central and Eastern Europe, the political revolution in South Africa, the pressures for economic development in India and China, and demographic pressure in Latin America.

Each volume in the Series will examine how systems of higher education are responding to this new and demanding political and socioeconomic environment. Although it is easy to overstate the uniqueness of the present situation, it is not an exaggeration to say that higher education is undergoing a fundamental shift in its character, and one that is truly international in scope. We are witnessing a major transition in the relationship of higher education to state and society. What makes the present circumstances particularly interesting is to see how different systems—a product of social, cultural, economic and political contexts that have interacted and evolved over time—respond in their own peculiar ways to the changing environment. There is no assumption that the pressures for change have set in motion the trend towards a converging model of higher education, but we do believe that in the present circumstances no understanding of "the idea of the university" remains sacrosanct.

Although this is a Series with an international focus it is not expected that each individual volume should cover every national system of higher education. This would be an impossible task. Whilst aiming for a broad range of case studies, with each volume addressing a particular theme, the focus will be upon the most important and interesting examples of responses to the pressures for change. Most of the individual volumes will bring together a range of comparative quantitative and qualitative information, but the primary aim of each volume will be to present differing interpretations of critical developments in key aspects of the experience of higher education. The dominant overarching objective is to explore the conflict of ideas and the political struggles that inevitably surround any significant policy development in higher education.

It can be expected that volume editors and their authors will adopt their own interpretations to explain the emerging patterns of development. There will be conflicting theoretical positions drawn from the multidisciplinary, and increasingly interdisciplinary, field of higher education research. Thus, we can expect in most volumes to find an inter-marriage of approaches drawn from sociology, economics, history, political science, cultural studies, and the administrative sciences. However, whilst there will be different approaches to understanding the process of change in higher education, each volume editor(s) will impose a framework upon the volume inasmuch as chapter authors will be required to address common issues and concerns.

This, the eighth volume in the Series, is written by David Watson, Robert Hollister, Susan Stroud, and Elizabeth Babcock. They offer a genuinely international perspective on a hot topic within current higher education policy and practice: the relationship between universities and their host communities, especially as it is refracted through the lens of institutional strategies for civic and community engagement. Among the novel features of their analysis are the following: an expansion of an Anglo-American-Australasian discourse to include perspectives from the global East and South; a sensitivity to the highly diverse economic, cultural and political circumstances faced by institutions in a wide range of national jurisdictions; and an informed coverage of the day-to-day challenges faced by institutional leaders and managers. They conclude by speculating about the presence and the prospects of an international movement of university–community engagement.

The current volume should also be read as complementary to the recently published volumes on universities' reputational positioning (see volume one edited by Ted Tapper and David Palfreyman), on academic identities (see volume four edited by George Gordon and Celia Whitchurch) and on international organizations and higher education policy (see volume three edited by Roberta Malee Bassett and Alma Maldonado-Maldonado). It adds an important new perspective to our coverage of the problems, prospect and performance of universities in the contemporary global polity.

David Palfreyman
Director of OxCHEPS, New College,
University of Oxford

Ted Tapper
OxCHEPS, New College, University of Oxford and CHEMPAS,
University of Southampton

Scott Thomas
Professor of Educational Studies, Claremont Graduate University,
California

FOREWORD

In universities around the world, something extraordinary is underway. Mobilizing their human and intellectual resources, institutions of higher education are directly tackling community problems—combating poverty, improving public health, and restoring environmental quality. Brick by brick around the world, the engaged university is replacing the ivory tower. A project of the Talloires Network, a global coalition of engaged universities, *The Engaged University: International Perspectives on Civic Engagement* documents and analyzes this exciting trend through studies of civic engagement and social responsibility at twenty institutions worldwide.

This trend has had an impressive impact on both community conditions and education, and it has even greater prospects ahead. The exchange of ideas and best practices, and objective documentation and research, are especially important during the early stages of a significant movement for change. I hope that *The Engaged University* will be a source of inspiration and guidance as well as a stimulus to further documentation and inquiry—that it will be useful for university administrators, faculty, and students, and also to their community partners and to governmental officials and development assistance agencies, and foundation officials.

To date, university civic engagement has not had nearly the visibility and recognition that its substantial results warrant. So I also hope that this volume will not only motivate and guide decision-making and action inside and outside the academy but will also elevate public awareness of, and support for, civic engagement in higher education.

All of the universities profiled here belong to the Talloires Network, which grew out of the first international gathering of the heads of universities on their civic engagement and social responsibility. That meeting, which I had the privilege of hosting in the fall of 2005 at the Tufts University European Center in

Talloires, France, brought together 29 university presidents, vice-chancellors and rectors from 23 countries on six continents. Together we drafted and signed a consensus vision statement and call to action, the Talloires Declaration on the Civic Roles and Social Responsibilities of Higher Education, and launched the Talloires Network to promote action around its principles, and to be a continuing vehicle of exchange and joint action.

Since then, the Talloires Network has grown six-fold and now counts 196 members in 59 countries, with a combined enrollment of over 5 million students. The Network's member institutions vary dramatically in their community and governmental contexts, and in their organizational structures, finances and traditions. Yet we share a common commitment to strengthening our civic engagement and social responsibility. As the Talloires Declaration put it, "Our institutions recognize that we do not exist in isolation from society, nor from the communities in which we are located. Instead, we carry a unique obligation to listen, understand, and contribute to social transformation and development."

In *The University and Urban Revival*, her compelling account of US universities as partners in urban revival, Rockefeller Foundation President Judith Rodin used the subtitle, "Out of the Ivory Tower and Into the Streets." The 20 profiles of civic engagement from around the world presented in the following pages could aptly be entitled, "Out of the Ivory Tower and Into the Barrio, the Baranguay, and the Township."

The Network works to raise the profile of university civic engagement, to strengthen the civic engagement work of member institutions, and to broker collective action. Members commit to strengthen their own engagement work, to foster effective partnerships with disadvantaged communities, to raise awareness about contributions of this movement, to share best practices, and to support other academic institutions and associations in this work. This book aims to help achieve each of these goals.

The global Talloires Network increasingly works in collaboration with regional and national higher education civic engagement networks around the world. We have developed formal partnerships with the Latin American Center for Service-Learning, the *Ma'an* Arab University Alliance for Civic Engagement, the Community-University Network in Russia, the Australian Universities Community Engagement Alliance, Campus Engage in Ireland, and Campus Compact in the United States. The Network is guided by a Steering Committee of higher education leaders from around the globe. Tufts University and Innovations in Civic Participation serve as secretariat of the Network (www.tufts.edu/talloiresnetwork).

On behalf of the Talloires Network Steering Committee, I would like to express deep gratitude to Sir David Watson, former Vice-Chancellor of the University of Brighton and now Principal of Green Templeton College, Oxford University, for initiating and leading this project. We also owe deep thanks to co-authors Robert M. Hollister, Susan Stroud and Elizabeth Babcock.

In addition, we wish to thank our colleagues from the 20 members of the Network that have contributed their experiences to this effort. Participating institutions have been active partners in this initiative—each responded to an extensive questionnaire and hosted a follow-up site visit with one of the co-authors. I salute the impressive achievements of these university administrators, professors and students, and their community partners, who are shaping their institutions into truly engaged universities. The experiences that are reviewed in this volume reflect tremendous vision and effort, and in many cases significant courage as well.

I would like to take this opportunity to express appreciation to the Institute of Education, University of London, the Jonathan M. Tisch College of Citizenship and Public Service, Tufts University, and Innovations in Civic Participation, which provided financial support for completion of the research upon which this book is based. In addition, we greatly appreciate the support for the Talloires Network that has been provided by generous foundations and organizations including The Omidyar Network, Banco Santander/Sovereign Bank, Walmart Foundation, Carnegie Corporation of New York City, MacJannet Foundation, Pearson Foundation, Rockefeller Foundation, Ford Foundation, Breidenthal-Snyder Foundation, Lowell Blake & Associates, and Charles F. Adams Charitable Trust.

I encourage you to join us in working to advance civic engagement in higher education. This work educates future leaders for change, mobilizes university professors and students to address pressing societal challenges, and builds public support for higher education. University enrollment worldwide is predicted to surpass 200 million by the year 2030. This book offers a glimpse of what these students, in collaboration with their teachers and institutions, can do to accelerate economic development and build healthy communities around the globe.

Lawrence S. Bacow
President, Tufts University
Chair, Steering Committee, Talloires Network
Medford, Massachusetts
October 2010

THE TALLOIRES DECLARATION ON THE CIVIC ROLES AND SOCIAL RESPONSIBILITIES OF HIGHER EDUCATION

In this century of change, we note with optimism that access to university education is increasing, that one-half of the students enrolled in institutions of higher education live in developing nations, and that the number of university students worldwide is expected to double between 2000 and 2025. The potential for social participation by students young and old, now and in the years to come, is massive. The extent to which this potential can be realized will depend on universities worldwide mobilizing students, faculty, staff and citizens in programs of mutual benefit.

We are dedicated to strengthening the civic role and social responsibility of our institutions. We pledge to promote shared and universal human values, and the engagement by our institutions within our communities and with our global neighbors. We urge the 100 million university students, and the many millions of faculty, staff, alumni and members of governing bodies throughout the world to join us in these initiatives.

We believe that higher education institutions exist to serve and strengthen the society of which they are part. Through the learning, values and commitment of faculty, staff and students, our institutions create social capital, preparing students to contribute positively to local, national and global communities. Universities have the responsibility to foster in faculty, staff and students a sense of social responsibility and a commitment to the social good, which, we believe, is central to the success of a democratic and just society.

Some of our universities and colleges are older than the nations in which they are located; others are young and emerging; but all bear a special obligation to contribute to the public good, through educating students, expanding access to education, and the creation and timely application of new knowledge. Our institutions recognize that we do not exist in isolation from society, nor from the communities in which we are located. Instead, we carry a unique obligation to listen, understand and contribute to social transformation and development.

Higher education must extend itself for the good of society to embrace communities near and far. In doing so, we will promote our core missions of teaching, research and service.

The university should use the processes of education and research to respond to, serve and strengthen its communities for local and global citizenship. The university has a responsibility to participate actively in the democratic process and to empower those who are less privileged. Our institutions must strive to build a culture of reflection and action by faculty, staff and students that infuses all learning and inquiry.

Therefore, we agree to:

- Expand civic engagement and social responsibility programs in an ethical manner, through teaching, research and public service.
- Embed public responsibility through personal example and the policies and practices of our higher education institutions.
- Create institutional frameworks for the encouragement, reward and recognition of good practice in social service by students, faculty, staff and their community partners.
- Ensure that the standards of excellence, critical debate, scholarly research and peer judgment are applied as rigorously to community engagement as they are to other forms of university endeavor.
- Foster partnerships between universities and communities to enhance economic opportunity, empower individuals and groups, increase mutual understanding and strengthen the relevance, reach and responsiveness of university education and research.
- Raise awareness within government, business, media, charitable, not-for-profit and international organizations about contributions of higher education to social advancement and wellbeing. Specifically, establish partnerships with government to strengthen policies that support higher education's civic and socially responsible efforts.
- Collaborate with other sectors in order to magnify impacts and sustain social and economic gains for our communities.
- Establish partnerships with primary and secondary schools, and other institutions of further and higher education, so that education for active citizenship becomes an integral part of learning at all levels of society and stages of life.
- Document and disseminate examples of university work that benefit communities and the lives of their members.
- Support and encourage international, regional and national academic associations in their efforts to strengthen university civic engagement efforts and create scholarly recognition of service and action in teaching and research.
- Speak out on issues of civic importance in our communities.

- Establish a steering committee and international networks of higher education institutions to inform and support all their efforts to carry out this Declaration.

We commit ourselves to the civic engagement of our institutions and to that end we establish the Talloires Network, with an open electronic space for the exchange of ideas and understandings and for fostering collective action.

We invite others to join in this Declaration and to collaborate in our civic work.

Talloires, France, September 17, 2005

INTRODUCTION AND ACKNOWLEDGMENTS

As described in the first chapter of Part II, at the heart of this book is the two-fold commitment of the institutional members of the Talloires Network: to the role of higher education in community development, and to self-study and self-critical reflection in pursuit of that goal.

To date, the literature about higher education civic engagement has been dominated by accounts of the experience of countries in the Global North—in North America and Europe. This book aims to help correct that imbalance, and to document and analyze the work of colleges and universities in all parts of the world, including many in the Global South. What can the Global North, and the whole world for that matter, learn from the civic engagement experience of universities in the Global South? Their experience adds substantially to the body of evidence about the positive impacts on civic engagement on community conditions, on student learning, and on public support for higher education.

The profiles that follow provide inspiring examples of civic engagement and social responsibility that are part of the very core mission of the institutions, rather than being a separate dimension of university operations. The experience of Southern institutions shows also that it is possible to elevate incentives for faculty performance, which is a universal challenge. The efforts of Southern universities in this regards are still modest and incipient, but they extend well beyond what Northern institutions have attempted. On balance, the Southern examples show a greater emphasis on goals of improving community conditions—because of the urgency of social and economic challenges. In addition, they indicate that it is possible to build and sustain substantial civic engagement and social responsibility programs with comparatively little money.

Our study confirms that higher education civic engagement truly is a global movement—global in is growing scale and fully international reach, in the nature and extent of its impacts, and in the common vision, strategies and programs of universities around the world. It also is a global movement in the patterns of growing interaction and collaboration—through regional and international associations and joint projects. The growth of the Talloires Network is further evidence of this movement, just as it also is influencing the trend. Each new member who joins the Network commits to our common set of principles and pledges to support the work of other members.

It is striking that this diverse group of institutions from all parts of the globe share a common vision of the engaged university and that they are pursuing similar strategies and programmatic approaches. Their social, political and economic contexts do indeed shape significant aspects of their civic engagement and social responsibility activities. At the same time, the commonalities transcend these differences in context. Virtually all of the participating institutions are committed to mobilizing their human and intellectual resources to address pressing needs of the societies in which they are located, and in the process to educate their students to be leaders for change.

The civic work of each of the participating institutions appears to be achieving substantial results. These are perceived and valued by a mix of constituencies—students, faculty, administrators, and community partners. At the same time, it is noteworthy that very few institutions systematically measure these impacts.

The cases illustrate the emergence of a new stage in the development of institutional mission—civic and community engagement as a new paradigm, as it has been conceptualized by David Watson. This paradigm builds upon and also moves beyond the historic models that emphasize liberal education, and professional formation, and in some instances, the university as research engine. It posits community engagement not as a separate kind of activity, but as a focus of the institution's teaching and research, and as a strategy for achieving greater quality and impacts in the institution's teaching and research.

Our cross-section of universities shows both consistency and variation in the goals that are the focus of their civic work. The majority of institutions emphasize the broad goal of addressing pressing community and societal needs, with considerable concentration on combating poverty, improving public health, and enhancing pre-university education. While some emphasize educational goals, aiming to develop students' leadership values and skills, for many of the participating schools this is an important, but lesser objective.

A hallmark of many of the institutions in this study is their substantial support for community partnerships. Developing and maintaining long-term working relationships with partner organizations—NGOs, government agencies and private businesses—is an essential component of their civic and social responsibility functions.

Almost all of the institutions aspire to not only sustain, but also to expand and deepen their civic engagement and social responsibility programs. Many seek to involve additional academic units in this work. They aspire to achieving greater impact on both their students and on their communities. Many aim to develop stronger, more extensive community partnerships. Many express a high interest in greater collaboration with other institutions of higher education in their region and/or internationally.

This study reaffirms the central importance of community partnerships in university civic engagement. In addition, they demonstrate a range of approaches and principles for the effective development and maintenance of partnerships. An important lesson from the institutions in this study is the powerful positive impacts that can be achieved by creating and supporting a high-level position and office to lead and coordinate the institution's civic engagement and social responsibility.

Our profiles describe key influences that drive and shape the institutions' civic and social responsibility activities: institutional leadership, financial constraints, government policies, political context, level of institutional prestige (schools that enjoy less prestige often are more pioneering and innovative in this realm), community needs and expectations, the academic rewards system, support from international agencies, and student expectations and leadership.

As authors, our most significant debt is to the leadership of the network, especially its convener and chair Larry Bacow, President of Tufts University, and to all of the members and supporters of the twenty profiled institutions who completed self-assessments, hosted meetings and visits, dealt with requests for supplementary information and, above all, responded fully and frankly in interviews. Absolutely critical to the success of this part of the project were the individual institutional contact persons, who dealt with our requests with professional skill and patience and enabled all the site visits to proceed smoothly and effectively (including occasionally in difficult, even dangerous, circumstances). In alphabetical order they are: Amira Badri, Samira Barghouthi, Ernesto Benavides, Roxana Cárdenas, Antonio Sánchez Chacón, Catherine Colohan, Linda Cuttriss, Chris Darling, Andrew Gaff, Saran Kaur Gill, Barbara Holland, Yoav Lavee, María Teresa R. de Leonardi, Joyce Nduna, Andy Nicolaides, Olexandr Pronkevych, Chandrakant Puri, Robert Sanane, Sajida Shroff, Noemi Silva, Amy Spring, Suzanne Tarlov, Sylvia Temu, Cecilia Vicentini, and Charles Webb. As our profiles in Part II emerged, their help was also invaluable in fact-checking and clearing interviews. Any remaining errors, however, remain our responsibility. Others who provided critical background information on higher education civic engagement globally included, in alphabetical order: Saran Kaur Gill, Barbara Ibrahim, Mónica Jiménez de la Jara, Andrey Kortunov, Paul Manners, Lorraine McIlrath, Janice Reid, Jerome Slamat, and María Nieves Tapia.

We also had faultless support from colleagues in our "home" offices: Alison Peacock at the Centre for Higher Education Studies (CHES) of the Institute of Education, University of London; Nancy Wilson, Joanne Minassian, Shenna Gianetta, and Veronica Leo at the Tisch College of Citizenship and Public Service at Tufts; and Kelly Fox at Innovations in Civic Participation (ICP) in

Washington, DC. The ICP office was the research hub of the project, with coordination by John Pollock and very significant input during the first year of the project from Hannah Ayers. John and Hannah undertook important background research, especially on the countries and institutions which we visited. Interns Alissa Brower and Jacquelyn Rioux also provided valuable assistance.

Several colleagues and friends listened to, read and commented upon our emerging ideas. We are particularly grateful to seminar groups and classes at the Institute of Education, University of London, the University of Oxford, Kingston University and the University of Brighton. Just before going to press our final section was enriched by a global, electronically mediated, dialogue arranged by Professor Budd Hall.

Rhonda Wynne has kindly given permission for the use of her "conceptions of citizenship grid" in Part I. David Watson's travel expenses were covered by the award of a National Teaching Fellowship from the UK Higher Education Academy in 2008. Other financial support came from the Institute of Education, University of London, and the Talloires Network.

Finally, we are grateful for the confidence shown in us by the editors of this burgeoning series, Ted Tapper, Scott Thomas, and David Palfreyman, and the representatives of our publishers, especially Alex Masulis, who were consistently encouraging from an appropriate distance. We trust that they are satisfied with the result.

David Watson
Robert M. Hollister
Susan E. Stroud
Elizabeth Babcock
October 1, 2010

PART I

University–Community Relationships
The Long View

1

HISTORICAL AND GEOGRAPHICAL PERSPECTIVES

For many in the business, a university is a library, while the library (in all its successive transformations) is the common denominator of all university-type institutions. Thus, most histories of the university as an institution like to start with the Alexandrian Library built by Ptolemy I in 306BC. In an interesting sign of the times, the Director of the Library and Ptolemy's modern successor, Ismail Serageldin, stresses not only its historical commitment to academic freedom ("the ancient library was about openness of knowledge, no taboos, questioning everything") but also its contribution to its contemporary community. In the words of a recent profile:

> He has helped establish the library as a learning complex, with a planetarium, art exhibitions, a children's learning center, a virtual reality chamber, and a museum chronicling the life of Anwar Sadat, the assassinated president. The library also operates as a cultural bully pulpit for Mr. Serageldin and like-minded scholars and regional leaders.
>
> *(Slackman, 2010)*

There is a truth here, which animates the analysis in this book. As a university-type institution, the Alexandrian Library has a community engagement strategy. Indeed, until the advent, in the late twentieth century, of company or for-profit universities, all university institutions grew in some way from the communities that originally sponsored them. These acts of foundation varied according to a range of local circumstances, in time and location. Many such founding commitments have been transformed—positively and perversely—over the ensuing years, but the familiar image of a university as somewhat separate from its community is curiously unfaithful to the historical record. Much of the current focus on the civic and community role of universities this represents acts of rediscovery and renewal rather than radical reorientation.

Most university foundations had an immediate element of service to the community in their agreed mission and purpose. The idea of responsiveness to social priorities was much more central to the founding goals of their institutions than many subsequent generations of university leaders and members have to believe. There is a pattern here, as set out below (this account is based on Watson, 2010).

A strong case can be made for the University as a quintessentially European institution. With the exception of idealized views of the Socratic dialogues and the Aristotelian *peripetea*, as well the Library of Alexandria, the models of a university most regularly appealed to as cultural icons are the late medieval foundations of Bologna, Paris, Oxford, and Cambridge. What is more, these models—properly understood—were anything but "ivory towers," set apart from the societies which founded them.

Here is Elizabeth de Burgh, Lady Clare, founder of Clare College, Cambridge, setting out a "mission statement" in 1359:

> Through their study and teaching at the University the scholars should discover and acquire the precious pearl of learning so that it does not stay hidden under a bushel but is displayed abroad to enlighten those who walk in the dark paths of ignorance.
>
> *(Shaw-Miller, 2001)*

And here is the Papal Bull of Innocent VIII establishing the University of Aberdeen in 1495:

> In the northern parts of the kingdom the people are ignorant and almost barbarous owing to their distance from a university. The city is near these places and suitable for a university, where all lawful faculties could be taught to both ecclesiastics and laymen, who would thus acquire the most precious pearl of knowledge, and so promote the well-being of the kingdom and the salvation of souls.
>
> *(see: www.neadvent.org/cathen/01042a.htm)*

The "pearl" is a particularly evocative metaphor, and draws upon a rich seam of medieval allegory (notably in the work of the fourteenth century "Pearl poet," probably also the author of *Sir Gawain and the Green Knight*). It requires grit to get it started; it is created in a relatively sealed environment; but it only achieves a real value once it leaves that protected environment. What's more, that value can be of various kinds: aesthetic and symbolic, as well as a tradable commodity. There is much more poetry here than in the concept of the "third leg" (or "arm" or "mission").

TABLE 1.1 The Pattern of University "Foundations"

Late medieval specialist communities
Regional and national institutions serving post-industrial society
Public "systems" of HE
Curriculum and institutional innovation
The "dual sector"
"For-profit"

If we then fast-forward to the early twenty-first century, European governments (like those on every other continent) see universities as vital parts of modern, competitive knowledge economies. The context has changed, but the expectations of communities that founded and maintain institutions of higher education remain constant.

In between these chronological points, higher education has developed differently in differing regional and national contexts, but a broad pattern can be discerned, in which, again, Europe took a lead. Fundamentally, the modern university developed in six stages, with each new wave of foundations overlaid on the previous, which continues to operate underneath, almost like geological strata.

Universities and Communities Phase One: Specialist Communities

The early foundations were specialist communities, such as the late medieval colleges for poor scholars in England (Oxford and Cambridge) and for urban professionals (such as Bologna and Paris in continental Europe). Three centuries later, a similar trajectory was followed by the American colonial seminaries, many of which subsequently became not only research universities but also expensive private schools in the United States, including the heart of the Ivy League. In 1643, a pamphlet called *New England's First Fruits* explained the mission of Harvard College as follows:

> To advance *learning* and perpetuate it to posterity; dreading to leave an illiterate Ministry to the Churches, when our present Ministers shall lie in the dust.
>
> *(Reuben, 2010: 27)*

By the seventeenth century, in Europe, the professional focus was reorientated: to serve the emerging state. Rosemary O'Day has demonstrated this set of developments in seventeenth century England:

> To say that the universities lost control of the professions is too simple and far from accurate. They maintained a firm grasp on preparation for careers in the church and the civil law. New professions grew up outside

the universities' formal control. However, the new professions were influenced by the universities in many ways, some formal and some informal. Leadership of the new professions often rested in university-educated men who revered learning. The ethos of the gentleman (which had developed at least in part in the universities) spread to the professions.

(O'Day, 2009: 99)

Historians like Stephen Lay point out that what distinguished all of these foundations from their ancient predecessors was the presumption of independence from the state, or what has subsequently become termed autonomy (Lay, 2004: 109).

Universities and Communities Phase Two: National and Regional Institutions Serving Post-Industrial Society

After a further fallow period, the next significant wave of foundations took place in the nineteenth century. These grew similarly out of perceived social and economic needs, but in the radically different context of industrializing societies. Examples are the University of Berlin in 1810, the national universities founded by newly-created European states, the late nineteenth century "civic" universities in the UK and the Land Grant universities of the American West and mid-West. The latter were progressively leavened by specific, primarily research-based institutions on the German Humboldtian model, such as Johns Hopkins.

It is often helpful to go back to the founding acts or charters to see what was intended. For example, the 1905 royal charter of what is now the University of Sheffield, when the city was the center of the British steel industry, of which some extracts set out below. Here, the emphasis is firmly on practical knowledge. There is also a strong sense of place. Other clauses enshrine gender

TABLE 1.2 Extracts from the Charter Granted by Edward VII in 1905, to Convert the University College of Sheffield (founded 1836) into the University of Sheffield

To provide for:

Instruction and teaching in every Faculty.

Such instruction in all branches of education as may enable students to become proficient in and qualify for Degrees Diplomas Associateships and Certificates in Arts Pure Science Applied Science Commerce Medicine Surgery Law and all other branches of knowledge.

Such instruction whether theoretical technical artistic or otherwise as may be of service to persons engaged in or about to engage in Education Commerce Engineering Law and especially the applications of Science. Metallurgy Mining or in other industries or artistic pursuits of the City of Sheffield and the adjacent counties and districts.

Facilities for the prosecution of original research in Arts Pure Science Applied Science Medicine Surgery (University College Charter, 1905: Para. 14. For the full document, see: www.shef.ac.uk/calendar/incorp.html)

equality (not just the absence of a religious test) and the importance of professional accreditation.

Meanwhile, one of the great mysteries of university history is exactly when and how in America what were essential religious seminaries (in which the college president invariably gave a senior seminar on moral philosophy and in some of which a "conversion experience" was a required part of the curriculum) turned themselves into scientific research machines structured around Enlightenment values. Judith Reuben reminds us that "Harvard was created not just to save souls, but to sustain a righteous community" (Reuben, 2010: 27).

Universities and Communities Phase Three: Public "Systems of HE"

In the next wave of development, the twentieth century saw the development across Europe of technical university or college systems, sometimes regionally planned as with the English polytechnics and American state systems (of which the archetypes are Wisconsin and the Californian Master Plan). These were equally specifically tied to expectations about relevant education and training, with a new element of ensuring both access by groups previously under-represented, and of progression.

In many countries, the result was to create what came to be known as binary systems of higher education: a group of traditional university institutions contrasted with a more local, apparently more locally-accountable, and apparently more responsive pattern of provision.

The "binary question" is a hugely important one. In his 2008 lecture for the Higher Education Policy Institute in London, Yves Mény, President of the European University Institute, sees this division as largely constructed around the separate realms of research and teaching. It reached its highest form (and one of the rare instances in which teaching is seen as more significant than research in reputational terms) in France:

> In fact, in most continental countries this strict division of labor was put in place rather late and mostly after the Second World War. Indeed in France for instance, where the Napoleonic model was imposed in a radical way, the fundamental division was not so much between teaching and research but between the university system on the one hand and the professional schools in charge of educating and training the future civil servants of the State.
>
> *(Mény, 2008: 2–3)*

Around the turn of the twenty-first century, this juxtaposition posed real dilemmas for policy makers dealing with the advent of mass higher education. Those with binary systems felt that they had run their course; those without them felt that the only way to re-inject mission diversity was to try to create a polytechnic-style counterpoint to unresponsive autonomous universities; others who had tried the change decided they needed to change back. (Australia is an example, with a number of "de-mergers" in recent years; South Africa may follow suit.)

Universities and Their Communities Phase Four: Curriculum and Institutional Innovation

To return to the *schema*, these were followed by late twentieth century experiments in curriculum, pedagogy, and a further drive towards accessibility. Examples here are the pioneering of open access, or admission of adults without formal qualification by the UK's Open University and New York's City College system, and their imitators around the world. At the same time, developing nations began to establish the mega-universities, as analyzed by John Daniel, making use of open and distance learning technologies (ODL) to speed up participation, and to cut costs. The Indira Ghandi National Open University, founded in 1985, had 1.4m enrolments in 1996, and the Islamic Azad University had 1.2m (Daniel, 1996). The notion of community interest is thereby dramatically expanded, although it has to depend upon a much more attenuated concept of the university community itself (not that all such large institutions abandon the sense of "membership": for an example, see the profile of the Open University in Part II below).

However, even the experiments in ODL built upon traditional foundations. In 2008, the University of London's external degree scheme (which was celebrating 150 years of such business) supported 43,000 students in 183 countries (Kenyon Jones, 2008: 35–50). One of the intriguing features of this design is that it separates teaching from examining. Local institutions all around the world prepare students for examinations of the awarding university (just as Colleges at Oxford and Cambridge will help to prepare students for examinations set and marked by the faculties of the University). In an interesting twist, this essentially nineteenth century model is being held out by leaders of the UK's new coalition government (2010) as a way of maintaining access while cutting costs (Willetts, 2010).

Universities and Their Communities Phase Five: Blurred Boundaries and the "Dual Sector"

Next, the latter part of the twentieth and beginning of the twenty-first centuries has seen significant action on the frontier between compulsory education, optional tertiary provision, and the initial rungs of higher education. Examples are the UK phenomenon of "higher education in further education" and the vitally important American Community College network: the former especially in the provision of intermediate qualifications such as the Higher National Certificates and Diplomas and Foundation Degrees, and the latter through two-year (when taken full-time) Associate Degrees. The latest descriptor of activity in this borderland is that of "dual sector" provision. There are not yet significant Continental versions of this model, although it is under consideration in parts of Germany.

Australia (followed in some respects by Canada, with their new system of Polytechnic-style universities) is the country that has probably taken this concept furthest, and several Australian cities now have "educational precincts" in which universities, Technical and Further Education Colleges (TAFE) and sometimes specialist training institutions (for example, for police or fire officers) are deliberately co-located. There are also five "dual sector" universities which have been established by the respective state and territory statutes to include both levels of provision (one is Charles Darwin University, profiled in Part II) (University of Ballarat, 2010; see also Garrod and Macfarlane, 2009).

These latter two waves of developments illustrate that as communities have changed—most recently in response to global communications—not only have existing universities had to respond, but also the acts and intentions of foundation of new institutions have adapted.

Universities and Their Communities Phase Six: The "For Profit" Sector

The "pattern" is rounded out by the most recent wave: that of the "for-profits" (perhaps the first university "type" not to see the need for their own libraries).

"Private" higher education, in the sense of major funding streams coming apart from the state, have always been part of the system, and indeed the patterns set out above were largely independent of government funding until the nineteenth and twentieth centuries. However, the philanthropic and religious motives for investment were a long way away from any considerations such as creating a realizable dividend. Many national systems—like Poland and Japan—have had strong parallel, even majority private sectors. Any profits (or surpluses) were invariably ear-marked for reinvestment in the enterprise.

The question of reputation is also very variable across different jurisdictions. In some, the "public" institutions command the highest respect (and hence levels of demand); in others, it is the private. In several (such as the United States and Japan) the "apex" institutions represent a mixture of public and private.

The global expansion of participation in higher education has predictably encouraged more strictly-business interests. The tradition of "private, not-for-profit" higher education has now been supplemented around the world by enterprises that are emphatically, "for profit." In many cases, this has been tolerated, or even encouraged because of shortage of public funding. As Jay Kubler and Nicola Sayers conclude in their invaluable survey of research on higher education "futures":

> At present, the private sector is much more active in developing and emerging economies, where they have been able to capitalize on high demand and limited supply, often combined with moiré open regulatory systems. In Africa and Asia, private provision is a major growth industry. India already has the third largest higher education system in the world and is planning expansion on an unprecedented scale, and private providers are seen as playing an important part in this process.
>
> *(Kubler and Sayers, 2010: 29)*

The picture that has emerged is, however, much more complex than simply a new stream of competition.

At one level, there is strong competition from in-company and professional accredited training, not necessarily calibrated against or seen as contributory to standard academic qualifications. Moving beyond this (to qualifications classed as "degrees" or membership of an institution called a "university") depends critically on the regulatory framework (normally at national level). For some companies, the cost on entry and maintenance of quality against objective tests may be too high. In these circumstances, the most characteristic development is of some form of partnerships between a company (normally in the educational publishing or communications field) and an established institution. Other possibilities include off-shore or transnational developments (including overseas campuses, often with substantial local or indigenous economic interests), where one of the main assets brought by the "mother" institution is the accredited or validated degree. Other tensions can arise when the initial partner company is bought out or transferred to new ownership.

Meanwhile, governments, as the architects of the regulatory framework (whether directly or through "academic" proxies), have not been slow to realize the potential of an independent stream of higher educational provision in order to meet both social demand and economic strategic objectives. Managing the process has, however, proved complex and frequently contentious, especially when following a surge of expansion a national system may wish to constrain or re-regulate the domain. De-regulation is relatively simple; re-regulation is much harder, as has become apparent in China. The outcome of a recent overview of developments in the UK is as follows:

> Our general conclusion is that the private sector is here to stay and will grow, but that it offers both opportunities and threats which will depend on where individual universities stand in the marketplace and how government policy responds.
>
> *(UUK, 2010: 6)*

As this brief account hints, the pathway of private, for-profit higher education has not been smooth or straightforward. Because of the profit motive, it has an ambiguous relationship to the question of civic and community engagement. It has, however, become a major element of the kaleidoscope of HE provision, and weaves its way in an out of the stories of several of our profiled institutions.

What these waves underline is the vital and continuing influence of "foundations"; of universities, as well as of organizations that become parts of universities. An act of higher education "foundation" creates a kind of DNA, which it is very hard for subsequent members (and especially managements) to suppress. Often that DNA is strengthened when it is combined with other strands. To conclude with another example, Queen Mary University of London (QMUL) is an independent university in its own right, with about 16,000 students and 3,000 staff, working across the full range of higher education disciplines and professions. It is also part of the federal University of London, comprising about 40 institutions and over 120,000 students. QMUL today brings together strands represented by:

- London's first medical school, the London Hospital Medical College (1785);
- St Bartholomew's Hospital Medical College (1843);
- Westfield College, one of the genuine pioneers in higher education for women (1882);
- the original Mile End foundation of Queen Mary College, as the People's Palace, dedicated to educational and cultural support for East London (1887).

Its contemporary mission statement seeks to capture all of these, with a particular sense of place (balancing its "global commitment with a serious engagement with its diverse and rapidly changing London environment"). Overall, it aims:

- to produce research of the highest quality which places it in the top rank of universities;
- to teach its students to the very highest standards, drawing in creative and innovative ways on its research; and
- to transfer the knowledge it generates to business and the community, regionally, nationally and internationally (see: www.qmul.ac.uk/about/mission/index.html).

The argument is that this pattern of foundations constitutes a robust, empirical shape for university foundations all around the world. Different societies, and their national systems, can be shown to join in at various points, but they generally follow the same sequence of events from the point when they do so. The UK, much of Europe, and the United States (through the colonial seminaries) can claim to have been there from the beginning. Several currently developed economies can claim to join in phase two: for example, Australia with its "sandstone" universities, and the Imperial Universities of Japan. Many other societies, including those with "colonial" and "independence" heritage, experience the "publicly planned" approach of phase three. The "innovations" of phase four spring up all over the world, particularly in societies with ambitions for rapid growth (like the mega-universities of the sub-continent and parts of Asia), but also in "developed" contexts. The "blurred boundaries" of phase five emerge around the turn of the present century, partly as a legacy of the "binary" thinking referred to above, partly as an attempt to "democratize" tertiary education, and significantly as a recognition that alternative routes for post-compulsory education increasingly need to be planned and delivered together. The newcomer (the "for-profit" approach of phase six) is significantly dependent on a favorable regulatory environment. There is also evidence that it works best when the relevant private bodies are able to work in partnership with established (including publicly-funded) institutions. Like several of the innovative approaches of phase four, it also has a distinct global reach.

To track forward, our 20 profiles examined below fall into the categories as follows:

Phase One

- Georgetown University (USA).

Phase Two

- Petro Mohlya State University (Ukraine)
- University of Melbourne (Australia).

Phase Three

- SNDT Women's University of Mumbai (India)
- Universidad Metropolitana en Caracas (Venezuela)
- Portland State University (USA)
- Notre Dame of Marbel University (Philippines)
- Ahfad University for Women (Sudan)
- University of Winchester (UK)
- University of Dar es Salaam (Tanzania)
- Universiti Kebangsaan Malaysia (Malaysia)
- University of Haifa (Israel)
- University of Western Sydney (Australia).

Phase Four

- Open University (UK)
- Cape Peninsula University of Technology (South Africa).

Phase Five

- Charles Darwin University (Australia)
- Aga Khan University (Pakistan)
- Tecnológico de Monterrey (Mexico)
- Al-Quds University (Jerusalem).

Phase Six

- Universidad Señor de Sipán (Peru).

Perhaps predictably, the majority are from the great era of publicly-planned higher education. It will also become clear from the profiles that these are leaky categories. Each layer is deposited on the stratum below it, and absorbs both possibilities and prejudices from its under-soil. Equally, the established institutions learn from the newcomers and will imitate their approaches to the market, to the curriculum, and to modifications of their founding purposes. It is for that reason that telling the story of institutions is so complex.

Grand Narratives

The narrative history of universities is capable of sustaining several "Whig" theories, encapsulating contending views of progress and development towards a preferred vision of the present. These include:

- the *liberal* theory of higher education as self-realization and social transformation, including latterly an element of social mobility and meritocracy (perhaps reaching its height, and certainly retaining its most important talisman in Cardinal John Henry Newman);
- the *professional formation* theory, identifying universities and colleges as providers of expertise and vocational identity, in some continuous (law, medicine and theology) and in some new (engineering, science and public administration) areas;
- higher education as a *research engine*, allied to regional and national ambitions for economic growth (in this area contemporary governments have rediscovered, rather than invented, priorities that were high over a century ago)—variations on this theme include higher education as a source of *business services*, and of *national pride*.

Each of these narratives (or theories) can, of course, be re-cast in a dysfunctional or negative light. The liberal aspiration can become a means of social selection and exclusion. Aggressively individualistic notions of advancement can lead to discrimination. Professionalism can lead to narrow and self-interested instrumentalism. Research can ignore some of its wider ethical responsibilities, and national pride can convert into short-term state priorities. And so on.

In *Managing Civic and Community Engagement* Watson has tried to re-formulate and endorse another consistent theme of value and identity for the higher education tradition and legacy: that of *civic and community engagement* (Watson, 2007). Meanwhile, as Stephen Lay concludes in his elegant survey of this long history for the *Observatory for Fundamental University Values and Rights* (otherwise known as the *Magna Charta Universitatum*): "the university should be valued as an intellectual resource of inherent social usefulness and admired as the model of a reasoned approach to life" (Lay, 2004: 111). His recommendation is that the "expectation of public service" should be added to the Charta (*ibid.*: 109).

These narratives matter: to leaders and members of universities and to those who attempt to steer them from outside, including governments, funders and public opinion more generally. As an "opt-in" organization, the Talloires Network would clearly endorse Lay's recommendation above. As contributors to this book, our 20 profiled universities have indicated their readiness to think through the implications structurally, organizationally, and in terms of the commitment of resources. There will, however, be natural nuances that produce variations even across as focused a sample as we now present.

2

TYPES OF CAPITAL AND CITIZENSHIP

One such variation can be approached by asking what kind of capital higher education sets out to create.

At its heart, the university is a reservoir of intellectual capital: its most fundamental purpose is about the creation, testing and application of knowledge. As a consequence, the twenty-first century preoccupation with knowledge management ought to be highly congenial to the higher education enterprise. To probe this further, it is helpful to assess the types of intellectual capital apparently preferred (and potentially privileged) in the wider society.

Traditionally, the battle lines have been drawn between an economically-focused preoccupation with *human* capital, seeing qualified manpower as an essential element of growth, and a community-focused desire for enhanced *social* capital, seeing education at all levels as a way of solidifying cohesive norms of mutually satisfying behavior.

A new kid on the block is the theory of *creative* capital, associated in particular with the work of Richard Florida. Yet another recent invention is *identity* capital—comprising the attributes individuals need to "intelligently strategize and make decisions affecting their life courses." Governments have also begun to get involved, for example through the British government's "foresight" exercise on "mental capital and wellbeing." Finally, the ex-British Prime Minister, Tony Blair, has promoted "spiritual capital" as the core concept for his new interfaith Foundation.

This section updates and develops the analysis in Watson's *Managing Civic and Community Engagement* (2007) from pages 14–17, focusing on the following features of competing concepts of capital, and the role of higher education in delivering them:

- The characteristic mode of production
- The chief values implied
- Preferred performance indicators
- Key objectives
- Form of trust or mutuality involved (see Smith, 2005).

Human capital in the works of Gary Becker and others is fundamentally an economists' construct, aimed at understanding how skills and a trained workforce can add value. It proceeds largely by aggregating the assets accumulated by individuals, either through qualifications or the duration of the educational experience. The main outcome towards which it is directed is increased productivity and national or regional economic "edge." In so far as it about a form of trust, it emphasizes calculation and predictability: the kind of trust you would have hoped to have in your bank.

Social capital is almost single-handedly the construct of Robert Putnam, and has attracted interest and admiration all around the world for what it appears to say about the power and resilience of communities. Rather than qualified individuals, it focuses on networked relationships and their shared norms and values. The key values that emerge are in terms of developing mutual obligations and a strengthened sense of civic society. The trust appealed to here is one closer to membership than contract. For this reason, it deals less well with opposition, otherness and difference, and much of its initial promise has dissolved in the face of the problems not just of divided societies, but also cultural diversity. This defect is becoming more and more apparent, as set out in this critique:

> The basic lesson that emerges from Putnam's research is that high levels of diversity currently have impact on levels of social capital . . . Relative to a more homogenous community, Putnam's research concludes that greater diversity means that a community will exhibit less trust, sociability, political participation and interclass mixing. Social capital, it would seem, thrives in places where 'diversity' has been effaced.
>
> *(Hallberg and Lund, 2005)*

Florida's *creative capital* tackles the issues of difference and otherness head on. It has proved much more persuasive at the local (including metropolitan) levels than when scaled up to regions, nations or global regions. Here the focus is on voluntary associations and "clusters" of like-minded or similarly motivated people: the "super-creative core" of Florida's more general "creative class" of brain-workers. Tolerant and diverse host communities seem essential; there's a premium on bohemianism and gay-friendliness. Formal entry barriers are more-or-less nonexistent; it is what you can do and how innovative your ideas are that counts, not what qualifications you have. Innovation is the goal, and fluid experimentation the key. Fluidity also applies to the communities themselves; they will dissolve and form at will. As a consequence, the type of trust on which they depend is personal, direct and highly affective.

Côté's *identity capital*, like human capital, begins with the individual, but in this case is ultimately not about aggregate economic impact as much as individual life-courses. The drive is towards self-reliance, self-confidence, and self-efficacy. What works for one individual may not work for another, but the goal is a personal story, based upon sound and informed decision-making, and an ultimate trust in the individual to get it right, eventually.

As an "official" formulation, *mental capital* is interested in the twin goals of economic competitiveness and social cohesion; it is about prosperity and peace. In this sense, the goal is to ensure that members of the society can contribute productively and happily. Mental health and its reciprocal, mental incapacity, are thus critical. Perhaps understandably, the key inputs are seen as public policy-related, and the trust sought is trust that elected representatives and other authorities will do the right thing.

TABLE 2.1 Types of Capital (1)

Human capital	Social capital	Creative capital
(Gary Becker)	(Robert Putnam)	(Richard Florida)
See Schuller et al. (1998)	See Hallberg & Lund (2005)	See Florida (2002)
Individual agent	Networks and relationships	Clusters of creative people
Economic rationality	Shared values and norms	Diversity and tolerance
Educational duration/ qualifications	Mutual obligation; Civic engagement	"Low entry barriers for people"
Individual income/ productivity	Quality of life	Rates of innovation
Self-interested trust	Normative trust	Affective trust

TABLE 2.2 Types of Capital (2)

Identity capital	Mental capital	Spiritual capital
(Côté)	(GoS "Foresight")	(Tony Blair)
See Côté (2002)	See Beddington et al. (2008)	See Blair (2008)
Individual agent	Individual *and* social benefits	Organized religion
Self-confidence and efficacy	Economic competitiveness and social cohesion	"Compassion and help for others," "not exclusionary identity"
Individual decision-making	Mental health across the life-course	Multi-faith societies
Satisfactory negotiation of the life-course	Effective policy interventions	Education about "each other's faith and traditions"
Trust in self	Trust in national political stewardship	Education about "each other's faith and traditions"

Spiritual capital will be attractive to those who see revealed religion in particular as the source of appropriate behavior. It will also have resonance for those with a non-dogmatic ethical approach. However, in the hands of Tony Blair and others, it quickly reduces to a bland confidence in inter-faith harmony. Blair's analysis is all about the old-fashioned merits of understanding the other point of view—provided it is brigaded within the disciplines of organized religion, and structured around common denominators like the golden mean or the Kantian categorical imperative. The trust is that knowing more about the other will reduce tension and spread sweetness and light.

A tabular analysis of these variables is on the previous page.

They may sound abstract, but these theoretical models matter. They represent a way of capturing priorities for the higher education enterprise that will have resonance for governments, for communities, and for the members of universities and colleges. Crudely (and in terms of their major emphases—of course these interests overlap): governments want human capital; communities want both this and the cohesive capital associated with social capital; meanwhile, modern students and their teachers are increasingly interested in creativity and breaking the mould.

For most of our group of institutions, it is the dialectic between human and social capital that engages them most, especially under the (sometimes divergent) pressures of civil society and the state. Meanwhile it is a significant set struggle with their own peculiar versions of both creative and spiritual capital: the former usually in response to perceived market opportunities and the latter through deference to their foundations.

The Question of Citizenship

Another fruitful approach is to consider conceptions of citizenship appealed to or actively promoted by universities in different contexts. Members of the Talloires Network are at the forefront of universities claiming that an effective higher education will assist not only in preparing future leaders but also responsible citizens. Other groups have emphasized this element of the community engagement agenda even more directly. These include the "International Consortium for Higher Education, Civic Responsibility and Democracy," in association with the Committee on Higher Education and Research of the Council of Europe, Construye País in Chile, and the Australian Universities Community Engagement Alliance. In its mission, the International Consortium for Higher Education, Civic Responsibility and Democracy seeks to "document, understand, and advance the contributions of higher education to democracy on the campus, in the local community, and the wider society." The European and North American founder members have subsequently been joined by South Africa (through the Joint Education Trust), Australia and South Korea. The consortium itself has sponsored a pilot study on "universities as sites of citizenship and civic responsibility." In June 2006, a further version of the Declaration was affirmed by 150 university and government leaders in Strasbourg under the aegis of the Council of Europe Forum on Higher Education and Democratic Culture.

One of the sticking points is that universities will always have an ambivalent role towards any tightly defined national concept of citizenship. The groups outlined above have a strong commitment to a view of higher education as a quasi-political rite of passage, now undergoing a revival that binds together moral and democratic sensibilities in the effort to construct positive qualities of "character" in both students and graduates. In terms of the "narratives" set out above, this would be closest to the Newmanesque "liberal emancipationism."

Such a concept has been threatened on a variety of fronts in the United States; not least through the "culture wars," critiques of American foreign policy, and a sense (inherent in the critique of "social capital") that it can be reductionist and oppressive. There are, however, distinct signs of revival. For example, Elizabeth Kiss and Peter Euben report on a conference held at Duke University to discuss whether or not universities "have quit the business of explicit efforts to shape the moral and civic lives of students" (Kiss & Euben, 2010: xi).

Their answer, broadly, is that a number of trends point to a revival of interest in exactly such a business. Their "twelve trends" include new academic interest in "normative questions," a "re-emphasis on higher education's responsibility to prepare women and men for democratic citizenship," the growth of a curriculum and pedagogy that bridges "action and reflection" (especially through service learning and community-based research), as well as parallel interests in "spiritual exploration" and "practical wisdom." They also acknowledge that several of these trends make "many in the academy deeply uneasy" (*ibid.*: 9–13); a reservation echoed by Patchen Markell's observation that teachers approach these issues with both "a wariness about moral education" and "a sense of the inescapability of the ethical" (*ibid.*: 187). On this, the most telling comments in the volume come from James Murphy, writing about schools, not higher education. He observes the general failure of "deliberate instruction aimed at inculcating civic virtue," noting simultaneously that (in the tradition of John Dewey) "academic education is itself a kind of moral education" (*ibid.*: 171–172).

In Great Britain, the ambivalence is much stronger. As John Ahier and his collaborators have shown, in a study of two very different universities (Cambridge and what is now Anglia Ruskin) contemporary students are redefining mutuality:

In their speech, our respondents recognized four circuits: (i) those of student peers; (ii) the intergenerational; (iii) that of imagined 'abstract others' as recipients of state welfare; and (iv) the formal constitutional dimension of their relationship to state and government. These circuits were governed

by principles such as fairness, altruism, reciprocity and responsibility that
we will sum up in the more general term, 'mutuality.' . . . The moralizing
of extended relationships in this manner counters both the fears of those
who believe that the absence of a language of formal citizenship indicates
privatized withdrawal and those who would wish to celebrate the primacy
of calculative individualism.

(Ahier et al., 2002: 141)

Echoing Murphy, it is possible that citizenship education, at both the higher
education level and in schools has got it wrong. A brittle, nationalistic, quite pos-
sibly politically colonized view of what it is to understand and project rights and
responsibilities as a member of a democratic and inclusive society is unpersuasive
to many of that society's members (particularly youth and minorities of various
kinds) and has been allowed to disguise a much more generous, contemporary
sense of what it is to be a citizen. The scholarly literature points to several dangers: a perennial "deficit" model (especially where young people are concerned),
a rhetorical trend that moves very quickly and uncritically from rights to duties,
a presumption that obedience and patriotism are inviolable, and a consequent
ceding of the case for change to extreme groups of both the right and the left
(Banajai, 2008: 557; see also Younge, 2009).

Universities were central, for example, to Prime Minister Gordon Brown's
conception of "Britishness":

The qualities of British life—the notion of civic duty binding people to
one another and the sense of fair play which underpins the idea of a proper
social order—come together in the ethic of public service [leading to] the
great British public institutions admired throughout the world [among
them] our universities, including the Open University.

(Brown, 2004)

Interestingly, in a book of essays, in which he was instrumental in commission-
ing, and in which he talked about a "foundation of values that can be shared by
us all," the majority of the contributors expressed skepticism and about this
triumphalist and reductionist approach (D'Ancona, 2009: 27). The political
scientist Anthony King, for example, talks about how "Britishness has survived
for more than three centuries substantively as a blur, on the whole an amica-
ble blur," while the broadcaster June Sarpong states that "there's something
poignant about how our cynicism makes us both strong and vulnerable" (*ibid.*:
183, 113).

Elsewhere in the countries covered by our profiles, there are other dominant
orientations: the Latin American focus on "solidarity"; the South African drive
for "transformation"; the Australian concern for "closing the gap"; and so on.
Meanwhile, several important conversations are taking place across national and

continental boundaries. For example, a Development Research Centre (DRC) has been established by the Institute for Development Studies at the University of Sussex, with support from the UK Department for International Development (DFID) to support a network across seven countries—the UK, India, Bangladesh, Nigeria, South Africa, Mexico and Brazil—examining citizenship, participation and accountability. The results are rich and, as stated in the conclusion, "citizenship is always under construction in practices and processes of contestation, not simply handed down from above as a given status" (Brown & Gaventa, 2008: 27). The UK Open University, profiled below, plays a coordinating role in a similar network across the enlarged European Union.

All would agree that the university occupies a critical role within civil society. According to Michael Edwards, formerly of the Ford Foundation, "as a concept 'Civil Society' speaks to the best of us, and calls upon the best of us to respond in kind"—and so should the university (Edwards, 2004: iii). There is a corollary: when it becomes over-identified with the political interests of the state, it has probably lost its way. The sticking point is well articulated by Michael Daxner, former Rector of Oldenburg University and post-war EU Education Commissioner in Kosovo. "East of Vienna," he has said, "the role of universities is in society-making, not state-making." Universities are needed, he says "because of our dangerous knowledge." At a conference of the European University Association and the American Council of Education in 2004, he went on to explain how this instinct can easily become masked:

> No wonder that most of the harmonizing structures in higher education refer to pure scholarship, administration, government, and institutional autonomy, whereas the basic notions of the university as the 'lead institution' in civil society—republican legitimacy, democracy, and citizenship—are rarely included in modern concepts of academic freedom, or treated only nominally in the mission statement of universities.
>
> *(EUA/ACE, 2004: 68)*

The notion of "dangerous knowledge"—that is of being critical as well as supportive of activities across civil society leads to moral injunctions for both states and their universities.

Just as in the discussion of "capital" there is clearly a spectrum of possibilities for conceptualizing citizenship. Here is a useful typology from the work of Rhonda Wynne (Wynne, 2010). Wynne's overarching concept is of a choice between more politically "civic," more locally "communitarian," and more networked "commonwealth" approaches. Her individual cells cash out the implications all the way down to pedagogic approaches of courses and institutions. Across our profiles we can see such choices being made, by and for universities. Sometimes, of course, they are in tension.

TABLE 2.3 Conceptions of Citizenship Grid

Conception	Civic	Communitarian	Commonwealth
Citizenship as:	Status	Practice	Activity
Citizen as:	Voter/Worker	Community member	Civic producer
	Consumer	Volunteer	Public worker
	Patriot		Activist
Citizen is:	Personally responsible	Participatory	Justice-oriented
Spectrum	Minimalist		Expansionist
	Passive: *Civic Slug*		Active: *Civic Spark Plug*
	Individual	Community	Collective
	Individual rights, freedoms, responsibility, morality	Community as locus of solidarity Associational Life	Public good Common good Civic responsibility
Purpose	Status quo	Maintenance	Renewal
Citizenship education:	Societal reproduction	Maintain/rebuild civic life	Systemic critique and reform
	Uphold cultural values	Strong communities	Political literacy
	Social cohesion		Social inclusion
	Social moral responsibility		Identity and recognition
	Conformist		Deliberative participation Civic identity/efficacy/ agency
Educational approach	Traditional; Mainstream	Progressive	Advanced; Transformative/Critical
Practice	Citizenship courses	Service-learning	Critical pedagogies
Domain	Content/Knowledge	Doing/Action	Self/Identity
Focus of programs	Formal/legal aspect of citizenship:	Substantive dimension of citizenship:	Affective dimension of citizenship:
	Laws, fixed rights	Rights and duties	Identity and recognition
	Government Voting and representation	Civic engagement Common good	Macro-level critique Political forces
	Democratic values		Systemic reform
	Symbols, icons, heroes		Social justice
	Personal morality		Structural dynamics
	Character education		Root causes
			Solidarity, pluralism

Pedagogy	Didactic	Participatory	Critical pedagogies
	Content/Knowledge transmission	Group work	Inquiry
	Teacher as expert	Volunteer initiatives	Critical thinking/ reflection
	Understanding	Enactive learning	Critical literacy
	Mainstream academic knowledge	Problem-solving	Critical discourse analysis
		Service-learning	Participatory research
		Responsibility	Action research
		Experiential learning	Transformative academic knowledge

See: Wynne (2010).

3

CONTEMPORARY DRIVERS

The higher education sector is undergoing massive transformation worldwide. Competing demands from government, the private sector, civil society organizations and local communities have forced many higher education institutions to rethink their mission and place in society. A report produced for UNESCO's World Higher Education conference in 2009, *Trends in Global Higher Education: Tracking an Academic Revolution*, outlined many of the key drivers affecting the higher education sector overall: massification of tertiary systems everywhere, the "public good" versus "private good" debate, the impacts of information and communications technology, and the rise of the knowledge economy and globalization. Add to these factors the global economic crisis beginning in 2008 and resulting increases in global poverty, economic distress of local communities and increasing demand to access higher education for retraining or further education, and the pressures facing the higher education sector become apparent.

Underneath these pressures, another set of drivers is helping to move the higher education sector towards greater public engagement, as universities increasingly recognize the importance of this aspect of their mission. This trend, which for many is a return to founding principles and modes of activity and for others is uncharted territory, is gathering momentum worldwide. While expressed in unique ways that follow cultural, political and economic influences, most universities now understand the need to place greater emphasis on extension, outreach and engagement.

In difficult economic times, higher education is being scrutinized for its value and relevance. Public funding has decreased in many countries and regulations and expectations have increased. In the past, this might have led to a redoubling of focus on purely economic dimensions of the contributions of higher education: building human capital, research output and technological innovation, and industry partnerships. Today, however, there is increasing recognition of the importance of social and civic contributions to development. In 2007, the Observatory of the European University proposed adding social factors such as contracts with public institutions, involvement in social and cultural life and public understanding of science to assess the relevance and impact of higher education institutions. As Jean-Marie De Ketele argues in her contribution to the GUNI series "Higher Education at a Time of Transformation," "The first and last criteria for assessing higher education should be social relevance" (*Higher Education and the World* 3, 2008). It is clear that this push for greater social relevance leads universities to engage more with local, national and regional public institutions, civil society groups and communities. In many places, these kinds of activities remain separate from partnerships with industry, though Malaysia is a pioneering example of integration of economic and social activities through its offices of "industry and community partnerships."

Higher education now makes an appearance in virtually every "strategy" set by public authorities at all levels. Thus there will be a role for higher education in economic development, in supporting the compulsory phase of education, in health and social care, and in criminal justice in governments at the local, regional and national levels. Often these roles extend to the cultural, sporting and recreational fields. Sometimes they will stress the role of higher education in conflict resolution, in community relations and in social cohesion.

Following a targeted push in the last 20 years to increase investment in primary education as a means to promote national development, many development banks greatly decreased their support for higher education as a proportion of their total investments in education. "For example, from 1985 to 1989, 17 per cent of the World Bank's worldwide education-sector spending was on higher education. But from 1995 to 1999, the proportion allotted to higher education declined to just 7 per cent" (Bloom et al., 2006). In the last decade, however, the international development community and governments have realized that building just, democratic societies capable of innovation and growth requires a robust higher education sector.

In a speech in 2000 in Ghana, former Secretary General of the United Nations, Kofi Annan, emphasized the many important roles higher education can fulfill:

> The university must become a primary tool for Africa's development in the new century. Universities can help develop African expertise; they can enhance the analysis of African problems; strengthen domestic institutions; serve as a model environment for the practice of good governance, conflict resolution and respect for human rights, and enable African academics to play an active part in the global community of scholars.
>
> *(United Nations Press Release, 2000; www.unis.unvienna.org/*
> *unis/pressrels/2000/sg2625.html)*

The multi-faceted thinking about the role of higher education in social and economic development has led to a slight reversal in trends for investment in higher education, though the full effect of the economic crisis on this change is at present unknown. The expectation for higher education today is that the sector will begin to look more seriously at local, regional and national development concerns and adjust research and teaching accordingly. This has necessitated the adoption of partnership strategies to build internal structures, policies and programs to respond to various social needs. These strategies often integrate service and extension with teaching and research in innovative ways.

Innovation in information and communication technology is also driving global recognition of the importance of greater public engagement in higher education. A key reason for this is the increased sharing of successful models of community engagement around the globe by active students, faculty, staff, and higher education leaders. Innovations in curriculum design, teaching pedagogy, public partnerships for research and models of community service are shared by practitioners around the globe. For example, the Latin American Center for Service-Learning based in Buenos Aires runs a password protected area for members of their networks to share community engagement research, syllabi and policy documents (this forum can be found at: www.clayss.org.ar).

Cross-fertilization between the global North and South and across regions is increasing. Latin America, for example, has a long history of public engagement by its universities. This knowledge has been shared through various connections with universities in Spain and the United States for the last decade. The Latin American Center for Service-Learning has, since 1997, hosted an international conference for university practitioners and scholars of service-learning and engagement. Participants have been able to use online forums and file sharing software to keep in contact and exchange knowledge in real time.

Information and communication technology also increases rates of change and makes institutions able to respond more effectively to innovations in curriculum design or research strategies. Collaboration is also facilitated by communication. Open source courseware is a phenomenon that allows resource poor institutions to develop innovative new approaches. The Massachusetts Institute of Technology has posted virtually all of its course content online at: http://ocw.mit.edu/about/. In fact, some have argued that the open source movement in technology has had huge implications for the higher education sector, both in its production of knowledge and its systems and operations. David Wiley, in his article "Open Source, Openness, and Higher Education," states that "the greater use of open source software in education has unfolded hand-in-hand with the development of open course content and open access research, . . . this more comprehensive shift towards 'openness' in academic practice is not only a positive trend, but a necessary one in order to ensure transparency, collaboration, and continued innovation in the academy" (Wiley, 2007; http://innovateonline.info). This trend in open communication and knowledge exchange is positively affecting the movement in higher education community engagement.

Young people around the world have embraced technological innovation and new forms of learning. Many global youth-focused organizations, operating both within higher education systems and externally, are using technology to connect students to provide educational and service opportunities. Additionally, students in many parts of the world, though not all, are increasingly asking for more experiential education that is directly linked with contemporary social needs. While one component of this trend is young people's need to prepare for and obtain employment, other important social factors are also driving this demand. Young people are urgently concerned with pressing social issues facing communities around the globe. In many instances, they have spurred movements to respond to these issues. The environmental sustainability movement within higher education was largely driven by student activism.

Entrepreneurship has been embraced by the social sector and universities have responded by combining traditional business school curriculum with social innovation and engagement. Ashoka U is one example of how universities are responding to the demand by students and civil society to engage in socially relevant teaching. Ashoka U, a program of the non-profit Ashoka, is working with many US universities to "provide a road map for universities that seek to create best-in-class social entrepreneurship programs that blend theory and practice" (http://ashokau.org/about/what-we-do/). Their social entrepreneurship curriculum focuses on achieving positive social change through innovation. Their experience draws on over 2,500 social entrepreneurs from around the world. Other global organizations, like Students in Free Enterprise (SIFE), work to create "a better, more sustainable world through the positive power of business" (www.sife.org). Students in SIFE participate in competitions to advance innovative solutions to social problems.

These types of learning experiences are essential to combat outdated curricula emphasizing rote learning, which is present in many universities around the globe. Barbara Ibrahim, Director of the Gerhart Center for Philanthropy and Civic Engagement at the American University in Cairo, has called service-learning the "Trojan horse" of curriculum reform in the Middle East.

In a world that is increasingly confronted with large, complex problems that often require multidisciplinary expertise and innovation to solve, it is not just students who are asking if higher education is up to the job. Scholars and higher education leaders are examining how to restructure their institutions to be more interdisciplinary, socially responsive and relevant. Many institutions have created programs that focus on big problems and questions rather than disciplines. For example, the University of Chicago, with a reputation as a quintessential ivory tower, has instituted an interdisciplinary "big problems" cap-stone course. The United Nations University fulfills its mission to "resolve the pressing global problems that are the concern of the United Nations, its Peoples and Member

States," by focusing its research on global health, population and sustainability, and human socioeconomic development and good governance. University College London has also created a research program called Grand Challenges that focuses on global health, sustainable cities, intercultural interaction and human wellbeing. Many universities around the world have responded to the question "Can we solve big problems?" by instituting transformation educational reforms and developing new modes of knowledge production for society.

Despite the urgent needs of many communities across the globe, younger generations seem to be expressing more optimism about social change. They also are more action oriented and somewhat less political than previous generations. In March 2010, the Talloires Network gathered higher education leaders from around the globe at the Rockefeller Foundation Bellagio Center to discuss future developments in community engagement. Russel Botman, Vice-Chancellor of Stellenbosch University in South Africa, emphasized that younger generations in South Africa were no longer interested in old political battles, but in new forms of engagement and development. In citing Paolo Freire's *Pedagogy of the Oppressed,* he stated, "We must move from the pedagogy of the oppressed to the new pedagogy of hope. We must believe in the triumph of possibility over limitations" (Talloires Network, www.tufts.edu/talloiresnetwork/). It is this essential shift in thinking about the university mission that is driving transformation at Stellenbosch University and so many others in South Africa and across the globe.

In Part II of this text, we will move to exploring examples of university engagement from around the world. The local context, including economic and political systems, culture, language and history, all interact with these contemporary drivers to produce unique, local approaches to the implementation of community engagement policy and practice.

PART II
The Engaged University

4

THE PROJECT

This research project examines an enduring and also changing dimension of higher education—its civic engagement and social responsibility goals and activities—in a wide range of geographic settings. Though we have identified the historical foundations for engagement and global drivers that are moving universities to embrace (or rediscover) more engaged models of teaching and research, it is critical to explore the experience of different kinds of higher education institutions in very different contexts and in all parts of the world. Our study examines the extent to which the founding missions of these institutions shape their current civic and social responsibility activities, and we analyze how a series of other driving forces—both reinforcing and constraining—determine the approaches and experiences of individual institutions. Alternative conceptions of capital formation are a guiding framework for this analysis, with an emphasis on the interplay between human capital formation and social capital formation. We reflect on how these diverse examples illustrate alternative higher education narratives—liberal theory, professional formation theory and the university as research engine. The research includes examples that represent the full spectrum of phases in the relationship between universities and communities: specialist communities, national and regional institutions serving post-industrial society, public systems of higher education, curriculum and institutional innovation, blurred boundaries and the dual sector, and the for-profit sector.

Scope

We have set out to address the following questions about colleges and universities in diverse parts of the world:

1. What are the commitments of institutions of higher education to their host societies and communities? How do they define their civic mission and responsibility? What are their most important goals for this area of their work?
2. How do the institutions' engagement activities inform and influence their other core functions—their teaching and research programs?
3. What are their primary civic engagement and social responsibility programs, activities and policies? How are these functions organized and supported?
4. What are the roles and responsibility of faculty members, other staff, students and external partners with regard to the engagement agenda? Who are major stakeholders and what are the roles that they play, and what are the expectations of each?
5. What are the most significant achievements and impacts of this work? Are these results documented and measured systematically, and if so how?
6. What factors influence the nature of university civic engagement work and its impacts? How?
7. What are the common challenges that the institutions encounter in this area of activity?
8. What are the institutions' future plans and opportunities for their civic engagement and social responsibility functions?

Why This Study?

Working in conjunction with the Talloires Network, the authors have undertaken this study because higher education civic engagement and social responsibility activities and programs appear to have grown rapidly in scale and also in impact. It is important to document and understand not only large-scale, global pressures in higher education, but also national and regional influences on policy and practice. Furthermore, it is notable that to date, there has been comparatively little systematic objective description and analysis of these activities. The written material that exists frequently is purely descriptive and often mostly self-promotional. Indeed this field of endeavor is long on rhetoric and short on objective analysis. If in fact the impacts of this work are significant, then it is problematic to have such a limited supply of credible data about it.

The research on this topic that does exist (in English) concentrates primarily on the experience of the global North and of more economically advanced countries. While that information is useful, it may not represent fully or accurately the experience of other parts of the world where university civic engagement is expanding and seems to hold high potential. In order for less economically advanced countries to pursue effective strategies with respect to this dimension of higher education, it is essential that decision-makers have access to data that accurately represents the present realities and future possibilities in those societies.

An additional reason why this project is timely is that the potential value of the findings is high during the present, early stage of development of this movement. As President Bacow's preface indicates, it is precisely in the early phases of significant new trends and period of innovation that accelerated exchange of experience—about what works and what does not—and assessment of the merits of alternative approaches, is particularly useful. In times of innovation, experimentation and expanding activity and possibility such as this one, fresh objective information can be particularly helpful—to individual colleges and universities, to ministries of education and other governmental agencies, and to prospective sources of financial investment.

Project Goals

With the rationale and questions summarized above, our project seeks first to document and analyze the experience to date of a broad range of institutions of higher education around the world. Second, it aims to provide information that can help to improve and strengthen university civic engagement. We hope to generate findings that are useful to all stakeholders that care about the societal roles of higher education institutions of higher education. Third, we wish to reinforce the work of the Talloires Network—the work of its individual members and of the Network overall. Finally, we would like this initiative to stimulate and guide subsequent research. In a context of limited information about an important phenomenon, our project will make a contribution to the purposes noted above, but at best it can make only a beginning. The importance of this movement and the diversity of contexts in which it operates argue strongly for substantial additional scholarship. We hope that our research demonstrates the value of such inquiry and that it motivates and guides future research.

Methodology

We decided that the most productive approach to addressing our questions would be to look in depth at the experience of individual colleges and universities. These are the logical units of analysis. Studying the actual behavior of these organizations clearly would be the best way to illuminate the issues that motivated our inquiry. While in theory we could have gathered information with less attention to institutional context, we were fundamentally interested in the behavior of the institutions themselves and in how to influence and support their future decision-making and practice.

Having determined that institutional profiles would be the best approach, we then had to decide how to select the participating universities. We began this process by deciding to limit the universe to the membership of the Talloires Network. Would it not have been more scientifically respectable to construct a random sample of higher education institutions? In theory, yes. But in practical terms, this was not a real option. We wanted to look at institutions that had accumulated substantial experience, which would by definition be a subset of the entire universe of higher education institutions. In addition, we were concerned about issues of access and cooperation. By focusing on institutions that were members of the Talloires Network, we could count on having their active cooperation and to secure full access to their experience. This indeed proved to be the case, first because sharing one's experience with other members is a responsibility to which institutions committed themselves when they joined the Network. In addition, participating in this project would be advantageous to them because communicating their experience could potentially help them to sustain and to build the support of internal and external constituencies. An additional consideration was that organizing the project through the Talloires Network would facilitate dissemination and use of the eventual findings—through the Network's website and other communications vehicles, conferences, and other programs.

We started by identifying the set of variables that would be important to explore. These included geographic location, policy context, size, and type of institution. An essential element of the process was to conduct background research about the national policies, geographic content, finances, policies, and culture of the countries in which each participating institution is located. Then we reviewed the current list of members and sought to identify individual institutions that would represent a broad spectrum in terms of these dimensions of variation. Thus, we developed an illustrative sample, not a representative one. The profiles are, of course, institutions that have a comparatively high commitment to university civic engagement and social responsibility. Their high level of interest in this topic after all is why they joined the Network in the first place. This is obviously both a strength and a limitation—a strength because the research would be enriched by the greater amount and depth of data available about universities with substantial civic experience and track record, and a limitation because it would be less revealing about why other institutions do less in the area of civic engagement. The vast majority of institutions that we invited to participate agreed to do so. Four of the institutions that we approached ultimately were unable, for a variety of reasons, to be involved.

The resultant sample includes public and private universities, sectarian institutions, and some with religious foundations and affiliations. The group represents a wide range in size, institutional prestige, educational and research priorities, and community context. Geographically, the group spans Asia (4 institutions), Latin America (3), Africa (3), Europe (3), Middle East (2), Australia (3), and USA (2). There are some significant gaps. It does not include universities from some key large countries—in particular, China, Brazil, and Japan or from Scandinavia. It also has only very limited representation of the largest state universities.

This methodology combines participatory research and independent analysis; it integrates self-study by the participating institutions and the more arms-length observations of the authors. We followed a four-step process. (1) Each institution responded to a detailed questionnaire (see Appendix I for a copy). (2) One of the four co-authors conducted a site visit to verify and also to build upon the information that was provided by each institution. Most of these visits were for two days and included interviews with the full range of stakeholders—institutional heads, other administrators, faculty members, students, civic engagement program staff leaders, and community partners. (3) The co-author responsible for a given institution then prepared a draft profile, based on steps one and two above. Subsequently, she or he asked the subject institution to review the case study for accuracy, and incorporated corrections and clarifications. (4) The fourth step was reflection by the team of authors on the data revealed by the profiles, in light of the historical and theoretical literature about university–community engagement, in order to generate not only comparative insights but also pointers to effective policy and practice.

This project represents the perspective of active participants in the global higher education civic engagement movement. Representatives of the participating institutions—the individuals who responded to the questionnaires and also the people who provided interviews during the site visits—are active practitioners and proponents of the engagement movement. The same is true of the co-authors. For each of the co-authors, university civic engagement has been a central focus of their professional careers. The institutional representatives and the co-writers have sought to be objective as well as supportive; thus many the institutional profiles incorporate critical observations, as well as documentation of positive achievements.

The 20 institutions, listed alphabetically by country, are as follows:

*   Charles Darwin University (Australia)
*   University of Melbourne (Australia)
*   University of Western Sydney (Australia)
*   SNDT Women's University of Mumbai (India)
*   University of Haifa (Israel)
*   Universiti Kebangsaan Malaysia (Malaysia)
*   Tecnológico de Monterrey (Mexico)
*   Aga Khan University (Pakistan)
*   Al-Quds University (The Occupied Palestinian Territories)
*   Universidad Señor de Sipán (Peru)
*   Notre Dame of Marbel University (Philippines)
*   Cape Peninsula University of Technology (Republic of South Africa)
*   Ahfad University for Women (Sudan)
*   University of Dar es Salaam (Tanzania)
*   Petro Mohyla State University (Ukraine)
*   Open University (UK)
*   University of Winchester (UK)

- Portland State University (USA)
- Georgetown University (USA)
- Universidad Metropolitana en Caracas (Venezuela).

Of these, 14 are "public" universities, as generally understood and six are "private." Three have specific religious denominational allegiance. Three are rural and 17 metropolitan. The oldest was founded in 1689 and the newest in 2003. Student enrollments vary between about 4,300 and over 180,000. Income per FTE student varies from $1,305.64 to $64,926.69. These characteristics are summarized in Table 4.1.

TABLE 4.1 Profiled Universities Comparison

Profiled Universities	Country	Public	Private	Religious	FTE enrollment	Funding per FTE student	Year established
Charles Darwin University	Australia	X			NA	NA	2003
University of Melbourne	Australia	X			33,639	$29,249	1853
University of Western Sydney	Australia	X			36,376	$12,337	1990
SNDT Women's University of Mumbai	India	X			75,564	NA	1916
University of Haifa	Israel	X			17,912	$11,682	1972
Universiti Kebangsaan Malaysia	Malaysia	X			24,733	$1,343	1970
Tecnológico de Monterrey	Mexico		X		58,291	$14,362	1943
Aga Khan University	Pakistan		X		2,475	$16,800	1983
Al-Quds University	Palestinian Territories	X			12,000	$2,941	1995
Universidad Señor de Sipán	Peru		X		7,500	NA	1999
Notre Dame of Marbel University	Philippines		X	X	4,548	$602	1955
Cape Peninsula University of Technology	South Africa	X			22,690	$6,627	2003

Ahfad University for Women	Sudan	X		5,420	NA	1966
University of Dar es Salaam	Tanzania	X		14,648	NA	1970
The Open University	UK	X		78,110	$7,834	1969
The University of Winchester	UK	X	X	4,640	$12,702	1840
Petro Mohyla State University	Ukraine	X		3,275	$1,305	1996
Georgetown University	USA		X	X	15,389	$64,926	1789
Portland State University	USA	X		16,614	$14,102	1946
Universidad Metropolitana en Caracas	Venezuela	X		8,000	$4,651	1944

Completed self-assessments provided reasonably standard information related to civic engagement and social responsibility on issues such as:

- mission and goals;
- governance, leadership and management;
- main lines of activity;
- availability and allocation of resources;
- relevant partnerships;
- range of impacts (inside and outside the university).

As indicated above, between June 2009 and March 2010 fieldwork was undertaken to get inside some of these more formal categories, to gather personal testimony and to examine, among other things:

- cultural specificities;
- reputational implications;
- prospects of sustainability; and
- potentially transferable initiatives.

The approach here has been to understand, validate and ideally extend the self-assessments. We arranged in advance meetings with (a) senior leadership, (b) staff involved with "cited" activities, (c) students similarly involved, (d) representatives of community partners. (Opening questions are set out in Appendix II.)

During this 10-month period there were, of course, major changes in political, economic, social and environmental circumstances around the world. There were also changes within our 20 university communities (including some significant changes in top leadership). We believe, however, that we have succeeded in providing one of the first genuinely global pictures of university civic and community engagement at the level of the day-to-day struggles and joys of individual institutions.

5

THE PROFILES

Australia and its Higher Education System

Australia has a population of 22 million, an average life expectancy for men of 79 and for women 83, and ranks 28th out of 173 in the Media Freedom Index. Its adult literacy rate is 99%; it has 2.5 doctors per 1,000 population and an adult HIV/AIDS rate of 0.1% (*Guardian* "World Fact Files," 2009). In 2005, Australia spent $12,416 per student, compared with the OECD average of $10,655 per student and the WEI average of $4,451 per student (OECD/UNESCO WEI, "Table 2.13: Annual expenditure on educational institutions per student," 2005).

As a country, contemporary Australia has to deal with the tensions between three powerful cultural streams: its responsibilities to the "first nations" of Aboriginal and Torres Strait Islander people; its largely Anglo-Saxon inheritance of public and governmental institutions; and the reality of Asian economic and cultural power. The combination poses a range of questions connected to the discussion of "southern theory" as set out in our final section. It also deeply influences the goals and strategic positioning of Australian higher education (HE).

Despite its large geographical size, Australia has a relatively small population that is highly urbanized and concentrated in certain regions of the country, mainly the Eastern seaboard. The low population density across much of Australia's land mass leads to particular issues in maintaining provision of the full range of services, including higher education, to regional, rural, and isolated communities (Department of Education, Science and Training, 2007: x).

There is significant variation among States and Territories with respect to educational participation. The Northern Territory has the lowest participation rate, being less than half the national average, while the Australian Capital Territory has a substantially higher rate than any other State or Territory. This higher participation rate for the Australian Capital Territory is largely due to students from other States and Territories attending Australian Capital Territory universities (Department of Education, Science and Training, 2007: 11).

There has been a strong and sustained focus on equity and access in higher education within Australia that involves monitoring and supporting the access, participation, success, and retention of identified equity groups. The equity groups so identified are: people from socioeconomically disadvantaged backgrounds; Aboriginal and Torres Strait Islander people; people suffering disadvantage because of gender; people with disabilities; people from non-English speaking backgrounds; and people from rural and isolated areas. Generally, participation in higher education by equity groups has remained relatively stable. While access for those with a disability rose in 2005, access for other target groups declined marginally. Preliminary student data for the first half of 2006 showed that the number of Indigenous students grew by 7% from 7,000 in the first half of 2005 to 7,500 in the first half of 2006 (Department of Education, Science and Training, 2007: xii).

The total number of students in higher education from rural and isolated areas has grown steadily since 1991. In 2004, rural students constituted 17% of domestic students and isolated students were 1% (a total of 18% from rural and isolated areas). This compares with approximately 30% of the Australian population living in rural areas and isolated areas, thus demonstrating that participation by rural and isolated students is less than expected from their population share. Put simply, current estimates suggest that, on a per capita basis, for every 10 urban people who attend university, there are roughly six Australians from rural or isolated areas (Department of Education, Science and Training, 2007: 23).

Universities are established legislatively by the States (each institution has its own "law"), although (following a Faustian pact between university leaders and the government) largely funded by the Commonwealth (national government). As summarized by the representative body (Universities Australia):

> Apart from the Australian National University, which is constituted under an Act of the Federal Parliament, all of Australia's universities are established or recognized under State or Territory legislation.
>
> The Federal Government has principal responsibility for public funding of the 37 public universities, although universities are increasingly seeking funds from the wider community, in part as a result of the Government's stated intention to alter the public-private funding mix for universities.
>
> The formal governing body of each Australian university is the Council, Senate or Board of Governors, presided over by a Chancellor elected by the members of the governing body. Members are drawn from government, industry, the community, academic staff, graduates and students.
>
> The chief executive authority rests with the Vice-Chancellor (increasingly also called the President), who is accountable to the Council, Senate

or Board of Governors and is responsible for the academic and administrative operation of the institution.

(see: www.universitiesaustralia.edu.au/content.asp?page=/
universities/overview.htm).

Along with the United States and the United Kingdom, Australia is one of the top three countries recruiting students from overseas, and has probably approached these markets most systematically and aggressively.

At the time of writing, Australia is preparing for a snap election (in August 2010). It is unclear how the outcome will affect higher education, which has recently (since 2008) been subject to a number of "reviews" (e.g., the "Bradley Review of Australian Higher Education"), together with related investigations into support for research and innovation, as well as student unionism. The expectations, based on current (Labour) government policy, are that the system will be allowed to continue to expand (with the modification of an "over-enrolment cap"—together with the removal of an "under-enrolment" safety-net) but with a strong emphasis on meeting equity targets.

Australia is the only country in our sample that contributes three profiles. Together they cover the full spectrum, from Melbourne (the only unambiguously "elite" or "apex" institution, recognized in "world-class" league tables); through Western Sydney (a strong regional and comprehensive university taking responsibility for the full range of tertiary education requirements in a locality); to the "frontier" challenges of the Northern Territory met by Charles Darwin University (the Territory's only university).

Two-Way Learning

Profile of Charles Darwin University (Australia)
By David Watson (based on field visit August 13 and 14, 2009)

Origins and History

Charles Darwin University (CDU) is the only university in Australia's Northern Territory (NT). It was founded in 2003 from four existing tertiary institutions. Its founding Vice-Chancellor, Professor Helen Garnett, described it as working in a "tough environment." This remains true, on all of the possible dimensions: social, economic, political, cultural and physical. Its nine campuses serve over 170 communities across the Territory, including the provision of Mobile Adult Learning Units (MALUs). Current Vice-Chancellor, Professor Barney Glover, states that "we are everywhere" throughout the Territory.

Professor Glover also points to the "deep sense of ownership" the community has towards the University. This is partly connected with political aspirations for statehood; it is even more grounded in a sense that the University holds the key to important aspects of economic and social development. As part of the self-styled "top end" of the country, it has national strategic importance, including as a gateway into Asia (notably through East Timor and Indonesia).

Research is strongly focused on what is relevant to the region. Stable and high-performing programs have been established in the following areas:

- Natural and Cultural Resource Management
- Human Health and Wellbeing
- Teaching, Learning and Living
- Community, Development and Identity.

Learning and Teaching has rapidly developed over the past five years to incorporate distance learning and to respond to community needs for flexible study (including to fit in with work and family responsibilities). As part of its overall strategic plan, CDU has adopted the following definition of community engagement: "Community Engagement is key to all of CDU's activities, characterized by two-way relationships in which the University forms partnerships with its communities to yield mutually beneficial outcomes."

Linda Cuttriss is Coordinator of Community Engagement. She described her role as "brokering across a very broad canvas." Working with a Secondary Schools Liaison Officer and Remote Field Officers, she is both the first point of contact and the progress-chaser and "closer" for the myriad individuals and groups who see working with the University as a source of assistance. Through her efforts, and those of her colleagues, CDU has become one of the leaders of the national dialogue about community engagement, not least by hosting the AUCEA Conference in Alice Springs in 2007.

Closing the Gap

A total of 30% of the NT's 210,000 population are Indigenous Australians. In 30 years, it is predicted that they will constitute a majority of its citizens. Of CDU's student body of 18,000, approximately 4,000 are Indigenous (matching this proportion), but only 400 of these are on higher education courses. Only 5% of the staff are Indigenous. The University's collaboration with the Batchelor Institute for Indigenous Tertiary Education, including creating on campus the Australian Centre for Indigenous Knowledge and Education, is designed to tackle this gap. In the words of its longstanding strategic alliance with the Northern Territory Government (NTG), one of CDU's main missions is to "close the gap" between Indigenous and non-Indigenous educational outcomes and life-chances. This agreement is now in its third iteration, covering the years 2007–2012. Rachel Shanahan described her experience in the NTG Secretariat with responsibility for the partnership, as highly positive, while noting some of the predictable points of occasional tension: around intellectual property, infrastructure, different language and building government–university relations further down both organizations.

The University's own *Futures Framework*, running from 2007–2016 was described by Senior Deputy Vice-Chancellor Charles Webb as covering five areas, in which performance will be carefully benchmarked:

- Indigenous participation and relevance, combined with a focus on "what it means to be a student in this community" (including through compulsory "common foundation units" such as "Northern Perspectives"), as well as a drive for "community-based learning in the curriculum";
- Pathways for learning—in particular, flexing the University's comprehensive vocational as well as academic curriculum and awards to "scaffold" both progress and changes of direction for individuals;
- Professional, globally-orientated education and training—in a context of rapid expansion of external and distance learning, and including means to draw such students into felt membership of the university community;
- Doing relevant research;
- A strong commitment to "being good at partnerships"—both within and beyond the territory (natural alliances are not only with Batchelor and the organs of government, but also on research and development with Australian National, Adelaide, James Cook and Flinders Universities).

A total of 25% of the NT population also "churns" each year; largely as a result of short stays by professional and higher income families. Of the university-age population, 20% chooses undergraduate study outside the state (not least because of perceptions of comparative quality), although in the Australian context, this is not an unusually high number for "out of catchment area" enrollment (CDU is, of course, the only university-level option in the NT). The University has ambitious plans to develop a private senior secondary school on its campus in Darwin, with a private partner, in order to provide options for what could be called the "oil and gas parents" who are both prosperous and potentially mobile. This will open in 2011.

The "Helping Professions"

A total of 50% of the CDU student load is in courses preparing for the "helping professions." Some 70% are female and the same proportion part-time and mature (over the age of 25); 80% of them are based outside the capital of Darwin. In the words of Paul Fitzsimons, Director of RemoteLink and responsible for CDU's extensive footprint throughout the NT, "the school-leavers are not a significant cohort" for the University overall. Bill Wade, Head of the School of Creative Arts and the Humanities, described the institution as a kind of "Open University," and distance and external study has certainly grown apace. David Price, Coordinator of the Law course, explained how 90% of his students were online "all over the world" while also pointing to how this discriminates against communities without broadband access.

This academic agenda, together with the University's drive to improve educational standards and reputation in a geographically, socially, culturally and economically complex environment, necessitates working in partnership. Retiring PVC Don Zoellner (whose portfolio responsibility for Community Engagement will pass to Professor Webb) described the historical success of working in "niches" and of a "loose-tight" management structure. In this way, the University has been able to make use of its "devolved identity" (the legacy of the nine campuses), to respond to change in an agile fashion, and to allow individuals to take responsibility for what are necessarily highly context-specific negotiations and outcomes.

Professor Sandra Dunn and Dr Greg Rickards are Co-Directors of the Graduate School for Health Practice, founded in 2005, as a joint initiative by CDU and the Northern Territory Department for Health and Families (DHF). They described a dramatic success story of improving professional standards, improving retention and delivering targeted services, as well international engagements in Samoa, East Timor and Papua New Guinea.

Not all subject areas can keep up at the moment. Partners working with some undergraduate courses expressed frustration, principally about issues related to resources. Sue Moore of Centrelink and Tony Barnes of the Department of Health and Families—both of whom are responsible for the supervision and induction of social workers—spoke of the pressure caused by vacancy rates and low student recruitment (although this is improving)—and the desire for more professional contact with University staff. Graeme Owen of the Department of Natural Resources, Environment, The Arts and Sport (NRETAS), who recruits both students and graduates to work in land-use mapping in particular, welcomed their technical skills in a field that has become significantly more sophisticated, but spoke of the supervisory burden associated with developing their essential "time in position." Debbie Hall of the NT Branch of CPA Australia (Certified Practicing Accountants) again regretted the missed opportunities for joint work with academic accountants, and the relative lack of preparation for professional life of international students in particular. Lorraine Corowa of the Department of Regional Development (and herself a CDU graduate, postgraduate student and member of a Course Advisory Group) was more positive about projects that had been achieved with students and staff, especially through individual contacts. The group sympathized with pressures on the University staff and students—notably around the high cost of living and student debt (and the need to work while studying)—and supported the attempts to leverage further CDU's unique location and role.

Other partners, who supplied written evidence, included Kelly Parker from "Good Beginnings Australia" who wrote about the high quality of the University team supporting the "Let's Start" program for young children experiencing difficulties in socialization (and their parents), and Marcus Finn from the Commonwealth Scientific and Research Organization (CSIRO) about the powerful and longstanding collaboration on Tropical Rivers and Coastal Knowledge (TRaCK). Dr Finn wrote in particular about the value of the partnership with CDU in helping with both "funding and the visibility of the research to the broader public."

Managing Expectations

One of the by-products of our discussion of partnership working was a detailed discussion of issues arising through and from work with Indigenous communities. Most importantly, as Paul Fitzsimons advised, it is necessary to "take the university from a deficit model of aiming to solve the poor education standards in communities towards empowering those communities." Bill Wade also spoke of the power of education in the arts and humanities as "avenues towards reconciliation."

Key elements of such partnership working include:

- the presumption of "two-way learning," from the community into the university as well as vice versa;
- the importance of negotiating protocols;
- the need for imagination in applying and "re-profiling" funding streams (e.g., in getting past an external drive towards "training for training's sake" into what are much more important sources of community cohesion and progress, such as confidence, health and wellbeing);
- the necessity of creating paid employment opportunities for community members.

Professor Michael Christie has been working for over 15 years on a program of Yolngu Studies, with the communities of North-east Arnhem Land. Matthew Campbell and Professor Michael Christie have produced a detailed guide to *Indigenous community engagement* (CDU 2008). This report details some of the unique elements of engaging with Indigenous communities, including how different traditions of knowledge making must be acknowledged and accommodated if the university is to achieve the mutual benefit community engagement promises.

Another powerful example is the School of Education's "Growing Our Own" program, as outlined by Alison Elliot, Head of the School. This joint project between Catholic Education NT and the School is designed to boost the number of Indigenous teachers working in remote communities. It draws particularly on existing teaching assistants and other support workers within the communities to enable them to continue working in their own schools while experiencing the benefits of mainstream professional teacher education. Professor Elliot spoke of the essential element of "shared design" in the development of this course, which took over 12 months of consultation.

"Dual Sector" Provision

CDU stretches the definition of a classic "dual sector institution," i.e. bridging the gap between technical and vocational, "further" education, and higher education. The University runs courses all the way from Certificate Level 1 (e.g., English language for immigrants) to PhD Graduation ceremonies on the University's main campus characteristically include students and their families from across this spectrum. It is a Registered Training Organization (RTO) and provides 85% of the vocational education and training (VET) in the NT.

Student Engagement

In the absence of a Student union (these were dissolved by federal legislation in 2006), the University has supported the student body in using the Talloires Network as an organizational device. The "CDU Talloires" student group, which meets weekly in term-time, has operated on a number of fronts. I met with a core group who described an impressive set of projects. These ranged from Law student Kevin Kardirgamar's leadership of a "Model UN" (drawing in international students to work with those from many communities of the territory), through a global poverty day, to a proposed "community garden" (for which significant resources—in cash and kind—have already been secured). They have made good contact with students in other Talloires universities, including face-to-face at the Clinton Global Initiative (CGI) International Conference in New Orleans in March 2008.

They also described connections with their academic work. Maria Kambouris —now undertaking a Masters by Research, and a CGI award-winner—had developed her work from "life-memory resource books" (to assist dementia patients and their younger carers) out of a placement on her Social Work course, and was exploring its wider significance in the community. Several were studying the University's new course in Humanitarian and Community Studies, described by Dan Baschiera, its academic leader, as the "first in Australia," with a unique mixture of academic ("questioning the political contract") and practical work (the latter involving placements throughout the Territory, Australia, and overseas). Student Matt Haubrick spoke of how working with the Talloires group had "broadened and filled in" his course. Anjea Travers (who is working one day a week on the community garden project) talked of how it provided a source of "hope and positivity" and had given students the confidence to pursue their own ideas.

Cultural Services

CDU's main campus is described by the Vice-Chancellor as a "vibrant cultural precinct." It supports cultural activities across a broad range: from western music (it hosts the Darwin Symphony Orchestra—just celebrating its 20th anniversary), a variety of youth music and arts initiatives, and a distinguished scholarly and curatorial contribution to aboriginal art. An example of the latter is the University's support of the annual Garma Festival: one of Australia's most significant cultural exchange events, which has won several awards. This is a powerful cultural affirmation of the University's development of its relationship with the Yolngu people of North-east Arnhem land referred to above.

Conclusions

There is still a distinct "frontier" quality to many of the challenges facing CDU, now supplemented by a sense of contributing to a national project of knowledge enhancement and application. CDU's value to the comparative analysis of the project rests on three of its distinctive characteristics.

First, there is the major commitment to serving the interests of an Aboriginal and Torres Strait Island population, described by the former Batchelor Institute Vice-Chancellor Professor Jeannie Herbert (interviewed on August 17) as "a group without a voice." CDU's commitment is, of course, to facilitating such a voice. This is maintained alongside meeting the needs of a number of other communities and accepting an obligation to a "comprehensive" higher education institution with a national as well as a regional presence.

Second, there is the acceptance of a fully-fledged "tertiary" agenda. CDU operates enthusiastically from "entry" to postgraduate level. As a result, there are significant challenges of "joining-up" the contributory elements, and of overcoming dead-ends.

Third, there is the commitment to a rich variety of cultural streams. This confirms an approach to academic activities across the spectrum of teaching, research and service underpinned by a philosophy of "two-way learning" that is exemplified but not exclusively confined to Indigenous education.

Sharing Knowledge

Profile of the University of Melbourne (Australia)
By David Watson (based on field visit August 10 and 11, 2009)

Origins and History

The University of Melbourne (founded 1853) vies for status with the University of Sydney (founded 1852) as Australia's most prestigious university. Its current Act (1958) is unusual in explicitly combining state, national, and contexts for its work. The objects include: "to undertake scholarship, research and research training of international standing and to apply that scholarship and research to the advancement of knowledge and to the benefit of the well-being of the Victorian, Australian and international communities."

The University of Melbourne is a huge presence: locally, regionally, and nationally. This is reflected in its economic, cultural, and physical presence. It has over 7,000 full-time equivalent staff, approximately 46,000 students, and a budget turnover of Aus$1.5bn. With this power comes a number of dilemmas:

- How to respond to the range and depth of expectations, inside and outside
- A presumption of leadership, and of being a role model
- The possibility of unintended as well as intended impact of policy and practice
- The power of tradition.

In other words, the University has an immense capacity to make a difference; it also has a potential in-built resistance to change.

Being There

In these circumstances, the University plays a major role in what is described as "first order engagement" with society: "just being there" (Watson, 2007: 132–133). The Vice-Chancellor, Professor Glyn Davis, describes it as a "public-spirited university." In the University's 10-year strategy (from 2005), *Growing Esteem*, this idea is unpacked as follows:

> As a public-spirited institution, Melbourne declares its intention to make research, student learning and external engagement serve public ends. This includes taking up pressing societal problems in research, producing graduates prepared for responsibility and promoting inquiry and open debate based on evidence and reason.

Professor Davis concedes that the result is a "slightly different" strategic approach to community engagement from many of the Talloires signatories, identifying less direct focus on social inclusion and civic relations, and more detailed attention to elements such as the following:

- the "scholarly end" of institutional presence—i.e. libraries, collections and galleries rather than professional sport;
- a "suite of initiatives" with students;
- technology transfer as a "public good" (i.e., as more than an income stream); and
- a focus on the "community-facing role of academics."

The then Deputy Vice-Chancellor for Global Relations, Professor John Dewar, glossed this by talking about an approach to engagement based upon "enlightened self-interest." He estimated that only between 10% and 20% of external activity is connected mainly or exclusively with profile-raising (an example was the University's annual "Festival of Ideas"). The rest is deeply embedded in what he called "better and more powerful teaching and research." All of the senior staff stressed the importance of "telling the story" of this broader concept of knowledge transfer.

Partly as a consequence of reorganization of the higher education sector following the Dawkins reforms of the 1980s, the University also inherited responsibility for a small number of rural and agricultural colleges. It has kept faith with these communities not least through a series of programs with the Indigenous community in the Golburn Valley, reflecting this commitment in the establishment of the Murup Barak—Melbourne Institute for Indigenous Development (www.murrupbarak.unimelb.edu.au/), which coordinates a range of partnerships in health, sport, and education.

Knowledge Transfer

"Civic engagement and social responsibility" is incorporated in the University's current (2009) Strategic Plan under "knowledge transfer." This in turn is presented as part of a "triple helix:" a "tightly-bound set of core activities," in which "knowledge transfer" relates to both research and teaching and learning, and is defined as the university working "with communities and industry to ensure a vibrant and continuous exchange of ideas and expertise."

Knowledge Transfer (KT) is a contested concept. Some members of the University have suggested moving to the more circular, iterative associations of terms like "knowledge exchange" or "engagement." In a discussion paper on "refining" the University's strategy (May 2009), the alternative of "knowledge exchange" is mooted, not least because it "avoids the 'social service' flavor of expressions such as 'community engagement.'" Helen Hayes, Executive Director of Knowledge Transfer and Partnerships has established a taxonomy of purposes for KT at the University, which incorporates the following examples:

- to foster partnerships to advance research;
- to foster partnerships that enhance teaching and learning;
- to enhance students' readiness for professional life;
- to raise aspirations for tertiary study;
- to produce cultural engagements;
- to develop the standing and practices of the profession;
- to develop better policy and governance;
- to commercialize our intellectual capital;
- to attract additional funding;
- to foster intellectual discourse and knowledge dissemination;
- to meet our responsibility to the greater public good;
- to improve our reputation and public standing.

Outcomes will often be in terms of genuinely cross-university initiatives (Professor Phil Batterham spoke of the VC's success in creating a "situation in which the walls just don't exist"). A powerful such case is the multiprofessional, multi-disciplinary initiative to examine and contribute to Bushfire Recovery, incorporating working groups on: reconstructing the built environment; environmental renewal; health, wellbeing and education in communities; and policy and governance.

Professor John Wiseman, Director of the McCaughey Centre, and his colleagues have suggested "knowledge translation and exchange," as a further alternative to KT, reflecting the current interest in "translational research." The Centre—supported by the Victorian Health Promotion Foundation (VicHealth) and the University's Faculty of Medicine, Dentistry and Health Sciences—is a prime example of what can be achieved by "boundary-spanning," especially through "consultative and collaborative work with external partners." The Centre also hosts the "Community Indicators Victoria" project, which collects and integrates a set of indicators on community wellbeing across the state.

Contribution to activities like these is now incorporated in both annual reviews for staff and promotion criteria.

Several interviewees reflected on the fact that the current strategy—and notably the KT aspect—is a work in progress. There are cold as well as hot spots, and in some places the double-helix of research and teaching continues to trump the triple variant.

The "Melbourne Model" and "Academic Enrichment"

Students at Melbourne are now recruited to the "Melbourne Model" of the curriculum: a two-cycle framework which concentrates on breadth of knowledge as well as disciplinary depth at the undergraduate level (in 3-year Bachelor's courses) and professional and vocational application (through 2-year Masters). Significantly, this is designed to be compliant with the Bologna agreements on the mutual recognition of European degrees. The first students were recruited in 2006 and the full array of first and second cycle courses will be in place in 2011. One consequence is intended to be that graduates have a rounded set of "graduate attributes," as set out below.

Another strong focus is on an institution-wide goal of "academic enrichment." The Australian Universities Quality Agency (AUQA) has already indicated that it will wish to examine these aspects of the Melbourne Model when they undertake their periodic audit next year.

Professor Phil Batterham, Associate Dean of the Faculty of Science, outlined how these priorities were affecting the student experience within his Faculty and across the University. In particular he stressed how only two of the desirable graduate attributes could be delivered within the lecture hall or laboratory. The

TABLE 5.1 Attributes of the Melbourne Graduate

Academically excellent:
  Have a strong sense of intellectual integrity and the ethics of scholarship
  Have in-depth knowledge of their specialist discipline(s)
  Reach a high level of achievement in writing, generic research activities,
  problem-solving and communication
  Be critical and creative thinkers, with an aptitude for continued self-directed learning
  Be adept at learning in a range of ways, including through information and
  communication technologies
Knowledgeable across disciplines:
  Examine critically, synthesize and evaluate knowledge across a broad range of
  disciplines
  Expand their analytical and cognitive skills through learning experiences in diverse
  subjects
  Have the capacity to participate fully in collaborative learning and to confront
  unfamiliar problems
  Have a set of flexible and transferable skills for different types of employment
Leaders in communities:
  Initiate and implement constructive change in their communities, including
  professions and workplaces
  Have excellent interpersonal and decision-making skills, including an awareness of
  personal strengths and limitations
  Mentor future generations of learners
  Engage in meaningful public discourse, with a profound awareness of community needs
Attuned to cultural diversity:
  Value different cultures
  Be well-informed citizens able to contribute to their communities wherever they
  choose to live and work
  Have an understanding of the social and cultural diversity in our community
  Respect indigenous knowledge, cultures and values
Active global citizens:
  Accept social and civic responsibilities
  Be advocates for improving the sustainability of the environment
  Have a broad global understanding, with a high regard for human rights,
  equity and ethics.

From the Learning & Teaching Management Plan (UGC 2007).

University has been both imaginative and entrepreneurial in developing such opportunities. For example, Professor Batterham explained how it became the first university to develop a structured relationship with the Duke of Edinburgh's Award Scheme, in recording and accrediting student service activities.

Pat McLean, Director of Student Enrichment Services, and Di Rachinger, General Manager of Student Engagement, explained the pattern of support for programs and initiatives. They explained how the goal was to ensure that "all students have some extra-curricular experience."

We reflected together on the three senses in which "student engagement" is discussed in the research literature—as engagement with the other members of the university community, with the community outside, and with academic study—and noted the sense of mutual reinforcement between these that the University sought to inculcate. Prime examples are the longstanding Student Ambassador Leadership Program (SALP) and the recent consolidation of related activities into LIVE (the Leadership, Involvement and Volunteer Experience Unit). I discussed with Richmond Glasgow, the President of the Melbourne chapter of SIFE (Students in Free Enterprise) how students have responded. He not only told a moving personal story of how he found the opportunity to contribute part way through his course, but also reported the strength of the University's support—administratively as well as through Faculty advisors. He confirmed that the University's "branding" of the Melbourne Model—under the heading "Dream-Large" (and seeking to attract students who "want to change the world")—has real resonance among the student body.

There is further early evidence that the new curricular model is changing the pattern of student application and enrollment. Numbers from private schools have declined, and the "inter-state" undergraduate enrollment (including a number of highly-qualified students from deprived backgrounds) has increased to 20% (a remarkably high figure for Australia).

Choosing Partners

Vice-Chancellor Davis confirms that the University "doesn't enter into partnerships lightly." With the professional input of the Knowledge Transfer and Partnerships Office a disciplined methodology is applied to current activity and future options to assess both strategic fit with the priorities of the University and sustainable mutual benefit. Notably strong current examples are with:

- The Federal Defense, Science and Technology Organization (DSTO—especially in modeling current and long term security concerns);
- IBM (focusing on four project areas of Water, Life Sciences, Learning Spaces, and Technology for Emergency Response);
- The City of Melbourne, and especially the Carlton Community (where the University is located);
- World Vision (on a range of themes including Global Health, Economic Development, and Aid/Development Policy);
- The Brotherhood of St Laurence (notably on early childhood interventions); and
- Department of Health and Department of Human Services North and West Metropolitan Region.

Looking to the future, Professor Dewar pointed to the potential for University participation in systematic but fluid "clusters" of collaboration and co-location with external enterprises, very much along the lines of the UK's National Endowment for Science Technology and the Arts' (NESTA) report on the "connected university" (*The Connected University: Driving Growth and Recovery in the UK Economy* April 2009).

I discussed the role of the University within the Carlton Connected Community Group link with its Chair, Susanna Bevilacqua of the Bendigo Bank. Putting this group's activities alongside the City government's coordination of the "opportunities for Carlton" project several themes come together from the University perspective: sensitivity to the needs of the neighborhood; academic leadership in scoping and designing interventions; student participation through volunteering and leadership programs; and coordination of a response through the Knowledge Transfer and Partnerships Office. On March 1, 2009, the Office managed "Carlton Community Day," in which community members of all ages and backgrounds were invited on to the campus, with a particular focus on residents of the nearby public housing estates, especially recently arrived people from the Horn of Africa. The objectives were to:

- make the campus more accessible to the residents of Carlton;
- break down its image as remote from the local community;
- raise aspirations for the children of attendees to become future students of the University; and
- establish a basis for an ongoing and productive relationship with the Carlton community.

Activities ran the gamut from academic "taster" sessions through drumming and face-painting. The elastic of knowledge transfer stretches a long way.

Conclusions

The University's resulting policy and performance raises a vital question for the project in comparative terms: for certain universities within the Talloires Network, is it possible for civic and community engagement successfully to be conceptualized and delivered largely as a consequence of "being there"?

The case also tests to the limit the use of "knowledge transfer" as an organizing conceptual framework for social partnership and impact.

The "Melbourne Model" represents a valuable "work-in-progress" from the perspective of liberal undergraduate education as a springboard for both thinking about and acting within a context of civic and community engagement.

Finally, Melbourne represents the only "apex" institution in our sample. It is unusual in our sample in that it has no ambition to grow further. What it wants to do, is able to do, and actually achieves in terms of community engagement, puts a marker down at one end of an internationally recognized spectrum.

Personal Declaration

I have collaborated for a number of years with members of the University of Melbourne's Centre for the Study of Higher Education (CSHE), including giving seminars and public lectures. Through the Institute of Education and its MBA in Higher Education Management, I also have a link with the L.H. Martin Institute for Leadership and Management which is hosted by the University.

A University Without Walls

Profile of the University of Western Sydney (Australia) By David Watson (based on field visit August 4 and 5, 2009)

Origins and History

The University of Western Sydney (UWS) was created in 1989 as a coalition of three existing higher education institutions across Greater Western Sydney (GWS). The oldest, an agricultural college, was formed in 1891, and the younger two in the 1970s. In 2001, the partner institutions merged, creating what is now, in government-funded student places, the fourth largest of Australia's 39 universities. Its six campuses draw from a catchment of almost 10,000 square kilometers. In the words of the Vice-Chancellor and President, Janice Reid: "The University of Western Sydney was founded to provide high quality and accessible higher education and research in a region historically under-resourced and under-valued." Its mission is captured in its motto, "Bringing Knowledge to Life". It thus has a powerful sense of both place and purpose.

There is strong evidence that it has succeeded in its aims. The Australian Universities Quality Agency (AUQA) concluded an audit in 2006 by describing it as "a university of the people." The Pro-Vice-Chancellor (Engagement), Barbara Holland, appointed in 2007, has been able to draw on scholarly and practical experience in the United States and elsewhere, to reinforce civic and community engagement as a highly distinctive feature of the University's policy, practice and performance. In its research and teaching, the University is addressing key issues of social, economic, and environmental sustainability as they affect a rapidly growing urban area.

GWS is the third largest regional economy in Australia (behind the neighboring Sydney city and Melbourne). It is one of the most culturally diverse regions in Australia, with the highest percentage of urban Indigenous residents, newly arrived refugees, and resettled migrants and their descendants in the State of New South Wales. It has significant pockets of both urban and rural deprivation, but also hosts the headquarters of 150 of the nation's largest 500 companies. It is growing quickly: Sydney's population is anticipated to grow from its present 4 million to 5.5 million in the next 15 years, and two-thirds of that growth will be in GWS. This combination of growth and diversity presents constructive challenges to an engaged university on a number of fronts, among them:

- student recruitment and widening participation;
- social justice, integration and inclusion;
- accommodating difference and diversity;
- complex local politics (with stakeholders across 14 local authorities, 28 State Parliamentary electorates, 14 federal electorates, and two federal Senators);
- substantial areas of high unemployment, poverty and social disadvantage;
- salience within the national policy framework; and
- its standing as a relatively young university.

The large footprint of the University brings benefits and challenges. Long-serving Deputy Vice-Chancellor, Rhonda Hawkins, said that its oft-cited aim of "making a difference" captures its values and has informed successive plans and budgetary decisions. UWS is one of very few universities in Australia whose legislation mentions its regional mandate. However, she also reflected on the demands of working productively with more than 40 politicians from different parties, who are important supporters and conduits to government, but can be energetic critics when they think the University has failed any of their constituents. "It's an exquisite juggling act of local interests, ideologies and expectations," she said, and also demands tactful judgment calls when election campaigns overlap with politicians' visits to campuses and advocacy for the University.

Among the several imaginative initiatives that UWS has devised to meet its challenges, the following stand out:

- A Schools Engagement Strategic Plan, which has a coordinated focus on a region of more than 900 schools and is guided by a Schools Engagement Reference Group, composed of external education leaders and stakeholders and convened quarterly.
- A Refugee Action Support program developed by teacher Loshini Naidoo, and recognized with a national citation for excellence. It currently involves 85 Master of Teaching students mentoring 200 refugee school students, primarily from war zones in the Sudan and Middle East.
- A standing University Indigenous Advisory Council and an Indigenous Engagement and Employment Advisory Board, and dedicated courses of study for Aboriginal students.
- The Whitlam Institute, which is named after the reforming Prime Minister whose electorate was in the region. It offers programs on contemporary social issues such as the "What Matters?" schools writing competition, judged by established authors, for which students are invited to write short essays on what matters to them in today's world.

- SMExcellence (www.smexcellence.com.au), a free interactive learning platform, designed and maintained by students and staff mentors. The project sets out to improve the business skills of the region's myriad small business owners and managers, estimated to be in excess of 240,000, working closely with the Commonwealth and State Governments and private sector.
- UWSCollege, a not-for-profit University-owned company that provides academic pathways into the University for students not fully prepared for first-year study and for international students who need to gain appropriate English language and study skills, as well as specific vocational courses and an Adult Migrant English Program (AMEP).
- The Badanami Centre under Dean Michael McDaniel, which coordinates outreach and support of Indigenous students and coursework on Aboriginal social history and culture for students in mainstream degrees. Badanami also offers dedicated teacher education bachelor awards for Indigenous students.
- A program to recruit Indigenous trainees and interns to work at UWS and with willing partners in industry and government, developed by its Director of Indigenous Employment, Melissa Williams, in collaboration with the elders. It provides a culturally-sensitive mentoring program and work experience for those who would otherwise struggle to enter and succeed in the workforce, encouraging them in turn to become role models for others.

The University's Research Centers embody priorities that begin with the region and its needs, notably:

- Cultural Research;
- Contemporary Muslim Societies;
- Plant and Food Science;
- Urban Research;
- Citizenship and Public Policy;
- Complementary [including traditional Chinese] Medicine;
- Civionics Research;
- Educational Research; and
- Auditory and Cognitive Research.

The Pro-Vice-Chancellor (Research), Andrew Cheetham, estimated that together these Centers supported 360 jointly-funded collaborative projects with community, industry and government, and many more applied research partnerships primarily resourced by UWS.

It is significant that the University incorporates a Medical School, which opened in 2007. The Vice-Chancellor has stressed the politically contingent nature of the sudden decision of the Commonwealth Government to fund its establishment, rather than increasing student numbers in the two long-established medical schools in the city. The rapid development of this new facility not only rounds out the comprehensive nature of the UWS engagement portfolio, but also recognizes UWS' public responsibility to respond to the urgent shortage of doctors, especially within the GWS region.

Unlike the more prosperous eastern part of the Sydney basin, the region has always suffered acute shortages of general practitioners and medical specialists, and, consequently, over-stretched health services. One of the factors considered in assessing applications from prospective medical students is a demonstrated understanding of, and commitment to, the region and its health challenges. This has resulted in up to 70% of students each year coming from the region and praise from experienced clinical teachers for their commitment, educated common sense and ease with the varied patients they meet in hospital and community settings.

In its present form, the University is celebrating its 20th anniversary. Its prehistory is, however, important. The Deputy Vice-Chancellor (Academic and Enterprise), John Ingleson, describes how, for at least two decades before its establishment, the local community "knew that they wanted a university," and lobbied hard for it. They now take palpable political and community pride in "our" university. It is also his view that one of the challenges for the University is to overcome a "dated" view of what it can offer, particularly in comparison with long-established universities, as its standing, and the breadth of its disciplines and research continue to grow. In this context, the Dean of the College of Arts, Wayne McKenna, emphasized the reality and importance of having a "mission-driven university," that regards its mandate as opening the doors to higher education for many who would otherwise not have the chance to study at university.

Strategic Integration

UWS attempts to meet these challenges by ensuring that the priority and practice of engagement is thoroughly embedded across its strategic objectives and carefully monitored. It is described as a "whole of university agenda." The Pro-Vice-Chancellor (Quality), Geoff Scott, emphasized what he called the "triple bottom line" of "social, economic and environmental sustainability," and the University's responsibility as one of the largest organizations in the region to model best practice in infrastructure development and greening of its campuses and work environment.

The Director of the Urban Research Centre, Phillip O'Neill, put the integration and sense of mutual reinforcement well when he described his and his colleagues' responsibility for "research, professional training, and public discourse." The Centre was formed *de novo* to bring greatly needed educational expertise and applied research in urban planning and management to the region. Recently, for instance, it was commissioned to provide advice for the development of strategies to generate 280,000 net additional jobs in GWS by 2030, to support the re-engineering of the region's urban structure away from a job-poor sprawl towards economic competitiveness and an improved quality of life.

At the same time, the University's approach to developing teaching and research which is engaged is to consolidate and focus on a carefully selected set of over-arching themes. These are intended to draw on expertise and resources across the University and to promote step-wise and strategic "multi-year" initiatives. At present they focus on:

- schools;
- the environment;
- cultural understanding; and
- small and medium-sized enterprises.

However, these areas of focus do not limit the freedom of academic staff nor the efforts of the University to pursue a wide array of community engagement activities. To capture these, a sophisticated tool for "Tracking and Integrating Community Engagement" (TICE) has been developed to record the great diversity of "academic partnerships" in teaching and research, as well as "public service" activities. A second instrument to capture community partner feedback and impact data is under development. Geoff Scott underlined the drive across the University for robust "user-centered data" to support continuous improvement and the measurement of outcomes.

"Making the Difference"

One of the strategic goals of the university is that there should be "experiential learning in every course of study." It is well on the way. The College of Business has incorporated "engaged" units into its largest undergraduate courses, which will see the current cohort of more than 5,000 students undertake a work-related community project in their final year of study.

The School of Education also requires its students to undertake community service placements in schools or working with young people that are additional to their standard classroom teaching practices. These include, for example, tutoring in community homework centers, assisting with gifted and talented student education programs, mentoring disadvantaged youth in leadership, buddying with students of non-English speaking backgrounds to increase their academic and cultural skills in the Australian setting, working with children with special needs and helping with primary-to-high-school transition programs.

The testimony and evidence of students, staff and community partners underline the "engagement" dimension of this educational priority. They also affirm that it is a two-way street: the University is as keen to learn from the community as it is to take its skills and knowledge outside. It is the spirit in which students have begun working with the "Street University," a not-for-profit drop-in centre for disengaged young people in one of the poorer city neighborhoods. It is this objective of mutual benefit and genuine partnership that characterizes the UWS engagement agenda.

A powerful example is the contribution over the past eight years to the "Students in Free Enterprise" scheme (SIFE). Somewhat at odds with its name, SIFE is part of "Learning through Community Service," an elective academic subject open to UWS undergraduates in nearly all programs, where teams of students undertake one- or two-semester community projects in areas as diverse as empowering children to "read for life," running school drama and performance programs, working in community language centers and helping young refugees and newly-arrived migrants understand their educational and employment options. As explained by students Lauren Chapman and Marny Yu and their academic mentor, Diana Whitton, the UWS SIFE operates not only with local and regional groups (like "résumé rescue" for recently arrived migrant groups and "pins and needles" for an African sewing group) but also international projects, such as raising funds for a school in Ghana or helping to sell Cambodian women's handicrafts in Australia.

Similar projects are also directly bound into the curriculum across many disciplines. Ned Doyle, an academic staff member in Marketing, described how his course marshals over 200 students in teams of five to help local enterprises (including some not-for-profits) with their promotion and marketing functions. Computing students spend 120 hours each helping local schools and not-for-profits with IT systems operation and maintenance.

During the site visit, a group of 10 students from across the University reflected on the pattern of self-interest and altruism involved in these types of curriculum-based engagement activities. They saw themselves as both contributing to and learning from the community. They also valued a "grown-up" relationship with their teachers, born of working alongside them in many of these projects. Anna Krjatian, a media and arts student who had worked in television through the University's community TV station said "they treat us like equals."

The reach of the University is wider than just the region. For instance, the University hosted Australia's 2009 *Power Shift* Conference in partnership with the Australian Youth Climate Coalition. This was one of a series of national conferences held across the world in the lead-up to the UN Climate Change conference in Copenhagen in December 2009. UWS media students filmed the speakers and their material was uploaded to You Tube, bringing the highlights to youth across the world.

Reflecting the multicultural mix of the Sydney population, UWS also hosts the Aurora Music Festival which celebrates music composed by people from the wide range of communities and language groups in Sydney. In the *Cantata Project*, Associate Professor Hart Cohen worked with the Ntaria Indigenous Ladies Choir in central Australia to bring a cantata in the Aboriginal Aranda language to the Sydney Opera House, which was filmed by the ABC, the national public broadcaster and beamed to a national audience.

Additionally, many students volunteer for community service activities where no academic credit is involved, recognizing the benefits to the community, the university and their own personal and professional development. Students from a range of disciplines became volunteer mentors to senior high school Indigenous students in 2009 because they wanted to learn more about Indigenous culture, and make a positive difference to local Indigenous communities.

One of the explicit goals of the University is to foster student self-confidence, especially in those whose opportunities have been limited. For example, Robyn McGuiggan explained how the University's Parramatta Community Law Clinic, working in partnership with local law firms and with the patronage of the Attorney-General's Department provides experience for students whose background might not provide the social capital to find placements themselves in private law firms. They in turn support and advise, under the supervision of qualified volunteer lawyers and their teachers, clients who lack the resources to commission legal advice. Such experiences mean, as Julianne Christie, Senior Policy Advisor for Economic Development at one local government Council (and herself a UWS graduate) stated, "UWS graduates hit the ground running."

Tom Urry, the Regional Director of the South-west Sydney region of the State's Department of Education and Training (DET) described a "genuine partnership" with the University, "not a master-servant relationship." His counterpart from Western Sydney DET Region, Gregory Prior, observed that "the University had read the demographics and responded appropriately." John DeCourcy, a senior Catholic education manager and member of the UWS Schools Reference Group, talked about "a real partnership," not least in the areas of innovation and pedagogical development. From the UWS side, Anne McLean, the Manager of Schools Engagement has outlined how a "trusted relationship" had been built up, based both on over 160 successful projects and the use of the Schools Engagement Reference Group to explore together emerging and often complex or difficult educational issues.

The University and its partners are prepared to take shared responsibility for tough and sometimes intractable issues. One such issue is the perceived deficit in mathematical and scientific skills among students at all levels and in the workforce. Mark Grady, the Coordinator of Lachlan Macquarie College, a specialist secondary college of DET in Western Sydney, described how the University and College work together on STEM (Science, Technology, Engineering and Mathematics) programs for school students, university students, school teachers and faculty members.

An "International Framework"

UWS is a proudly multicultural institution. Its student body (domestic and international) comprises students from 170 countries. It is one of the most ethnically and religiously diverse communities in Australia. Alongside the more than 4,000 international students, a third of the Australian students are from non-English speaking backgrounds. Across both groups about 10% are Muslim. In recognition of international tensions and in order to build trust and respect locally, the University has created a collaborative Muslim Harmony Group and, among other initiatives, funds a community Iftar feast at the end of Ramadan each year. Its undergraduate prospectus states that the University is "about the community and making a difference all over the world." In the words of John Ingleson, "we must ensure that UWS develops graduates with a strong sense of global citizenship."

A University or a "System"?

The six campuses of the University are not only widely spread throughout the region, but are also the sole higher education providers. They take their "neighborhood" role seriously, with a senior staff member appointed as "Provost" to each to look after not only campus life but also local community liaison. Genevieve Savundranayagam, a postgraduate student working on a civic engagement strategy for the Medical School, pointed to the symbolism of the removal of perimeter fences, which had previously seemed to "protect" and separate the Campbelltown campus (in one of the region's most deprived areas) from its neighbors.

These campuses are also one of the University's major economic assets, together comprising a land bank of approximately 1,850 hectares. This provides significant opportunities for partnership development. For example, the University has numerous community "tenants" and activities on its sites, and is involved with the new Western Sydney Australian Rules Football national franchise for development projects on and off campus with future players, support staff and the junior squads. UWS also works across the full tertiary range, from VET (Vocational Education and Training) in its affiliated pathways college and educational linkages with public technical colleges, to post-graduate and doctoral studies. Putting this alongside its various engagement activities it is emphatically an "all-through-life" learning institution.

National Leadership and National Policy

Janice Reid has been one of the strongest advocates for community-oriented higher education, and is a staunch critic of the "implied stratification" which seeks to present the 'third wave' universities formed in the federal reforms of the late 1980s, often in the less prosperous urban frontiers or rural locations, as being of lesser status. She described the fitful emergence of a national movement in the direction of greater recognition of outward-facing university missions that was now gaining strength, not least because of a stronger alignment with current national political priorities. Both she and Barbara Holland played key roles in establishing in 2004 and then hosting the Australian Universities Community

Engagement Alliance (AUCEA) at UWS. AUCEA has attracted most Australian universities to its membership and is now working to recruit international members, particularly in Asia, through the Talloires Network.

Such a generous and widely applicable definition of university engagement does not, in the view of UWS, yet animate national policy nor, notably, funding for higher education. They have felt somewhat embattled against a highly traditional definition that focuses almost exclusively on "knowledge exchange" (and within that broad field on "technology transfer" or commercialization), but see a growing acceptance throughout the Australian sector of the need for a sharper focus on knowledge partnerships which align university expertise with community needs, challenges and concerns.

In responding to the sweeping 2008 Federal Review of Higher Education the Labor government declared that it would expect 20% of university students to come from disadvantaged backgrounds and 40% of Australians aged 25–34 to have a degree by 2025. UWS already exceeds the national target for students from low socioeconomic backgrounds. One-third of the students are aged over 25, and 40% are the first in their families to go to university (the latter is also true of 52% of its first 100,000 graduates). Some expressed a concern that the belated designation (with a change of Government in 2007) of the recruitment of disadvantaged students as a funded national priority, might favor those universities that are well below this target but can mobilize various strategies, notably monetary, to attract such students.

Conclusions

The main value of the UWS case to the project in comparative terms lies in its disciplined and thoroughly committed focus on civic and community engagement with the State of New South Wales and region (Greater Western Sydney), guided by a strategic engagement agenda embedded in teaching and research and supported by staff and dedicated funding. This is the lens through which all parts of the University view excellence. It thus represents a worked example of Rosabeth Moss Kanter's model of "world-classness" as achieved through "thriving locally" (Kanter, 1997).

Nor is there any evidence that this is a "default" or "second-best" choice. John Ingleson spoke of an explicit effort to encourage University members and their advocates to "stop apologizing" and to recognize the national leadership provided by the University. The proposition is that pursuing both equity and excellence in education and research is a fundamental, rational and achievable objective. (The Vice-Chancellor refers to this as "bi-modal" and HE as "twin-track".) Several members of the University reflected that the mass media conspired to make this difficult, regarding GWS as "the badlands," reporting almost exclusively on crime and sport and privileging higher education stories from more traditional universities closer to Sydney's Central Business District (CBD) and to the newspaper and commercial TV headquarters. However, the Head of the School of Communication Arts, Lynette Sheridan-Burns, put the point about UWS distinctiveness differently: following a classic design adage, she said, "if you can't hide it, you make a feature of it," drawing on the rich tapestry of people and places in the region. Stuart Campbell also referred to the University's growing reputation among young people: "our viral marketing is good." The Director of the Whitlam Institute, Eric Sidoti, stated that from his point of view, "the University is very brave", in nailing its colors to the mast of social responsibility, public scholarship and research partnerships. These comments reflect a University-wide determination to pursue its vision, even if this means at times going it alone.

A second striking feature is what was referred to by several interviewees as a "whole of university approach." Engagement is widely understood as core business of the University. A further key example of this would be the approach to the Indigenous community, which the Dean, Michael McDaniel, contrasted with that of other universities, describing it as responding to "guidance and leadership all across the University," in order that it should "not be about the education of Aboriginals; it's about the education of the nation."

A third strong theme is their contribution to what we call in our concluding chapter the "public service alliance". It was acknowledged that this also entails reputational risk, but is pivotal to the institution's role in educating future generations of professionals, such as school teachers and health professionals, and creating close alliances with public sector employers and policymakers.

Finally, there is the issue of breadth and comprehensiveness. UWS is fully prepared to work outside the conventional higher education envelope when this is indicated by a community need and, in so doing, champion the region and its future. In this sense it is genuinely, in the words of the Vice-Chancellor "a university without walls."

India and its Higher Education System

India has a population of 1.17 billion (second largest in the world), an average life expectancy for men of 65 and women of 67, and ranks 105th out of 175 in the Reporters without Borders 2009 Media Freedom Index. Its adult literacy rate is 61% (men 73.4% and women 47.8%) and an adult HIV/AIDS prevalence rate of 0.3%. The infant mortality rate is 49.13 deaths per thousand live births (*Guardian* "World Fact Files," 2009).

India has faced numerous challenges since it gained independence in 1947, including several wars with its neighbor Pakistan and the ongoing threat of terrorism. But according to the CIA's (2010) *World Factbook*, "Despite pressing problems such as significant overpopulation, environmental degradation, extensive poverty, and widespread corruption, rapid economic development is fueling India's rise on the world stage."

Indian higher education can be broken down into government institutions, private aided institutions, and private unaided institutions. According to the World Bank, in 2001, 33% of HEIs were government institutions (including SNDT), 42% were private aided institutions, and 25% were private unaided institutions. Of the 8.4 million students enrolled in tertiary education, 40% were in government institutions, 38% in private aided institutions, and 22% in private unaided institutions (World Bank "A Policy Note on the Grant-in-Aid System in Indian Education," 2003).

Enrollment in higher education has grown steadily from 3.75 million in 1986 to 6.84 million in 1996 (Kapur & Mehta, 2004) to 11 million in 2006 (Azam & Blom, 2008). The Educational Attainment Rate (percentage of those aged 25–34 who have completed a higher education degree) has increased from 4.4% in 1984 to 8.7% in 2004 (Azam & Bloom, 2008). India's gross enrollment ratio (those aged 17–24 enrolled in higher education) is 11%, which is more than twice the GER of its neighbor Pakistan (5%) but half of China's 20% (Asia One, 2010). There remain numerous access gaps based on gender, urban/rural, ethnicity, caste, religion, and income.

Indian higher education is overseen and funded at the federal level by the University Grants Commission, established in 1956. Government HEIs such as SNDT are primarily funded by the federal and state governments. In fact, traditionally, the financial resources available to public institutions were limited by "a severe prohibition on public institutions mobilizing private resources in any form—higher fees, licensing arrangements, or philanthropy," although these restrictions have been eased in recent years (Kapur & Mehta, 2004). The UGC provides most of the funding for central (national) universities, whereas most funding for state universities like SNDT comes from state governments with the advice of the UGC. Both the UGC and state governments provide some funding for the private aided institutions. Overall, India only spends about $400 in public funds per tertiary student, some of the lowest spending in the world (India Education Network, 2009). However, with private institutions accounting for a large percentage of HEIs, over half of tertiary funding comes from private sources such as tuition, fees, research contracts, and philanthropy (RNCOS Industry Research Solutions, 2008).

Indian universities overall have limited autonomy. For example, the UGC sets strict criteria for faculty pay and promotion, leaving limited flexibility for university independence in this regard ("Pay Order Regulations" 2006–2007). According to Christopher Koh, "The Indian higher education system is highly regulated by its government . . . Institutions lack the autonomy to offer new programs, change curricula and evaluation, or even to change policies" (Koh et al., 2008).

While this level of government control has limited autonomy, since 1977 the UGC has also enacted policies promoting community engagement work, referred to as "adult continuing education, extension, and field outreach" (University

Grants Commission, 2006–2007). The extension and field outreach work is to focus on the following areas:

- continuing education programs;
- communal harmony and peace education;
- human rights and rights of vulnerable groups;
- environmental issues;
- *panchayats* and development issues;
- health education for the community;
- women's empowerment;
- social issues and gender issues.

The UGC sets firm guidelines for such programs to receive UGC funding. For example, universities are called upon to establish a system whereby students involved in such programs can receive academic credit for their work. More generally:

> The university level extension should be qualitatively different from the NGOs and other departments and bear the stamp of university scholarship. Universities should take up extension with the purpose of developing innovative models of extension and generating documentation and try to link theory with practice and vice versa. As far as possible extension activities should be planned with the active participation of university community specially the students. All the extension activities should be systematically planned and well documented . . . and disseminated.
>
> *(UGC, 2007: 7)*

Overall, the relatively low level of tertiary funding combined with plans to massively expand the higher education sector mean limited public financial support for a range of higher education activities, including community engagement. The higher education policy environment for community engagement is encouraging, and the UGC seems committed to providing some financial resources for this type of work, but universities should work to identify new funding streams and innovative approaches to secure adequate resources for community engagement.

An Enlightened Woman is a Source of Infinite Strength

Profile of Shreemati Nathibai Damodar Thackersey (SNDT) Women's University, Mumbai (India)

By Susan E. Stroud (based on field visit December 8–9, 2009; December 8 at Juhu campus and December 9 at Churchgate campus)

History and Organization

The origins of Shreemati Nathibai Damodar Thackersey (SNDT) Women's University were in an ashram for widows and other vulnerable women that was established by Dr Dhondo Keshave Karve at Hingne near Pune in 1896. Dr Karve understood the importance of schooling for the women in the ashram as a means of breaking the barriers of gender, class and caste. In the early years of the twentieth century, Dr Karve became interested in providing higher education to women, but at the time there were no models in India upon which he could draw. Supportive colleagues sent him information about the Japan Women's University founded in Tokyo in 1901. He took inspiration from the Japanese university and subsequently created a college for women, which opened in 1916 with five students. With the financial assistance of Sir Vithaldas Thackersey, an industrialist, Dr Karve transformed the college into a women's university in 1920 and named the university after Thackersey's mother. Since that time, the University has been popularly known as SNDT Women's University. In 1936, SNDT moved from Pune to Mumbai and continued to grow until, in 1951, it was granted statutory recognition in Maharashtra state with a special exemption to be able to establish programs across India. SNDT was the first university for women in India and has retained a strong commitment to the empowerment of women through education.

The University's motto is *Sanskrita Stree Parashakti*—"an enlightened woman is a source of infinite strength" (see the SNDT website: http://sndt.digitaluniversity.ac). Outreach and civic engagement—with particular emphasis on the empowerment of women—have been central to SNDT's educational philosophy and curriculum since its beginning and continue to be a strong part of the University's culture and academic programs.

In 2009, student enrollment at SNDT and its affiliated colleges was approximately 75,564 students. Of the students, 35% belong to the 'reserved category,' and the majority are first and second generation university students (see SNDT website). SNDT operates four university campuses—two in Mumbai and one each in Pune and Ahemedabad. There are numerous affiliated colleges and schools in Maharashtra, Gujarat, Assam, Madhya Pradesh, Goa, Haryana, and Daman. Altogether there are 11 Faculties and 31 postgraduate programs. Four languages are used as the medium of instruction—Marathi, Gujarati, Hindi, and English. It offers courses in conventional classroom as well as distance learning modes (see SNDT website).

As a public university, SNDT operates under the guidelines of the Maharashtra Universities Act as well as the University Grants Commission (UGC), the national government body responsible for funding and quality assurance of all higher education institutions. The Vice-Chancellor of the University is Dr Chandra Krishnamurthy, a constitutional law expert, who, prior to becoming the Vice-Chancellor at SNDT, was on the Law Faculty of the University of

Bombay for many years. Dr Krishnamurthy has provided strong leadership for civic engagement at SNDT and speaks frequently at international higher education conferences on the topic.

The Mumbai Context

Mumbai is the most populous city in India with 14 million people and the second most populous city in the world. Including the metropolitan region, it is one of the most densely populated urban areas in the world—estimated to be about 22,000 persons per square kilometer. According to the 2001 census, Greater Mumbai has a literacy rate of 77.45%, higher than the national average of 64.8%.

Mumbai is an ethnically and religiously diverse city. The majority of the population is Hindu (67.39%), but there is also a significant Muslim community (18.56%). Other groups include Buddhists (5.22%), Jains (3.99%), Christians (3.72%), Sikhs (0.58%), and smaller populations of Parsis and Jews (Census of India, 2001). Sixteen major languages of India are spoken in Mumbai, the most common being Marathi, Hindi, Gujarati, and English. English is extensively spoken and is the principal language of the city's professional workforce.

Although Mumbai is considered the financial capital of the country (as it generates 5% of the total GDP), about 60% of Mumbai's population lives in slums (MMRDA, 2008). There is widespread poverty and unemployment, poor public health, and poor civic and educational standards for a large section of the population. Given SNDT's location in central Mumbai, many academic departments' outreach efforts are focused on improving the lives of people living in the urban slums, although there are also significant programs carried out in rural communities.

Civic Engagement, Outreach, and Extension at SNDT

The underlying philosophy for civic engagement at SNDT is based in Gandhian ideals.

> The holistic education of the head, the heart and the hands with the socialist understanding is best imbibed through action for social change. Knowledge of the social reality is not seen as received passively in the classrooms, but through community participation.
>
> *(SNDT, http://sndt.digitaluniversity.ac)*

This approach to higher education is contrasted with the perceived elitist model of higher education under colonial rule. The model Gandhi championed sought to make education an instrument of social change. According to information at SNDT, various national policy documents (Radhakrishnan Commission, 1948; Kothari Commission, 1966; New Education Policy, 1991) specify "University education should not remain uncommitted to the process of socio-economic and political transformation," and should be comprised of research (or the discovery of new knowledge), teaching (or the transformation of knowledge from one generation to another) and extension (i.e., becoming agents of social/political transformation) (SNDT website, Centre for Rural Development). Over time, SNDT has developed a model of "education for social change."

The special mission of the university has been the empowerment of women of all ages and stages of development. The academic programs of the university are in conformity with its founding mission. Multiple entry points are provided in both formal and non-formal education, facilitated by distance learning to women in remote areas and by multiple languages of instruction to facilitate access by many first generation higher education learners (National Assessment and Accreditation Council, India, 2007).

Academic courses at SNDT range from certificate to Doctoral levels. As an indication of SNDT's commitment to increasing access for women, all professional courses are available through distance learning and some short-term and graduate diploma courses are offered through adult and continuing education and extension work.

The University as a whole embraces the concept of Community Development Learning (CDL), which is carried out by blending theoretical knowledge and practical community-based experience. CDL at SNDT has several core objectives to uplift poor communities through sensitization to gender issues, education about rights and access to legal assistance and developing programs for economic empowerment (SNDT website). Departments, centers, and other academic units carry out specific projects with these objectives in mind and apply the lens of women's empowerment throughout their curricula as a whole. The following are brief summaries of information from some of the heads of departments with whom I met during my visit to SNDT.

THE CENTRE FOR RURAL DEVELOPMENT

Begun as a project of the Research Centre for Women's Studies in 1976, the Centre for Rural Development began research in 1976 in nine villages in rural South Gujarat. What began as a need-based survey of the rural area evolved into a set of programs for women on education, health, and income generation with a strong research component. In the time since, more programs have been added, further research conducted, and a platform for teaching and learning has been launched as a training site for students from a variety of disciplines at SNDT and other universities in the region. The Centre now works in 35 villages on projects that include a variety of income generating activities, including microfinance, training in management of small enterprises and banking, vocational training in different job areas, legal literacy and health awareness, and other activities. The Centre has worked with government at all levels to ensure that various social and economic development programs reach the women in the poor rural areas. Other departments at SNDT are involved for specific projects in health, domestic violence, family law, and other issues.

Law School

Law School students hold regular law clinics on Saturdays and during vacation times. The clinics involve lawyers, sociologists and other professionals to support students who are advising community residents. In the current year, training is planned for law students on the UN Millennium Development Goals, particularly those that apply to education and the rights of women.

Special Education

Students in Special Education focus on working with disabled people of all ages in urban slums and rural areas where few services are available. The research and assessment unit provides various services such as early intervention and education of children with intellectual and physical disabilities, parental training and counseling, remediation, community awareness, inclusion of disabled students in mainstream schools, enhancing of educational practices, and in-service training of teachers. The Special Education department maintains a robust research agenda and consults on the development of national and state policy.

Centre for Study of Social Exclusion and Inclusive Policy

Under the 11th national plan, the national government through the UGC funded centers on social exclusion at several universities, including the establishment of a center in 2009 at SNDT. Faculty and students associated with the Centre conduct participatory research on excluded groups such as Indigenous populations, marginalized farmers, denotified tribes and nomadic tribes in the state, domestic workers and other unorganized sector workers, women from excluded communities, and people with disabilities and to work with NGOs on action projects related to these populations. In addition to conducting research, the Centre staff is involved in carrying out activities to raise awareness about excluded groups, support activists working with excluded populations, and consult on national policy related to exclusion and excluded groups. The Centre has conducted several events at the national and regional levels on various issues related to social exclusion. Recently the Centre has developed the following three academic programs which are launched from the academic year 2010–2011: a Master of Arts in Social Exclusion & Inclusive Policy Studies, a Diploma in Social Exclusion & Inclusive Policy Studies, and a Diploma in NGO Management.

Home Science

Postgraduate courses since 1987 incorporate community work in order to sensitize students to the realities of the communities in which they eventually work and support the concept of social responsibility as a cornerstone of education. In courses at the MS level, students participate in community-based research and some courses include compulsory community-based clinical work.

Education

Faculty with whom I met repeatedly stated that they are educating teachers to be agents of social change. Undergraduates are required to work with socially deprived students, and community work in a variety of social institutions is a core component of the MA program.

Clinical Psychology

Students conduct counseling sessions in community organizations, hospitals and NGOs as part of an internship that is required in the undergraduate program.

Social Work

Students help to run non-formal courses for staff at NGOs on capacity building and leadership development. In another project, students and faculty work with an association of 5,000 rag pickers in Pune.

In addition to the civic engagement aspects of the academic program, students have the opportunity to participate in the National Service Scheme (NSS). The national NSS program falls under the auspices of the Ministry of Youth Affairs and Sports, and recent estimates are that nationally the program engages 2.6 million students in higher education institutions and senior secondary schools. Its motto is "Not Me But You." Among its stated objectives are "develop among themselves (students) a sense of social and civic responsibility" and "gain skills in mobilizing community participation" (NSS website, "Objectives").

About 10,000 students at SNDT and affiliated colleges participate in the NSS each year. Students take part in both regular activities to complete the requirement of 120 hours of service each year (70 of which must be in community settings and 50 in other settings such as a hospital or on campus) and 1-week camps that are held in vacation times in urban slums or rural areas. SNDT students involved with the NSS have identified a special focus on projects related to malnutrition, child development and adolescent reproductive health.

Other projects are in the area of disaster management, improving environmental quality, childhood inoculation against polio, and literacy. Students who successfully complete the requirements for participation in the NSS receive a government certificate which is looked upon favorably by potential employers and it increases the score for application to university. Although the NSS is a program of the national government, it provides minimal funding for the program. The NSS has been underfunded for many years and HEIs carry most of the responsibility for the program's management and financing out of a commitment to its goals. Business and service organizations in the community such as Rotary and Lions Clubs and institutional support from the Vice-Chancellor's office contribute most of the funding to the SNDT chapter.

Institutional Policies

The criteria for faculty promotion are prescribed nationally by the University Grants Commission rather than by the university. Although there are no specific criteria related to civic engagement for individual faculty, one faculty member responded to a question about incentives for the extensive outreach activity most faculty are involved in by saying that "the incentive structures are the same at SNDT and any other University in the state. The difference is the culture of the institution. SNDT attracts people with a strong sense of social responsibility."

One criterion for assessment of institutional performance of HEIs as set by the National Assessment and Accreditation Council is the extent and quality of extension work undertaken *in toto* by the university. In all of the departments with whom I met, examples were presented of how civic engagement is imbedded into both the theoretical and practical applications of the curricula.

Challenges and Observations

SNDT has a strong institutional culture that supports outreach and civic engagement. Over nine decades, the university has invested in developing the infrastructure needed throughout the various academic departments to carry out sustained community engagement activities that have research and teaching opportunities associated with them. Faculty raised several persistent challenges associated with this work. These included the frequent lack of capacity of community organizations to partner with the university, especially in rural areas. Over time the university staff and students have had to help develop the capacity of organizations they work with in order to have the necessary infrastructure for the work to be carried out. Academic schedules were also mentioned as a challenge—communities do not operate on semesters. Lack of continuity was also cited, which often results from the frequent turnover of students.

Several heads of departments mentioned that the trend is positive in terms of gaining more financial support, i.e., grants, for outreach projects and research focused on community problem-solving. This support comes from government sources, private foundations, international donors and—in a limited number of cases—from corporate sponsors. In recent years there has also been increased recognition for community-based activities at SNDT. As one faculty member observed, "Recognition may come in ways other than publications, for example being asked by government for advice and to draft policies or recognition by international organizations such as UNICEF and UNFPA, who ask faculty to evaluate programs."

Conclusion

SNDT's commitment to empowering women through education has made it a tremendous resource for local and regional development and gives it a unique niche in Indian higher education. SNDT's urban and rural outreach programs are a vital component of the struggle against seemingly intractable poverty in Mumbai. SNDT has leveraged its capabilities by developing the capacity of community partners and NGOs, thus building the civil society and human capital necessary for a sustainable effort at economic and social upliftment of women and marginalized groups.

Challenges remain, but overall SNDT presents a solid model for other Indian institutions to tackle various social problems. The UGC has long encouraged higher education outreach and extension and has set useful guidelines for these programs, but it has limited financial resources to devote to higher education overall and to community engagement in particular. Therefore, Indian universities will need to make community engagement a priority and identify other funding streams such as foundations and corporate sponsors. Given its strong institutional commitment to women's empowerment, development, and community engagement, SNDT appears poised to play a leadership role in such a movement.

Israel and its Higher Education System

Israel has a population of 7.3 million, an average life expectancy for men of 79 and women of 83, and ranks 93 out of 175 in the Reporters without Borders 2009 Press Freedom Index. Its adult literacy rate is 97.1% (male 98.5%; female 95.9%); it has 3.7 doctors per 1,000 population, an infant mortality rate of 4.17 deaths per

1,000 live births, and an adult HIV/AIDS rate of 0.1% (*Guardian* "World Fact Files," 2009).

Israel gained independence in 1948, and has faced conflicts with its neighbors since that time, including wars in 1948, 1956, 1967, 1973, 1982, and 2006. It now has full relations with two of its neighbors (Egypt and Jordan), but the Israeli–Palestinian conflict remains unresolved. Israel's population has grown significantly since independence, especially due to Jewish immigration. Poor in natural resources, Israel has developed a diversified economy, and has recently been invited to join the Organization for Economic Cooperation and Development (OECD).

Since the creation of the state of Israel in 1948, higher education has been dominated by public institutions, mainly large universities. In the 1990s, this began to shift, and other types of HEIs came into existence, including some privately-financed HEIs. In 2006, there were 61 accredited HEIs in six categories: universities (7), the open university (1), arts academies (2), comprehensive academic colleges (10), academic colleges of engineering (6), non-budgeted academic colleges (8), and academic colleges for the training of teachers (27). Of these, only the non-budgeted academic colleges are private institutions that do not receive public funding. Only 10.8% of the 250,000 Israeli HE students in 2006 were enrolled in the non-budgeted (private) colleges (Planning and Budgeting Committee of the Council for Higher Education, 2008: 8). About half of Israeli students are enrolled in the eight universities. Enrollment increased massively during the 1990s, but has somewhat leveled off in the past decade.

In 2005, the female Gross Enrollment Ratio was 66% and the male GER was 50% (UN Data, 2007). There remain significant access and achievement gaps in Israeli higher education. The gap in access between Arabs and Jews has been

TABLE 5.2 Enrollment at the University of Haifa and Universities Overall in Israel, 1979–2008

	1979–1980	*1989–1990*	*1999–2000*	*2007–2008*
University of Haifa	6,140	6,780	13,550	17,460
Total Universities	54,480	67,770	113,010	120,990

Central Bureau of Statistics (2008).

TABLE 5.3 Percentage of Israelis Aged 20–29 Enrolled in Higher Education (HE), Based on Their Father's Region of Origin

Father's region of birth	*HE enrollment of those aged 20–29*
Israel	9.8%
Europe, USA	12.1%
Africa, Asia	6.5%

Central Bureau of Statistics (2008).

shrinking over the past two decades, but it remains stark. The share of Arabs enrolled has increased from 6.7% in 1990 to 10.1% in 2005, but this remains well below their 20% share of the overall population (Planning and Budgeting Committee, 2008: 18). There is also a considerable gap between Jews based on region of origin, with Jews of African/Asian backgrounds tending to be underrepresented.

Israel's higher education system is overseen by the Council for Higher Education, established in 1958. CHE is chaired by the Minister of Education and has 25 members, of whom 17 are HEI professors and two are student representatives (Planning and Budgeting Committee, 2008: 6). CHE is responsible for accreditation, quality assurance, and funding higher education institutions. Overall, this system is what Gila Menahem calls a "state-sanctioned self-regulation regime" (Menahem, 2008).

The higher education budget is granted by the Ministry of Finance to the Council for Higher Education in five-year lump sums, giving the CHE considerable independence in how it allocates the funds. CHE's Planning and Budget Committee (PBC) allocates funds in three ways: block grant allocations (76%), earmarked allocations (20%), and matching allocations (4%) (Planning and Budgeting Committee, 2008: 9–11). In addition to public financing, all HEIs charge tuition, with the average annual tuition at public institutions at around $2000 (Planning and Budgeting Committee, 2008: 15). Overall, in 2005, 48.7% of HE financing came from the government while 51.3% came from private sources (34.9% of the total financing came from tuition). In 2005, Israel spent $10,919 per student in tertiary education, just under the OECD average of $11,512. (OECD, Indicator B1, 2008a).

Government policy does not promote community engagement in higher education. Quality assurance and evaluation guidelines are silent on community engagement, and there do not appear to be any funding streams specifically for this type of work.

Institution-Wide Commitment to Social Responsibility

Profile of the University of Haifa (Israel)
By Robert M. Hollister (based on site visit June 16–18, 2009, building on previous visit June 16–17, 2007)

Origins and Context

Although it is located several miles from downtown on a high hill above the rest of the city, Haifa University is hardly an ivory tower; it is a university that is highly engaged with its metropolitan area and the country as whole. From its inception, it has been deeply involved in efforts to address local, regional, and national needs. Social responsibility was an important part of the rationale for the

creation of this university in 1963; it was one of the justifications for the allocation of public funds to support it. At Haifa, the operative conceptual vocabulary
is "social responsibility," not civic engagement or public service. The university's
mission statement commits the institution to providing higher education opportunities for diverse and talented students from the region and the country as a
whole, to conduct research that benefits the country and the world, and to foster
social responsibility through applied research and community leadership. The
university views itself, and is seen widely by local officials and residents, as an
integral part of the city and its region.

With a student enrollment that is 20% Arab, the University of Haifa is significantly more diverse than in other Israeli universities. Many students come from
lower socioeconomic backgrounds and work full or part-time.

Overview

The University of Haifa has embraced social responsibility as an overarching strategic theme—an area of current strength and a priority for future programming.
This major dimension of the institution's work combines robust and pervasive student volunteer programs, and extensive faculty research and faculty-led programs
on community needs, ranging from poverty to public health and environmental
quality. In 2007, the University initiated a high-profile national conference on
social responsibility and national policy challenges, which it repeated in 2008, but
has been unable to continue due to financial pressures. The comparatively high
religious diversity of its student body makes bridging disparate elements of Israeli
society a defining aspect of Haifa's social responsibility role.

Haifa defines civic engagement as "the acquisition and development of social
consciousness within the university itself and the improvement of the society surrounding the campus, instilling a sense of social responsibility." The institution
aims to narrow the gaps between various sectors of the population and has established unique immigrant absorption programs that advance its goals of "enabling
success for students from underprivileged areas." Creating an institutional environment that enables disadvantaged students to thrive is therefore an important
part of the University's civic engagement efforts.

The University runs a variety of programs to build the capabilities of non-
student constituencies including non-governmental organizations. In addition, it
plays a critical role as a development partner to strengthen the economy and social
conditions in Haifa and the Galilee area more broadly.

President Ben-Ze'ev's Vision to Elevate Social Responsibility

In 2005, President Aaron Ben-Ze'ev, a professor of philosophy, decided to place
additional strategic emphasis on the broad theme of social responsibility. He concluded that social responsibility was already a significant asset of the institution

and that it also represented an area of special opportunity. He created the new position of Advisor for Social Responsibility to the President to strengthen and coordinate the university's work in this realm. Dr Irit Keynan filled this role with great creativity and entrepreneurial energy.

For three years the university expanded and deepened its social responsibility programming in multiple dimensions—academic work, community involvement, and campus life. Dr Keynan played a vigorous coordinating role, inventorying and communicating the broad range of social responsibilities of the University of Haifa. The national conference on social responsibility that the University hosted in 2007 and 2008 dealt with "the most crucial issues on the Israeli social agenda." This well-attended and broadly publicized conference showcased faculty research on pressing societal issues and provided a platform for debate on competing policy directions on issues such as children at risk, Arab-Jewish relations, health and housing policy. Internally, it encouraged professors to extend and apply their research to public decision-making and provided a vehicle for increasing the impacts of their scholarship. Externally, it built public interest and support for the University's social responsibility work. The conference linked university research to public policy-making, framing and elevating public dialogue. Then a funding crisis resulted in elimination of the Advisor for Social Responsibility position and suspension of the conference. Social responsibility remains a defining focus at Haifa, but many social responsibility programs have been reduced in scale.

A Broad Range of Student Volunteer Opportunities

Following elimination of the position of Special Advisor to the President for Social Responsibility, the Dean of Students has assumed a greater role as he continues to manage the program that predated the special initiative on social responsibility. Professor Yoav Lavee, Dean of Students and Associate Professor of Social Work, oversees and guides several substantial student service programs. Placing a strong emphasis on maximizing student learning outcomes, Dr Lavee's unit administers a program through which students can apply for academic credits for their volunteer work. This program operates through a system of demand from community organizations, supply by students, and academic oversight by departments. Community organizations list with the University their requests for student volunteers, students select among these community service projects, and a broad range of academic departments certify when the academic credit is appropriate and has been earned. In 2008–2009, 180 students were approved to receive this credit.

Lavee calls special attention to the University's policy of expecting recipients of financial aid to provide community service. In 2008–2009, a total of 190 students of Druze, Arab, and Jewish background received scholarships and participated in community programs through the Department of Social Involvement. This approach, says Lavee, is that "You get and you give." Lavee's office runs four separate leadership development programs—for Jewish, Arab, and Druze students, and a combined Jewish–Arab leadership program. A Program to Cultivate Academic and Social Leadership gives scholarships to students from peripheral regions chosen not only for academic excellence, but also for their leadership and community service abilities. The program includes leadership training and supports students to conduct service projects.

The Friends of Raveh-Ravid Fund, sponsored by a local accounting firm, strives to develop in participating students a combination of social leadership and academic excellence. Each year, 10–15 students are selected for their academic strength, leadership, and service record. They receive full tuition, participate in training in social leadership and identify a social problem to address together. In 2009 the topic was youth violence in schools.

Students participate in a wide variety of social responsibility opportunities within and outside of the academic curriculum. In some fields of study, like health and welfare, community work is a requirement, in others like life sciences, it is not.

Approximately 20% of University of Haifa students participate in Perach, a national program through which university students are trained and supported to serve as mentors to underprivileged children. They work 4 hours week, and receive partial scholarships (financed by the national government) or academic credit.

In two innovative programs, students live in poor neighborhoods and lead service initiatives in those areas. A flagship program is The Student Village, located in the Hadar Hacarmel neighborhood. Some 60 students live in apartments, receive additional scholarship assistance, and conduct service projects. They make a year-long commitment to provide 370 hours of service. In the second program, called Open Apartments, 19 students live in six apartments. In this cooperative effort of the University, Perach, the municipal welfare department and two local community centers, students receive scholarship assistance and free housing, and contribute to neighborhood community work with at-risk youth and senior citizens. Students from diverse backgrounds are assigned to live together. Some 70% of the participants in Open Apartments are still involved in community work, and 30% continue working in community centers or with welfare agencies.

Student Diversity is a Major Challenge and Opportunity

Educating its diverse student body is seen by university staff as an important dimension of the University's social responsibility. The extent to which the university prepares all segments of Israeli society to participate vigorously and successfully in its economy and political and social life is thus treated as a central part of its social responsibility mission. Several programs work to strengthen intergroup understanding and tolerance. For example, the Jewish–Arab Community Leadership Program facilitates dialogue and social interaction between Jewish and

Arab students, and engages them in joint service projects. This program develops in students the skills to be effective, inclusive community leaders, people with the ability to effectively build bridges and be collaborative among groups that so often are in conflict with one another.

History Professor, Danny Gutwein, states, "By its very existence the university is a kind of a laboratory for how Israeli society can work. In Israeli society different population groups lack meeting places. Here they meet in classes." He adds, "Civic engagement is seen not only as external fieldwork, but the field is here (within the university)." A University report summarizes, "The University's diverse population of students and faculty provides a model of a multicultural community. It is analogous to a social laboratory of the future, whether in Israel or elsewhere. This enables us to explore ways to use this diversity as an asset while simultaneously diffusing associated tensions that might impede the University's functioning."

To some faculty members, the most important aspect of social responsibility at the University is not a set of programs that formally address social responsibility goals, but rather how the institution does (or does not) "live" social responsibility in its own policies and practices. Professor Gutwein comments, "Universities are instruments for normalizing students to the market. Social responsibility is a contradictory message, a subversive and constructive paradox." He describes his role as a professor as being to "enlarge or deepen this paradox." Therefore, how the university deals with its own employees—for example, levels of compensation of cleaning women and security guards—is a key aspect of its social responsibility performance and of its informal educational impacts. In this view students' social activism is an important dimension of the institution's social responsibility behavior and record. Gutwein seeks to empower the more socially aware students, to help them to become constructive agents of change by organizing to change the university itself.

While the diversity of its students represents an educational opportunity, it presents a great deal of challenge as well, for relations among different population on campus at points are conflicted. During my site visit, an Arab student group, after lengthy argument with the University administration, had received permission to invite to speak on campus, a cleric who is a vocal critic of the existence of Israel. The cleric's presence sparked a protest march of Jewish student groups and stimulated sharp criticism of the University administration by national politicians. Even as he staunchly defends freedom of speech as a fundamental principle of the academy and a contributor to its educational process, President Ze'ev observes that the University's diversity reduces political, and ultimately financial, support to the institution in some quarters.

Extensive Faculty Initiatives to Address Community Needs

The University supports many long-term programs that connect its intellectual resources to community priorities. Several of these efforts are embedded in the academic curriculum and in faculty members' ongoing research and professional activities. These programs build upon and benefit from an extensive infrastructure of strong working ties between the University, local NGOs, and municipal government agencies. Notable examples include the Haifa Partnership Project, the social theatre program of the Drama Department, and a pair of innovative social indicators projects—the Social Justice Index, developed by Professor Arye Rattner, and the Index of Arab–Jewish Relations, developed by Professor Sammy Smooha. The indicators initiatives regularly gauge the status of hot political conditions and measure progress (or lack thereof) on these challenges, providing constructive background and stimulus for continuing policy debates.

Dr Roni Strier, School of Social Work, in 2006 initiated the Haifa Partnership Project, an innovative and ambitious learning and action initiative, in collaboration with the municipal Welfare Department. The Project organizes students, researchers, social service professionals, and impoverished families "to jointly combat the roots and consequences of social inequalities in the community." Students and staff provide direct services to poor families and work jointly with those families to develop proposals for change in public policies and programs. Participating students enroll in an undergraduate course that was designed especially for this effort. In addition the School of Social Work established a one-year training program for 30 field practice supervisors and social workers. The Project has organized seven regional conferences and several working committees to analyze the causes of inequalities, develop proposals for change, and to build support for these proposals. This ongoing effort is generating lessons "about practical work with and for families living in poverty and social exclusion, about how to train social work students for direct practice with clients living in poverty, and about factors that promote or hamper a partnership between academic and people living in poverty."

The Women Legal Leaders and the Legal Feminism Clinic, initiated by attorney Dana Myrtenbaum in 2004, promotes access to justice for women from disadvantaged communities and marginalized individuals. Committed to developing a new legal model based on feminist principles, the clinic "exposes law students to women's struggles and strengths and to the power of the law in the process of social change." This effort trains and supervises law students and a smaller number of social work students to represent female clients and to address women's legal issues. In addition, each year it trains 35 women who are not law students "to become legal leaders in their communities and policy advocates for change." The clinic won a third prize in the first year of the MacJannet Prize for Global Citizenship, a project of the Talloires Network to recognize outstanding university civic engagement.

Driving Factors

Haifa's social responsibility policies and programs are shaped by strong presidential and faculty leadership, its position in the city's institutional landscape, the priority needs in the city where it is located, the university's distinctive role in Israeli higher education, and the diverse composition of its student enrollment.

President Ben-Ze'ev has made social responsibility a defining strategic theme of the institution, reinforcing what was already a major focus of the work of many faculty members and departments. For a considerable number of senior and highly regarded professors, social responsibility lies at the core of their teaching and scholarship. Faculty incentives to do social responsibility work vary among departments. In some fields, such as Social Work, social responsibility performance is well supported; other academic disciplines provide less recognition. In combination, these factors make for sustained collective leadership in support of a highly engaged university.

Among Israeli research universities, Haifa is not only the newest, but also is seen as being the most diverse, the most politically liberal, and also the most focused on regional development. These founding goals and rationales of the institution are reinforced by the perceptions and expectations of Israeli opinion-leaders and decision-makers, both proponents and critics of the University. Haifa is an innovative outlier within Israeli higher education—it serves a more diverse student population, and has a greater commitment to local and regional development.

As has been discussed above, the composition of its student body is a major factor in the life of the University, one with profound implications for its social responsibility activities and aspirations. National policies and conflicts bear heavily on the University. Because it is heavily dependent upon funding by the national government, these budget allocations by definition have large effects. Some right-wing politicians view Haifa as "the Arab university," which negatively affects their willingness to support the university.

Future Directions and Reflections

Haifa's experience illustrates the positive potential of a university-wide strategic emphasis on the broad theme of social responsibility, addressed in research, teaching, and service activities. A broad cross-section of faculty, staff and students yearn for a return to the recent high water mark in social responsibility programming. The availability of funds will play a large role in determining whether and when this occurs.

Several programs whose effectiveness has been well-demonstrated—programs like Open Apartments—could be restored to earlier levels of participation and expanded. President Ben-Ze'ev would like to see a greater proportion of students participating in community work. Funding, of course, will also be a major factor with respect to this goal.

The diversity of its student body poses significant educational opportunities, and also social political challenges, both within and outside the university. Haifa's experience and its programmatic strategies may be informative to the many other universities around the world that are concerned about diversity challenges and opportunities.

The linking of scholarship assistance and community service work is an instructive part of the Haifa story. The University has had significant success in requiring and supporting recipients of financial aid to do community service. Providing scholarship assistance, leadership training, and taking part in community service can be a potent combination. This approach communicates an additional rationale for investing in financial aid, enhances students' development, and helps to meet community needs.

The Occupied Palestinian Territories and their Higher Education System

The Occupied Palestinian Territories (OPT) have a population of 4 million, and an average life expectancy for men of 72 and for women, of 75. The adult literacy rate is 93.5%, with 1.62 doctors per 1,000 population and an adult HIV/AIDS rate of 1.62% (*Guardian* "World Fact Files," 2009).

Palestinian higher education institutions operate in a complicated political context. First, they exist in a condition of ongoing conflict and occupation, which sometimes leads to university closures, loss of funding, and other challenges. The Palestinian National Authority (PNA) has a unique status with limited sovereignty. In addition, the West Bank is controlled by the secular political movement Fatah, while the Gaza Strip is controlled by the Islamist political movement Hamas. The status of Al-Quds University (AQU) is further complicated by the fact that, while it is based in the West Bank town of Abu Dis adjacent to Jerusalem, it also has facilities in East Jerusalem which was annexed by Israel in 1980. It traditionally has had cooperative relations with Israeli universities (unlike other Palestinian institutions), but Al-Quds University remains a public university under the Palestinian Ministry of Education and Higher Education. Therefore, this profile will focus on the Palestinian higher education system.

There are four types of Palestinian HEIs: 10 traditional universities (55% of total enrollment); one open university (34% of total enrollment); 13 university colleges (4%); and 19 community colleges (7%). These are further divided into government institutions (founded and funded by the government); public institutions (partly funded by the government); private institutions; and several schools run by the UN Relief and Works Agency (UNRWA) (Ministry of Higher Education, Palestine, 2005).

Tertiary enrollment in the OPT has increased dramatically since the Oslo Accords. For example, enrollment at AQU increased from 1,805 students in 1995 (just after the establishment of the university) to 10,371 in 2009 (Al-Quds University in Facts and Figures: University Annual Report, 2008–2009). This rapid growth has posed a serious problem due to lack of the resources and capacity to handle this influx. According to the Ministry of Education and Higher Education:

> Over the past half decade, Palestinian universities have not been able to train and recruit high level academic and administrative staff, acquire equipment, including computers, develop libraries and documentation centers, and upgrade facilities to accommodate the doubling of enrollments during that time. Nor are they prepared to deal with the possible flood of new enrollments that may arise from the projected burgeoning number of high school graduates.
>
> *(Ministry of Higher Education and Scientific Research & World Bank,*
> *2002: 21)*

The pattern of Palestinian higher education funding has been greatly affected by the Palestinian political context. During the 1970s and 1980s, most funding came from the PLO, expatriate Palestinians, and charities, allowing tuition and fees to be relatively low. However, when the Gulf States dropped funding for the PLO in the early 1990s, universities began to rely more heavily on tuition. Public support from the PNA declined steadily in the late 1990s, from $1,287 per student in 1996 to just $857 per student in 1999, and in 2002, just 0.3% of the GDP of the Palestinian territories was spent on public finance of higher education, compared to an OECD average of 1.3%. The share of university revenue from tuition went from 10% of total university income in the early 1990s to 55% in 2002 (Ministry of Higher Education and Scientific Research and World Bank, 2002). In the case of AQU, tuition went from being 46% of total university revenues in 1998 to 74% in 2001 (Al-Quds University Office of Research, 2001). Especially after the second Intifada began in 2001, PNA revenues plummeted, drastically cutting the public funds available for higher education. In addition to tuition revenues and receiving limited funding from the PNA, universities receive grants from foreign aid organizations such as USAID. The decline in public finance and increase in tuition has seriously hampered equal access to higher education: 37% of college graduates come from the upper 20% in income, while just 9.1% come from the bottom 20% (Ministry of Higher Education and Scientific Research and World Bank, 2002).

The HE system is overseen by the Ministry of Education and Higher Education, created by the Palestinian Law No. 11 for Higher Education (1998). In 2002, the Ministry created the Accreditation and Quality Assurance Commission, an autonomous body tasked with improving the quality of Palestinian HEIs (Accreditation and Quality Assurance Commission, 2008). Given the low level of public funding for HEIs, the Ministry has limited effective control over the higher education sector.

Given limited public sector involvement, many Palestinian universities independently adopted strong community engagement policies as early as the 1970s in order to tackle the range of problems faced by their society. A number of Palestinian universities have created community engagement centers and several require their students to complete a certain number of hours of community service in order to graduate. Al-Quds University is one example of this commitment to community engagement and service.

Education and Service for Political Change and Development

Profile of Al-Quds University (OPT)
By Robert M. Hollister (based on site visit June 14–16, 2009; building on previous visit March 15, 2007)

Overview

Al-Quds University was founded in 1984 through the merger of several existing Palestinian colleges. Organized in 12 Faculties, including Arts, Sciences, Medicine, and Law, over 1,200 faculty members (500 full-time) teach a student body of approximately 12,000.

Al-Quds operates in a context of harsh political conflict. One administrator commented, "We are a Jerusalem university, yet we are separated from Jerusalem." The University is located on the West Bank in Abu Dis which used to be a neighborhood of Jerusalem. An imposing 26-foot high separation wall defines one edge of the campus. (President Sari Nusseibeh led a major a major battle to keep construction of the separation wall from bisecting its campus.) The wall is both a significant obstacle to movement in and out of the Abu Dis campus, and it symbolizes powerfully the political division and power relationship between Israel and The Occupied Territories. In spite of the painful economic and political realities, Al-Quds students and faculty exude a very positive, optimistic spirit. In this besieged context, and functioning in an immediate environment of huge unmet social, health, and economic needs, Al-Quds plays an important community "anchor institution" role.

The institution is committed to promoting a culture of service throughout the university that encourages the development of personal and community responsibility, "assisting its students to develop into the powerful leaders of tomorrow."

The University hosts a vibrant set of national and international cooperative projects for the improvement of socioeconomic conditions in Palestine. Extensive student service programs focus on human rights and on pre-college education. In a university where the dominant form of pedagogy is traditional lectures and rote learning, students respond very positively to volunteer service as an opportunity for experiential learning. To date the university has embraced community service learning only to a limited extent and the number of community service learning courses is growing slowly.

A highly regarded public intellectual and forceful leader on issues of university social responsibility both within and outside the University, President Nusseibeh observes that Al-Quds' partnerships with Palestinian communities continue to grow in scale and importance. With respect to the societal role of university, he observes, "Sometimes universities can do things government cannot do."

Organizational Diffusion

Community service is promoted as a major theme throughout the university; it is not the focus or lead responsibility of a particular organizational unit or leadership position, but rather is built into the entire identity and fabric of Al-Quds. This decentralized and dispersed structure may be changing through the initiative of Dr Masa Bajali, formerly the dean of the faculty of dentistry, who in 2009 assumed the new position of Assistant to the President for Student Services. Dr Bajali is promoting student leadership development by training and supporting student to take a larger role in performing core administrative functions of the University, including admissions and course registration. Through this strategy, he aims to empower students and to build their organizational leadership skills in ways that will also enhance their effectiveness in doing off-campus service work.

Student Volunteering and Limited Curricular Integration

During their time at Al-Quds, all students are required to complete 120 hours of service, at least one-third of which must be outside of the university. Students in all fields of study do volunteer work on a broad range of community needs—tutoring elementary and secondary school students, helping farmers to harvest their crops, running blood drives, planting trees in local communities, and promoting environmental awareness. They often perform service that fits within their area of academic specialty, but they can work on other topic as well. Student volunteer service programs are organized by the Student Union and also by student forums, of which there is one in each of the 10 colleges, with the role of providing student voice and advocacy.

Many Al-Quds students are enthusiastic about their volunteer service work. They state a broad range of reasons why they and their peers volunteer—religious motivation ("to please God"), to address pressing societal needs, to improve their CVs and advance their careers, to connect with other students, and to fulfill the university requirement. Students appreciate the encouragement and recognition for community work that is provided by the Al-Quds administration. Dr Said Zeedani, Acting Vice President for Academic Affairs, asserts that the majority of students respond very positively to the requirement.

Students feel that their service work accomplishes a variety of things that they care about—bridging differences and building tolerance, enabling volunteers to discover their talents, building their self-confidence and skills (teamwork, leadership, and public speaking).

Common challenges that students perceive include frustration with respect to the levels of progress that their community work achieves on intractable community problems, limits on the kinds of work that women are permitted to do, insufficient preparation of some volunteers, a cultural norm that it is undesirable to work for free, and the demands of their academic work.

Students value highly their participation in volunteer service activities, both for the community service that they provide and also for what they gain in terms of personal and professional development. They express satisfaction in seeing young people whom they served in their community work later become students at Al-Quds.

Although several professors incorporate service learning in their teaching, the vast majority do not. Dr Zeedani comments, "We are moving in that direction and are expanding the number of internships that are available in many disciplines."

On-Campus Programs Serve Community Constituencies

Several academic programs engage community challenges through the direct provision of health services, applied research, education and sponsoring public forums. Hasan Dweik, Executive Vice President, emphasizes that a key part of the University's civic engagement and social responsibility work is the applied research activities of professors. Dr Dweik explains that many faculty members and several research centers are deeply involved in efforts to grow and strengthen businesses in the region, through training programs and also through their research projects. They contribute directly to the development and operation of business enterprises in the region, including chemical technology, plastics, rubber and fibers, and food technology. For example, the Chemical Analysis Center partners with area companies to develop technologies and to supplement their technical capabilities.

Dr Dweik adds that another major focus of Al-Quds engagement activities is applied research to inform public decision-making on important policy issues and conflicts such as water supply and quality. For example, on an ongoing basis University personnel analyze water quality in the region, and inform municipal officials and the general public.

The University exercises a strong commitment to improving pre-college education—by building the capabilities of practicing teachers as well as preparing future teachers. An important pivot to its educational activities is the Science and Mathematics Museum. Located on-campus, the museum provides in-service training to K-12 teachers and extensive workshops for K-12 students. In its extensive efforts to strengthen primary and secondary education Al-Quds seeks to foster creative and critical thinking, to help teachers move beyond the traditional didactic lecture formats. From its satellite campus in Ramallah, the University operates Al-Quds Educational TV, a network that serves the broad Palestinian community.

The Insan Center for Gender Studies offers a combination of academic courses, research, conferences, training for local residents, and action initiatives. Student enrollment in its courses is growing rapidly, and it sponsors 12-session long trainings for local community representatives. One research project, funded by Canada International Development, is studying the impact of the separation wall on women and families in Jerusalem.

In 2006 the Human Rights Clinic was established in the Law School of Al-Quds as the first Palestinian clinical legal education program. Students learn about human rights advocacy by practicing with lawyers and working with organizations, supervised jointly by staff members of partnering non-governmental organizations and of the clinic itself. Students participate in a year-long program of lectures, workshops, skills development, and practice. The Human Rights Clinic was awarded a third prize in the first year of the Talloires Network's MacJannet Prize for Global Citizenship. The clinic is organized to mutually benefit clinic students, low-income Palestinians, the law school, and Palestinian human rights organizations. Students provide legal services, monitor and report human rights abuses, and aid human rights organizations. In the Street Law Project they inform residents about their rights and represent them in legal proceedings. Group research projects include a study of torture in prisons and an analysis of a ring road proposal to link Israeli settlements that would further cut off sections of East Jerusalem.

Students speak very positively about their experience as volunteers at the Human Rights Clinic. Several relate that they first signed up assuming that this would be easy work, a perception that changed quickly. One reflects, "Our work through the clinic is very different—much more experiential—than our usual academic work where we take notes on lectures, study books, and take exams. The clinic involves us in diverse ways of learning. We learn how to deal with people and the practicalities of legal practice." Another adds, "It increases your belief that you can make a difference." Students attest that the experience sharpened their professional goals and heightened their interest in practicing human rights law. They would like to see this clinical, hands-on approach spread to other courses.

Off-Campus Community Centers Address Societal Challenges and Focus on Human Rights

The University also addresses Palestinian community needs through a series of centers and institutes located off campus, in community settings. These programs concentrate on human rights issues—women's rights, water rights, residency rights and travel restrictions, and civil and labor rights. Some of these units were established primarily to provide services to local residents; they all draw upon the skills of Al-Quds faculty members, but they vary in the extent to which they involve Al-Quds students and faculty members, and in the extent to which they contribute to students' education.

The Community Action Center, started in 1999 in collaboration with McGill University (Canada), plays a leading role in the university's civic engagement. Located in the Old City of Jerusalem, separate from the main campus at Abu Dis, the Center provides legal, social, educational and gender-based services to disadvantaged residents, with a major focus on women's empowerment. It "employs a unique social service model called the 'rights based community practice' that departs from a traditional social work center where impoverished individuals go to receive handouts." Operating out of an attractive facility, staff members manage a storefront walk-in information and referral clinic and do extensive outreach and community organizing both in Jerusalem and also in refugee camps. The Center offers civic education classes for 12–14 year olds in 17 schools, and coordinates 200 volunteers to provide education support services. Women's empowerment is a major focus. Modest numbers of students participate in the Center's work.

A second university program, also located in the Old City, the Community Development Center has as its mission to assist in the advancement and development of Palestinian civil society, to support and strengthen the role of Palestinian women and youth in the local community; and addresses pressing issues facing Jerusalem residents—social, economic, academic, and psychological. Primary programs include legal counseling, enhancement of school students' skills, psychological and parenting counseling, and youth leadership development. The Center's tutoring and training courses seek to strengthen the democratic process.

Like the Community Action Center, the Community Development Center places a special emphasis on women's empowerment. The Center "believes that women should have a prominent role within the community. Therefore, we have created capacity-building programs especially for women."

A flagship initiative of the Community Development Center is the Jerusalem Women's Parliament which involves women from all sectors of the community "to create a supportive network for women." It "seeks to give women the opportunity to participate in their community and develop their capacities. As well as strengthen women's national belonging, cultural and humanity, in order to build a democratic civil society."

A third off-campus center, the Center for Jerusalem Studies, situated in the Old City close to the Community Action Center, is devoted to preserving Palestinian culture and heritage. Originally envisioned as a forum and a think tank, the Center today focuses on elevating public knowledge about and respect for the city, from a Palestinian perspective. It offers to local residents, tourists, and Al-Quds students a broad range of intensive courses, tours, and cultural events.

Driving Factors

Al-Quds' social responsibility work is influenced greatly by the University's location, physical barriers to travel, community needs, presidential leadership, and severe financial pressures. The needs of the Palestinian community are a major determinant. Immediate and pressing, these needs are felt directly by students and faculty members and are regularly expressed by a network of community partner organizations. Al-Quds is so integrally part of Palestinian society that it does not need or employ special procedures to assess community needs. These realities are abundantly clear. Contributing to the development and wellbeing of Palestinian society is thoroughly woven into how University personnel and programs are designed and how they plan and operate their core functions.

The Israeli separation wall, check points, and restrictions on residency and travel have profound effects on the university's community work. These factors greatly impede the ability of students and faculty to participate in the work of community centers that are located outside of the home campus. In addition, they reduce the ability of those centers to contribute to academic programs of the university.

President Nusseibeh's high international stature and reputation is a major influence upon, and resource for, the university's social responsibility activities. Through his extensive international travel and visible participation in world events, he attracts support and creates new service-oriented collaborations.

Al-Quds faculty members and administrators cite financial constraints, but in their vigorous social responsibilities they are undeterred by the severe monetary pressures under which the institution operates. Dependent largely on student fees for its core operations, the availability of external sponsorship and external partners has a defining impact on Al-Quds' community service and social justice activities. Highly entrepreneurial in partnering with other groups to generate financial resources, Al-Quds personnel are adept at accomplishing their community service activities with very little money.

Future Directions and Reflections

The experience of Al-Quds is instructive with respect to the question, what does university civic engagement and social responsibility mean in a situation of intense social conflict? Civic engagement and social responsibility are not a choice for the university. Al-Quds by necessity is highly engaged. Its civic engagement and social responsibility work is manifest in a set of programs, but even more through its larger institutional presence and role in regional politics and development.

Because it operates with such severe financial constraints, external funding is especially important as a source of support for community programs. Al-Quds' success in brokering funded collaborations with other universities and with other institutions around the world is a powerful reminder of the potential for mutual support within the higher education civic engagement movement.

An important theme in this story that resonates with the experience of other universities is the relationship between off-campus university centers and students' education and service activities. Al-Quds is a good example of an institution that does a great deal of both and where there are significant, but also limited, connections between these realms. The University relies extensively on full-time staffed service programs in order to do a good job of responding to community needs. Serving community needs takes priority over providing educational opportunities for students.

At Al-Quds students' community service activities are a major corrective or supplement to the reliance of the curriculum on traditional lectures and rote learning. The university has an opportunity to implement community service learning more extensively; to what extent it will move in this direction is not clear.

Malaysia and its Higher Education System

Malaysia has a population of 26.2 million, an average life expectancy for men of 71 and women of 76, and ranks 131 out of 175 in Reporters without Borders' 2009 Press Freedom Index. Its adult literacy rate is 88.7% (male, 92%; female, 85.4%); it has 0.7 doctors per 1,000 population, an infant mortality rate of 15.37 deaths per 1,000 live births, and an adult HIV/AIDS rate of 0.5% (CIA, 2010).

Present-day Malaysia was formed out of former British colonies and protectorates established in the eighteenth and nineteenth centuries. In 1957, the British territories on the Malay Peninsula gained independence as the Federation of Malaya. Several other colonies, including Singapore, joined the federation to become Malaysia in 1963, although Singapore seceded in 1965. Malaysia's early history was marked by conflicts with neighboring states, a communist insurgency, and inter-ethnic violence. However, Prime Minister Mahathir bin Mohamad's 22-year rule (1981–2003) witnessed significant economic growth and development. Today, tensions still exist between the majority Muslim Malay population and minorities, especially ethnic Chinese. As the majority the Malays tend to dominate politically, although ethnic Chinese tend to have more economic power and wealth.

When Malaysia became independent in 1957, it had just one university, but soon began expansion of its tertiary sector. For the first decades after independence, higher education in Malaysia was dominated by government institutions. However, several reform bills were passed in 1996, including the Private Higher Education Act, which for the first time allowed the creation of private universities and allowed private colleges to gain university status (UNESCO International Bureau of Education, 2006). Private higher education expanded rapidly after this, although public education still accounts for about 60% of student enrollment (Ministry of Higher Education, Malaysia, January 2009). Today, the tertiary sector consists of "20 public universities, 33 private universities and university colleges, four foreign university branch campuses, 22 polytechnics, 37 community colleges and about 500 private colleges" (Ministry of Higher Education, Malaysia, January 2009).

Tertiary enrollment has expanded steadily over the past decade. From 2002 to 2007, private enrollment increased 24% while public enrollment increased about 37% (Ministry of Higher Education, Malaysia, 2009). Today, over 900,000 students are enrolled in higher education. In 2005, the Gross Enrollment Ratio for tertiary education was about 29%, a huge improvement over the 1990 GER of 7% (World Bank, 2008).

The Ministry of Higher Education (MOHE) was established in 2004 to oversee the country's higher education system. Several other agencies handle specific areas under MOHE's jurisdiction. These include the National Higher Education Fund Corporation, which provides student loans; and the Malaysian Qualifications Agency, which was established in 2007 by the merger of the National Accreditation Board and the Quality Assurance Division of MOHE. Until the late 1990s, the government provided most of the funding for public institutions, keeping tuition fees relatively low. However, starting in 1998 the government granted greater autonomy to some public universities and encouraged them to supplement their public funding through private sources such as "research contracts, consulting, business linkages with appropriate industry clusters, and . . . increased tuition fees at the graduate level" (Foong, 2008). Private institutions receive tax incentives but otherwise rely on private sources for their funding. Spending on higher education is fairly high, but has been criticized for inefficiency. For example, in 2000, Malaysia spent about 83.3% of GDP per capita on each tertiary student, while Singapore spent just 33.5% and Thailand 33% with better educational outcomes.

Community engagement in higher education remains a relatively new concept in Malaysia, but it is increasingly promoted by government policy. The Malaysian Qualifications Agency's first Code of Practice for Institutional Audit (COPIA), published in 2008, stressed community engagement as a requirement for higher education institutions. The second edition of the COPIA, published in 2009, states that "Teaching, research, consultancy services and community engagement are the core interrelated academic activities" and adds the following community engagement requirements:

- There **must** be a policy and programs for active student participation in areas that affect their welfare, for example, peer counseling, co-curricular activities, and community engagement;
- The HEP **must** encourage connectivity of its staff and students with the local community around it, including through cultural, social and community service activities;
- The HEP [Higher Education Provider] should actively participate in socioeconomic activities of the community in which it is located.

(Malaysian Qualifications Agency, 2008, emphasis in the original)

Community Partnerships to Address National Priorities

Profile of Universiti Kebangsaan Malaysia (Malaysia)
By Robert M. Hollister (based on field visit
January 7 and 8, 2010)

Overview

Universiti Kebangsaan Malaysia, the National University of Malaysia (UKM), was established in 1970 to preserve and promote the Malay culture and language. The University has also been entrusted with the important national agenda of unity and integration among ethnic groups, and it presently houses the nation's first ethnic studies institute. Over time, UKM has developed to become one of Malaysia's premier research universities with over 27,000 students, 13 faculties and 14 research institutes. Today UKM is a preferred choice for Malaysian students seeking tertiary education.

The University summarizes its civic engagement and social responsibility mission as follows:

> The university aspires to pioneer innovation and produce a society that is imbued with dynamic and civic leadership. We make available our intellectual expertise to serve the wider community at large and equip our students with the tools to be knowledgeable, productive and adaptable in today's complex world. We lay foundations for our students to become caring citizens. We work actively to contribute to nation building and to developing a body of research relevant to the global community, including the preservation of our environment.

Key societal challenges include disparities in income and wealth, increasing ethnic polarization, and environmental sustainability. The country is striving to "promote economic growth with equity."

UKM is notable not only for its civic engagement and social responsibility accomplishments to date, but also for its distinctively strong institutional leadership and organizational strategy. UKM is led by Vice-Chancellor Dr Sharifah Hapsah Syed Hassan Shahabudin, a forceful advocate of university–community partnerships to address national priorities. Dr Sharifah Hapsah Shahabudin, who also serves as President of the National Council of Women's Organizations, personally models civic leadership both within and outside the university. A major aspect of UKM's approach to civic engagement, and one that may be of special interest to other institutions, is its establishment of a high level position of Deputy Vice-Chancellor for Industry and Community Partnerships in 2007. To date UKM's engagement work has concentrated on initiatives that enhance and enrich the central roles of the university—research, education, and service.

Several research institutes are primary vehicles through which the university addresses societal needs.

The University places special emphasis on selected societal challenges, which include preservation of the Malay language and culture, sustainability and environmental preservation, and strengthening inter-ethnic relations. The institution has created an institute to lead its work on each of these issues—the Institute of the Malay World and Civilizations, the Institute for Environment and Development, and the Institute of Ethnic Studies.

UKM's civic education goals directly express the Prime Minister's vision expressed in a speech in Parliament (March 31, 2006): "Malaysia's future success depends on the quality of its human capital, not only in terms of intellect but also character. Therefore, in line with this thrust, the Government aims to undertake comprehensive improvement of the country's education system, from pre-school to tertiary and vocational institutions. A more enabling environment will also be fostered to encourage the R&D. At the same time, a heavier emphasis will be placed on the shaping of values to create more well-rounded individuals."

In 2009, UKM issued a publication titled "Strengthening Community Engagement: Nurturing Caring Citizens," that was both a vision statement and a report on substantial work-in-progress. It is notable that the publication report's subtitle communicates a key educational goal: "Nurturing Caring Citizens." The document summarizes the University's aspirations: "The expectation is that UKM will be a driver for the K-economy to fast-track Malaysia's development in an increasingly globalized world, to be a leader in creating human capital, producing graduates who are innovative and economically productive while being socially responsible citizens." It goes on to observe that in the tenure of Vice-Chancellor Sharifah Hapsah, "More academic staff and students have come to realize that quality education is not just about learning facts and figures, but also experiencing and responding to real life situations and challenges."

UKM aims to be a good institutional citizen through its own policies and practices in, for example, how it approaches the design of new buildings and through steps it takes to limit energy consumption. The University manages on the campus a forest reserve that is a living laboratory for research on biodiversity and tropical rainforest ecology. It maintains the country's only fernarium, the third largest in the world, which preserves endangered species and conducts research on them.

Community partnerships are a central dimension of UKM's civic work. It has a memorandum of understanding with MERCY Malaysia, a medical relief organization. UKM staff participate in MERCY Malaysia's medical relief missions. It addition, it collaborates with MERCY Malaysia on disaster relief and risk reduction research.

Vigorous Leadership from the Top

Civic engagement is a high priority for Vice-Chancellor Dr Sharifah Hapsah Syed Hassan Shahabudin. A regular participant in UKM community service activities, in her public communications Dr Sharifah Hapsah Shahabudin frequently emphasizes this dimension of the University's mission. In addition to serving as Vice-Chancellor, she continues in her prior position as President of the National Council of Women's Organizations. This major NGO leadership role reinforces what she is able to accomplish as the leader of UKM. In addition to promoting student volunteering, the Vice-Chancellor is a vigorous advocate of UKM's research capabilities and takes personal initiative to arrange specific opportunities for UKM centers and professors to address local and national problems.

Key elements in the Vice-Chancellor's strategy are her support for the Office of Deputy Vice-Chancellor for Industry and Community Partnerships, the creation of industry-community partnership coordinator positions in all faculties, the establishment of annual awards for outstanding civic engagement, and the elevation of civic engagement in the annual performance reviews of faculty members.

A well-known public intellectual, Vice-Chancellor Sharifah Hapsah Shahabudin writes a regular column in the *New Straits Times* newspaper. She views service to society as not only the university's responsibility to the national government, but also as a central element in its social contract with Malaysian society. Her perspective is that UKM must contribute its resources directly to serve pressing needs of the community, and also to do so through its research and educational programs. Student volunteer projects play an important role, but are not sufficient because there is only so much time that they have beyond their coursework.

The Vice-Chancellor forcefully expressed her vision for the societal role of UKM in one of her *New Straits Times* columns entitled "Universities as Conscience of Society" (August 18, 2008):

> Engaging in social change induces a cultural change in academia and society that allows independent thinking and opinion-making on societal issues . . .
>
> The university serves as critic and conscience of society. It reconciles ethnic traditions with state rationality and legitimizes them by founding a set of practices, a cultural image, a discourse, or an institution. This is also part of the social contract of universities . . . It is a way of providing evidence of value for the financing spent on universities.
>
> It is incumbent on universities to protect their cultural mission in this globalized age of the innovation economy, where universities are increasingly being viewed as economic producers of knowledge, innovation, technology and skilled workers. . . . It would be a shame for ethics and values to be inadvertently sidelined, because intangibles such as beliefs, spirituality, happiness, tolerance, mutual respect, sharing, caring and loving are marginalized.

The Vice-Chancellor constantly seeks opportunities to link UKM's research strengths to community programs. When the wife of the Prime Minister of Malaysia expressed concern about antisocial behavior by unemployed youth, the Vice-Chancellor organized UKM professors to develop policy recommendations to tackle the causes of this problem. More recently, the university secured substantial funding from the Sime Darby Foundation (YSD) to establish a Chair for Climate Change, one of UKM's niche areas of expertise. The Chair will be managed by the university's Research Centre for Tropical Climate Change Systems (IKLIM) which is part of the Faculty of Science and Technology. The Chair will be a platform to spearhead research that can identify the impact of climate change at local and regional levels, develop scientific findings to formulate policies for sustainable development and aid the development of mitigation measures and adaptation to climate change. Awareness and adaptation measures will be communicated to communities through UKM students who will be trained as climate change ambassadors.

The Vice-Chancellor sees participation in community service as another way to build inter-ethnic group cohesion, stating, "When we've common goals, we forget our differences. Civic engagement is a better laboratory for building intergroup understanding than the lecture halls."

An essential educational goal advocated by Dr Sharifah Hapsah Shahabudin is to enhance students' understanding of the value and importance of Community-Based Organizations. She observes that many graduates who ultimately work for government agencies, and also those who work for private companies, should know about and respect the role and contributions of CBOs in Malaysian society.

Creation of a University-Wide Office of Industry and Community Partnerships

The civic engagement programs of UKM are comparatively new. A major stimulus for strengthening and expanding them was a national government directive in 2007 that each of Malaysia's four research universities establish the new position of Deputy Vice-Chancellor for Industry and Community Partnerships. This high level position is filled at UKM by long-time faculty member Professor Saran Kaur Gill, a specialist in language and cultural policy and planning. She is defining this new university-wide role with high creativity and entrepreneurial drive. Her portfolio at UKM provides a structured platform of governance for the university to reach out and establish strategic relationships with industry and community. The Office works systematically and in a mode of mutual support with the Vice-Chancellor and Deputy Vice-Chancellors for Research & Innovation, Academic & International Affairs and Student Affairs & Alumni. The efforts and initiatives are directly supported by three engagement offices—the Industry Liaison Office, Office of University–Community Partnerships, the Chancellor's Foundation—as well as the Heads of Industry and Community Partnerships at 13 Faculties and Directors at the 14 Research Institutes.

Dr Gill and her staff are encouraging professors across all fields of the University to integrate community service in their teaching and research, are providing guidance and financial support to facilitate these changes, and are actively brokering collaborations with all sectors—business, government and nonprofit—to support effective public service-oriented research, scholarship and education. Their strategy for strengthening civic engagement at UKM is to both promote culture change within the institution and to build colleagues' capacity, always in alignment with core goals of the University.

The next stage in UKM's organizational strategy calls for the appointment of a Deputy Dean for partnerships in each of its 13 schools. These are three-year positions, to be filled by current faculty members. The result will be an unusually extensive infrastructure of support for partnerships, one that is embedded in the full range of disciplines.

Operating principles in the draft Industry and Community Engagement Strategic Plan 2010–2014 are:

1. Knowledge Exchange: Engagement involves a two-way follow of knowledge and experience between UKM and our partners. They learn from us and we learn from them to facilitate positive outcomes for all stakeholders.
2. Knowledge Eco-System: Industry and community engagement will largely be driven by UKM's niche research areas.
3. Supportive Role: Engagement initiatives support and enhance the three core activities of UKM—education, research and service.
4. Quality: UKM undertakes high quality engagement that contributes to building just and sustainable communities.
5. Human Resource Capacity: Engagement initiatives develop knowledge leaders in industry and community engagement throughout the university.

The Deputy Vice-Chancellor's office recently launched UKM's Industry & Community Engagement System (ICEsys), which will facilitate the process of consolidating, documenting and monitoring existing and new engagement initiatives across the university. Another major milestone for the Deputy Vice-Chancellor's office is the revamping of existing staff appraisal systems at the University to incorporate key criteria that recognize and reward efforts in industry–community engagement across the areas of research, education and service.

The Deputy Vice-Chancellor's office operates a web-based request-for-assistance system to match community demands for assistance and the university supply of the same. It addition, it provides University–Industry and University–Community Research Grants to encourage professors to conduct research that has direct and immediate societal impact. It provided seed funds in 2008 to four community-focused projects, for a total of almost US$150,000. These projects concerned community health, computer skills, a village community center and three schools in Johor, and development of an educational module for autistic children in a local community.

The Office maintains close collaboration with international student organizations such as AIESEC to provide students with opportunities for work-based training through national and international internships. Through targeted industry networks, this office also organizes programs to develop work-place skills, provide career advice and enhance job-placement opportunities for the graduates, and coordinates the placement of academics within industry and community organizations. Another important role of the Office is to develop strategic partnerships with key industry players for collaborative research that is driven by the university's niche research areas.

One example of successful collaboration between UKM's community partnerships and industry partnerships personnel was securing funding from the Exxon Corporation to expand community service uses of the University's large fernarium. Another positive example of the private sector supporting university service projects was the funding provided by pharmaceutical and telecommunications companies to the Lake Chini project. More recently, the Office of the Deputy Vice-Chancellor (Industry & Community Partnerships) led a successful collaboration with Sime Darby Foundation (YSD) that resulted in the establishment of an endowment Chair for Sustainable Development which is an area of critical concern in the South East Asia region. This will focus on researching on zero-waste technology for the oil palm industry. The Office also supports a Small and Medium-sized Enterprises Entrepreneurship Program through which Economics students mentor participating businesses, and learn in the process.

Dr Gill's division directors observe that many professors initially equate civic engagement with volunteerism. The Office of the Deputy Vice-Chancellor views its challenge as to demonstrate that civic engagement also consists of service that is integrated in academic courses and as conducting community-based research and applying research findings to community needs. The ultimate aim is to share and exchange knowledge, expertise, facilities and services with all partners to address economic, social and environmental challenges faced by communities, the nation and the region. All of this contributes to the development of human capital that meets the expectations of industry and the community and contributes to the wellbeing of the nation.

A Focus on Student Volunteer Service

UKM sponsors extensive student volunteering in order to serve society and to educate its students for social responsibility, which is a stated priority: "As part of the vision of pioneering innovation in knowledge, we recognize that we have a moral obligation to be the conscience of society and hence we endeavor to preserve values such as social responsibility . . . we need to equip students with the ability to respond to community challenges . . ." The Centre for Students Advancement supports and coordinates student volunteering. In 2008 the Center spent over US$90,000 on 308 student community projects. Since 2005, students have had the option of participating in a six-credit Community Services course that consists of doing a service project. An average of 900 students take this course each semester.

In response to a devastating flood in the Pagoh area of Johor province in 2007, UKM adopted a village where they are concentrating their relief and rebuilding efforts. The flood stimulated an outpouring of volunteer service and remains a significant focus of ongoing volunteer efforts. Accompanied by the Vice-Chancellor and many faculty members, more than 1,000 students volunteered to clean up the village in the period immediately after the flood. In what is now known as the Village Adoption Project, UKM has worked with village representatives to prepare a comprehensive development plan for post-relief action that emphasizes goals of reducing poverty, improving health, and environmental conversation.

Students participate in Youth Companion programs that are co-sponsored by the Youth and Sports Ministry. With its strong institutional commitment to the preservation of Malaysian culture, an important dimension of UKM student volunteering is the performing arts on campus and in the community. Through the Cultural Centre multiple student artistic clubs carry out community service that promotes and enhances Malaysian culture, especially traditional art and music. The University plays a similar role in the area of athletics. Its Sports Unit offers consulting services to community groups to operate and to improve their sports activities. Faculty and students collaborate with MERCY Malaysia on medical and humanitarian service projects in Malaysia and abroad.

UKM and the National Council of Women's Organizations have a strong partnership, reinforced by the Vice-Chancellor's continuing role as president of NCWO. The two organizations co-sponsor a program of home stays wherein UKM students of diverse ethnic groups live briefly with families of different ethnic backgrounds to promote intercultural understanding.

Students value the skills that they build through their volunteering—interpersonal skills, leadership development, building self-confidence, communication and teamwork, and problem-solving. Student service leaders claim that their peers' preoccupation with their academic studies is an obstacle to recruiting them to participate in volunteer projects.

Growing Faculty Initiative

A modest number of professors incorporate community service activities in their teaching. A larger number advise student volunteer programs. Many are involved in policy development activities through national committees, and the university encourages this participation. One professor stated, "It is part of our jobs, and increasingly is recognized in our yearly evaluation." Faculty members attest that

Professor Saran's new high-level position shows that the institution is committed strongly to her responsibilities. Those faculty members who are most active in community service would like to see community activities be better planned and conducted, with more funding. Professor Dr Wan Zurinah Wan Ngah, Deputy Director, Medical Molecular Biology Institute, states, "We are encouraging steps be taken to move from student volunteer projects that are ad hoc and one-off activities to projects that are sustained over time."

Due to feedback from employers that university graduates are lacking in "soft skills," UKM professors as well as administrators are concerned about the employability of their students. This concern translates into additional support for regional and international internships and community-based programs, which are seen by faculty members as an effective way to strengthen the development of participants' soft skills and workplace competencies.

All of the faculty in Community Medicine and in Family Medicine directly supervise the community practice activities of students and they also advise students as they plan volunteer service initiatives. All students are required to take co-curriculum modules, within which community service is an option. Medical students are required to complete eight-week postings in both a rural health facility and in a district hospital that emphasizes primary care. Students also are encouraged to select a community-oriented project for their required five-week elective posting. Students in the Dept. of Community Medicine conduct research in communities, for example, on how to encourage people to adopt a healthy life style. Medical faculty would like the continuity and sustainability of student service work, in order to increase community impacts and also to elevate what students learn.

In the Faculty of Law, first-year students are required to participate in a community service co-curriculum activity during their second semester. Faculty and students in the Faculty of Economics and Business are engaged with several corporations and agencies through an internship program and staff business mentoring program.

Research Institutes are Primary Vehicles for the University to Address Societal Needs

Key civic engagement roles are being played by several UKM centers that administer sponsored projects that link with and serve external constituencies. The University is concentrating on eight niche research areas: renewable energy; climate change; nanotechnology and advanced materials; health and medical technology; sustainable regional development; biotechnology development; content-based informatics; national identity, nation-state cultural diversity and globalization. Examples of recent research projects that contribute directly to pressing societal needs include: Managing Intellectual Property Rights for Malaysian Small and Medium Enterprises; Modeling of Junior Entrepreneurship Attitudes and Intention; A National Study of School Dropouts Characteristics; Risk Factors and the Development of Dropout Prevention Strategies. A Social Energy Research Institute project placed solar panels in remote Indigenous communities. It is also envisaged that the endowed Chair for Climate Change will emerge as a national and regional force in climate change research, sustainable development and knowledge generation.

The Lake Chini Research Centre, Faculty of Science and Technology, is collaborating with the Pahang State Government to restore the lake and its surrounding wetlands to achieve classification as a UNESCO Biosphere Reserve. The project is working to reduce water pollution and also to train Indigenous people in entrepreneurial skills. Team members come from a broad range of disciplines—they are environmental engineers, botanists, biotechnologists, health professionals, economists, business experts, and psychologists. In a second major environmental restoration project, the Institute for Sustainable Development and the Langkawi Development Authority collaborated to make Langkawi the first UNESCO Geopark in South-east Asia.

Associate Professor Datin Dr Norizan Razak directs the E-Community Research Center, established in 2001, which assists marginalized communities and aims to bridge the digital divide. A national center of excellence on this challenge, a recent project helped female entrepreneurs to develop their websites. Dr Norizan comments, "Our aspiration is to increase the university presence in the community. We both learn from the community and we share our expertise with the community."

Driving Factors and Challenges

As the publicly funded National University of Malaysia, UKM'S civic engagement work is guided explicitly by priorities of the national government, as they are expressed in annual and multi-year plans for education and development, including the National Higher Education Strategic Plan. Dynamic leadership by the Vice-Chancellor and the Deputy Vice-Chancellor for Industry and Community Partnerships are important drivers. The future employability of its students is a pervasive concern at the University and figures prominently in planning discussions about the next stage of its civic engagement activities.

Public service is rewarded in faculty and staff evaluation processes. In recognition of the importance of service and civic engagement, the University in 2009 increased the weight given to industry–community engagement contributions in annual performance reviews to a maximum of 20% (up from 5%) and for support staff to 10%. These figures include engagement with industry and community at all levels, across the areas of research, education and service. These are notably greater than the rewards in many other universities where lack of faculty incentives is a frequent complaint. Faculty members experience the common cross-pressures of the institution's increasing aspirations and expectations in the areas of research, education and service.

The University's civic work is shaped substantially by national and more local priorities. Its Board of Directors is appointed by the Minister of Higher Education. In addition, its work is guided by the National Higher Education Strategic Plan which is updated each year. Community input is secured through advisory panels that are specific to each faculty; the membership of these panels consists of representatives from industry and community-based organizations. As one of four research universities in the country, UKM is expected by the national government to contribute directly to the country's economic development.

Future Directions

A priority for Vice-Chancellor Sharifah Hapsah Shahabudin is to more fully integrate UKM's education, research and service activities and to develop multiple entry points for faculty and students to participate in these activities. She and her leadership team want to encourage and grow the number of professors who are integrating community service learning in their courses. The Vice-Chancellor cites as an illustration of successful integration, how faculty members' service work with the Adopted Village program led to subsequent research activities on energy production and environmental conservation. She also aims that innovative community interventions that prove to be effective be adopted by the government for broader implementation.

UKM appears to be poised to play a leadership role within other institutions of higher education in South-east Asia. The University is organizing an international conference on higher education–industry–community engagement in 2011, focusing on Innovative Practices and Strategic Partnerships that can impact social, economic and environmental development in the ASEAN community. The Talloires Network is a prospective partner for this effort, which could become a major focus of UKM's engagement initiatives.

Reflections

As was discussed above, a distinctive feature of UKM's approach is the creation of a high-level university office in charge of industry and community partnerships, accompanied by the creation of full-time deputy dean positions in each of the University's 13 colleges to advance the partnerships strategy within the primary academic units. This organizational approach represents an unusually comprehensive infusion model. Furthermore, the organizational co-location of responsibility for industry partnerships and for community partnerships creates promising possibilities for both program development and for financial support of community projects.

UKM's commitment to social responsibility is apparent in how the institution has visibly embraced the role of being "the conscience of society." As the Vice-

Chancellor expresses it, "We recognized that we have a moral obligation to be the conscience of society and hence we endeavor to preserve values such as social responsibility and taking the right actions."

Mexico and its Higher Education System

Mexico has a population of 107 million, an average life expectancy for men of 72 and women of 77, and ranks 140th out of 173 in the Media Freedom Index. Its adult literacy rate is 92.4%, it has 1.5 doctors per 1,000 population, and an adult HIV/AIDS rate of 0.3% (*Guardian* "World Fact Files," 2009). Mexico's Indigenous population comprises almost 30% of the total population.

Mexico faces numerous social challenges, the most pressing being high levels of poverty, social inequality, drug violence, and corruption. Approximately 14% of the population regularly experiences hunger. Economic development has been uneven and social problems continue to grow, resulting in a reduction in quality of life and a very high rate of violence. Conditions vary significantly from region to region, with the south-east of the country reporting the lowest levels of development.

On the other hand, Mexico has a significant population of highly educated and affluent citizens and very competitive industrial and business sectors. As the global economy becomes increasingly reliant on the development of new technology, Mexico seeks to increase the educational attainment of its citizens and decrease extreme poverty.

Higher education in Mexico is diverse with over 515 public institutions, including 45 universities, and over 735 private institutions. Private HEIs account for over 27% of undergraduate and 36% of graduate enrollment. The remainder of students attend public HEIs, with 52% of undergraduates and 48% of graduate students attending public universities and the rest attending other public HEIs. Although private HEI shares of undergraduate enrollments increased from 11.7% in 1975 to 27.6% in 1999, it remains well below Latin American averages. Most research is conducted by public institutions.

In 2005, Mexico spent $6402 per student in public HEIs, compared with the OECD average of $11,512 per student. From 1995 to 2005, public spending on state universities increased 43.2%.

Private HEIs get most of their funding through tuition and fees. Public HEIs get most of their funding through public finance. Federal universities receive funding from the federal government, while state universities receive both federal and state funding.

The legal framework for HE is provided by the Mexican Constitution and a number of national laws, including the General Education Law and the Law for Higher Education Coordination. The Mexican Constitution guarantees that: "Universities and other higher education institutions granted autonomy by the law will be empowered to and responsible for governing themselves."

The Mexican Secretariat of Public Education cites strengthening HEI autonomy as one of the guiding principles in its HE reforms, indicating that even the Mexican government admits that HE lacks an appropriate level of autonomy.

Mexican law states that all students should complete 480 hours of community social service in order to earn a baccalaureate degree. It is up to each individual higher education institution to manage and certify the observance of this requirement. These hours can be earned through a variety of activities including internships, employment on campus, or community service. Individual universities may choose to add additional layers to this requirement, for example, by stating that at least half of these hours are pure community service rather than pre-professional practice.

In May of 2009, legislators pushed for greater recognition for professional practice through Mexico's service hour requirement. Carlos Pedrero Rodriguez, president of the Youth Commission in Congress, pressed for changes to the Education Act that would allow students to gain more professional skills while serving the community. He said, "Our intention is not to eliminate social services but show that it has a dual purpose, enabling young people to provide a service to society, but also to help them gain work experience."

Mexico has many prestigious universities, both public and private. One of the top public universities is The National Autonomous University of Mexico (UNAM). Founded in 1551, UNAM claims to be the oldest university in North America. UNAM is also considered to be the largest university in Latin America. In 2005, *The Times* of London ranked it as the best in Spain, Portugal, and Latin America, and 95th overall. UNAM has an enrollment of 269,000 students, which makes it one of the world's largest universities.

The top private institution, profiled below, is the Tecnológico de Monterrey, or The Monterrey Institute of Technology and Higher Studies, abbreviated as ITESM. It is exceptional in both technology and research. The university's educational model redesigns the educational experience around technology and culture, knowledge production and social consciousness.

Cultivating Ethics and Citizenship

Profile of Tecnológico de Monterrey (Mexico)
By Elizabeth Babcock (based on field visit to Monterrey and Saltillo campuses February 10–11, 2010)

Background

The Tecnológico de Monterrey, also known as Monterrey Institute of Technology and Higher Education or Instituto Tecnológico y de Estudios Superiores de Monterrey (ITESM), was founded in 1943 by a group of Mexican businessmen in the city of Monterrey. It is a private, non-profit institution committed to social development and innovation. It has 33 campuses distributed throughout the country, and academic centers in Mexico and other Latin American countries; it also has international offices in North America, Europe, and Asia. Through its Virtual University, founded in 1989, it is present all over the world. The institution offers 54 undergraduate degrees, 54 Masters degrees and 10 Doctoral degrees. The current system-wide Rector is Rafael Rangel Sostmann, a class of 1965 alumnus, who has held this position since 1985.

The Tecnológico de Monterrey is one of the most highly regarded institutions in all of Mexico. One of the key founders, Eugenio Garza Sada, was a graduate of the Massachusetts Institute of Technology (MIT) and had a vision to establish an institution like MIT in Mexico to service the human and social development needs of the country. However, the economic development of Mexico was, and still is, so intricately linked with the United States that internationalization of the university was one of the first and most crucial institutional priorities. In 1950, it became the first foreign university in history to be accredited by the Southern Association of Colleges and Schools (SACS). This external accreditation process was extremely important for institutional recognition and development.

The Tecnológico de Monterrey explicitly cites the importance of civic engagement in its mission:

> The mission of Tecnológico de Monterrey is to form persons with integrity, ethical standards and a humanistic outlook, who are internationally competitive in their professional field and, who, at the same time are good citizens committed to the economic, political, social and cultural development of their community and to the sustainable use of natural resources.

This emphasis in the mission translates into a large array of programs and courses that emphasize ethics, citizenship and community service. The business school was ranked fourth in the world in business ethics and social-responsibility by *Business Week* Magazine in 2005. Roxana Cárdenas, Director of the Office of Social Education and Development, emphasized that "universities contribute both to personal and social formation. Because Tecnológico de Monterrey is private, they also have a larger obligation to fulfill this debt to society. Over 50% of students at Tecnológico de Monterrey have some scholarship and they work to expose students from privileged backgrounds to real community issues."

The university reviews its mission every 10 years in order to stay on the cutting edge of knowledge production and innovation. The current 2015 mission, revised in 2005, has the following strategic aims, to:

- promote the international competitiveness of business enterprises based on knowledge, innovation, technological development, and sustainable development;

- develop business management models to compete in a global economy;
- create, implement and transfer business incubator models and networks to contribute to the creation of enterprises;
- collaborate in professionalizing public administration; and analyze and propose public policies for Mexico's development;
- contribute to the sustainable development of the community with innovative models and systems for its educational, social, economic and political improvement.

The mission of Tecnológico de Monterrey has evolved over time to include a greater emphasis on community engagement, citizenship and ethics. Indeed, mission statements since 1985 have included some mention of developing professionals with ethical skills in order to be competitive in the marketplace and contribute to development. This objective was clarified further in 1995 to include social and community development. The most recent mission is the most explicit to date about the important of civic engagement to the education and professional development of its students. It also mentions sustainable development for the first time, echoing an important concern of the business sectors, as well as government.

Betting it all on Ethics and Citizenship

The Tecnológico de Monterrey has continued to seek its accreditation from the Southern Association of Colleges and Schools. When approached by SACS about choosing the focus of its most recent accreditation process, the university chose an unlikely and highly challenging topic: ethics and citizenship competencies of students. In fact, they were advised not to choose this focus as it would be difficult to measure and may put their accreditation in jeopardy. But they proceeded, with the conviction that these were key attributes they wanted in their graduates and the external pressure would push them to achieve their goal.

They have put in place the Quality Enhancement Program (QEP) in order to measure student knowledge, skills and behavior in ethics and citizenship. The QEP seeks to ensure that students develop ethics and citizenship competencies that they will carry with them throughout their professional careers.

The QEP is an institution-wide effort with the inclusion of staff, faculty and students from across the university system. When I spoke with Carlos Mijares, the Vice-Rector for Academics and Research, regarding the QEP parameters and measurement tools, he informed me that they are measuring student learning outcomes in these areas in multiple ways. They have sampled the general student population to ascertain trends and areas for improvement. They have also sought to measure individual student progress in order to provide feedback and guidance. In 2009, they surveyed over 10,000 students to evaluate their educational development around ethics and citizenship. Additionally, they will do longitudinal studies that follow students beyond graduation to determine the effect of this program on students' long-term choices in their careers, including measuring their public service.

The reaccreditation process is a difficult one, but Tecnológico de Monterrey is ensuring that they use this process to fully evaluate the quality of their ethics and citizenship curriculum across the entire university system. Luis López Monreal, the QEP Director, emphasized the "democratic nature" of their consultation process. They include the perspectives of all stakeholders, from academic directors on each branch campus, to faculty, students and community partners. This enhances the value of the information they gather and aids in implementation in a diverse multi-campus system.

Creating High Quality Community Partnerships

Mexican regulations for higher education state that all the students must complete 480 hours of community social service before graduation. It is up to each individual higher education institution to manage and supervise the observance of this requirement. As I learned in discussions with both students and faculty, not all Mexican higher education institutions have a rigorous process for counting these hours or ensuring quality experiences for students or positive impact in the community. Since 1998, the Tecnológico de Monterrey has worked to develop a more rigorous system for vetting community service opportunities and tracking hours earned by students. In the past, students from Tecnológico de Monterrey admitted to me that they had falsified some of their hours because they felt they could not complete them or did not have good quality experiences. The new monitoring process seeks to ensure this will no longer occur.

In order to increase the quality of the service experience, the Institute for Sustainable Social Development (ISSD) helps manage and evaluate community partners, such as NGOs, businesses or local governments. Tecnológico de Monterrey has over 400 official partner organizations in its central database. These partners are governments (federal, state, municipal), educational institutions (universities, school districts), private corporations, NGOs, and international organizations (Organization of American States, Inter-American Development Bank). They survey students who have worked with these organizations and maintain relationships with managers there. Students can only receive credit by doing their service hours with an approved partner. Of the 480 social service hours each student has to complete before graduation, 240 must be devoted to professional experience in their fields of expertise. Many students find it is possible to combine work in their chosen fields with community service.

The main ISSD office is located at the headquarters of Tecnológico de Monterrey, with a manager at each of the 33 branch campuses. In additional to monitoring community partnerships, ISSD also provides direct community services through further education opportunities for community members. It develops educational, training, and entrepreneurship programs and courses focused on topics such as entrepreneurship and microenterprise, legal counseling, and primary and secondary education tutoring. Tecnológico de Monterrey students take part in these programs in their area of study or because of a personal interest and are able to receive community social service hours. Faculty members guide and oversee the students' activities in these programs.

In addition to its responsibility providing and monitoring community service hours, ISSD performs several other important functions. It offers a program called Prepanet, an online high school program for individuals who, because of time, financial or geographical constraints, have not had the opportunity to pursue their high school studies through traditional channels. ISSD also runs two other national social programs: social incubators and community learning centers. The social incubators provide space for incubating microenterprise projects or starting community service organizations. There are 63 of these incubators located in 27 states of Mexico as of 2009. Community learning centers provide a broad range of courses in technology, business, law, education and other topics. These are frequently sponsored and operated with public and private partners.

Each year, the university publishes the University Social Responsibility Report. This report covers all social responsibility programs and outlines the number of internal participants and the social impact of the program. This report is submitted to all stakeholders of the institution.

The Debate: Mandatory Student Service Hours

I asked both students and faculty to weigh in on the nationwide graduation requirement of 480 service hours. This is always a contentious policy debate and there was certainly disagreement among both faculty and students on the merits of a policy requiring mandatory service. I found it striking that a majority of students supported mandatory service hours because they believed young people would not care or engage otherwise. Yet these students were examples of the possibility of engaging young people in meaningful service activities. Many of them mentioned they had completed far more than the number of required service hours because they loved the work they were doing.

There were compelling arguments supporting the policy of mandatory service. In Mexico, only 10% of citizens engage in service or volunteer activities. This is significantly lower than in the United States, which has the highest rate of volunteerism in the world at 47% (see: www.prospect.org/cs/articles?article=the_tocqueville_files_the_other_civic_america_5197). Students believed that by requiring their peers to do service, it would open their eyes to the reality of their country and the pressing needs of local communities in a more profound way than reading about it. They also believed that their peers would "get hooked" on volunteering once they had a positive experience.

Faculty also supported mandatory service, but for a wider range of reasons. They cited the importance of guiding young people through a learning experience with support from the university and its partners. They also cited the importance of connecting their professional development with service. Ernesto Benavides Ornelas, Director of the Program of Social Education, Citizenship and Community Service, emphasized to me the "process of personal discovery" that occurs for students throughout their service experience. He emphasized that both positive and negative or challenging experiences can lead to personal growth. However, there were some faculty members who dissented. Some felt the number of hours was too high, or had some concerns about the consistently ensuring quality experiences for students throughout their time in the university.

Additionally, the topic of what kinds of activity should count as service was brought up. Service-learning is being implemented in various courses across the curriculum and the faculty members I spoke with had volunteered to receive training on this teaching pedagogy. An average of 60–70 different service-learning courses, engaging more than 200 civic groups and reaching an average of 5,000 students per semester are now offered. At the time of my visit, students were able to receive both course credit and service hours for service-learning courses. Professor Maria del Carmen Villareal Erhard felt that it was not appropriate that students should receive both types of credit. She felt it was very important that students complete the full amount of service hours and that the course credit should be only for the learning that happens as a result of in classroom work and community service. Not all faculty members agreed and it was clear that this policy may be revisited as the number of service-learning courses expands.

Teaching with Purpose: Ethics, Citizenship and Service in the Curriculum

The Tecnológico de Monterrey has always emphasized an innovative curriculum, which includes problem based learning, case based learning and project oriented learning, and, more recently, service-learning. The academic rigor of the curriculum is managed centrally at the main campus in Monterrey and implemented across all 33 branch campuses in the system. In order to meet the goals of the QEP program, they have continued to strengthen the teaching of ethics and citizenship through the Citizenship Education Program. This program provides faculty training and lesson plan support, as well as monitoring over the course of the term to measure the quality of instruction. The program seeks to improve faculty members' ability to teach ethics and citizenship within any field or discipline.

All faculty members are encouraged to use problem based learning, case based learning, project oriented learning, or service-learning in their curriculum. This ensures that students are exposed to real-world scenarios they may experience in the professional careers, including questions relating to professional ethics.

Faculty members also found this type of teaching, based in practice, is very useful to them. One faculty member in the Saltillo campus emphasized that is you only teach theory, you will lose the skills you have as a practitioner. She believes case based learning and service-learning to be very effective for student development and keeping her professional skills sharp.

Each semester, more than 150 courses are taught using service-learning. This number will likely increase as more faculty members are trained in this teaching pedagogy. According to the questionnaire submitted by Tecnológico de Monterrey, of the 8,500 faculty members, about 10% assign at least 30% of their time to civic engagement activities. Additionally, over 150 faculty members teach subjects related to civic engagement. Many of them are actively involved in community projects and participate in community-based organizations. This constitutes a significant portion of the faculty body and overall course offerings that focus on ethics, citizenship or service.

Conclusion

Tecnológico de Monterrey is always innovating and embracing new, effective modes of teaching and learning. Their status as one of the top university's in Latin America lends weight to the approaches and techniques they emphasize in their curriculum. Their focus on ethics and citizenship education in the reaccreditation process elevates this role for higher education and will likely be influential for other institutions.

Their highly systematic approach to community service and pre-professional practice seeks to ensure high quality and to measure impact. An area of strength is their ability to measure learning and follow student progress over time. However, it was less clear in the course of my discussions if they have given similar weight to measuring community impact and outcomes. While they seem to work closely with approved community partners, it is also important to measure the benefits for recipients of their services.

Additionally, the level of sophistication in their measurement tools and tracking programs require significant financial resources and institutional support. Measurement of outcomes from service activities is almost always underfunded both at universities and in the nonprofit sector overall. Their ability to devote significant resources to this analysis is unique and likely not replicable at many other institutions, particularly in the developing world.

A striking feature of discussions with faculty and staff at Tecnológico de Monterrey was their compelling vision of what their graduates should look like. They have thought in depth about the kind of graduates they want to produce and the skills that will make them effective. They believe that service is a key component of their personal and professional formation. They also emphasized that employers in the public and private sector indicated the importance of formation in ethics and citizenship when making hiring decisions. Clearly, Tecnológico de Monterrey is responding to this urgent need in the public sector in Mexico, and also to business interests who have strong ties to the institution. The decision to emphasize this aspect of their students' education is not only driven by personal interests of the leadership of the institution or by belief in the "rightness" of these activities, but by external pressures and demands.

Pakistan and its Higher Education System

Pakistan has a population of 158 million (the sixth largest in the world), an average life expectancy for men of 65 and women of 66, and ranks 152nd in the Media Freedom Index. Its adult literacy rate is 54.9%: men, 68.7%; women, 40.2% (*Guardian* "World Fact Files," 2009). The infant mortality rate is 70.2 per thousand live births, down from 81.1 in 1998, but significantly higher than the world average of 55 deaths per thousand (IHSN, 2007–2008). The report of a UN Interagency Assessment Mission in 2008 found that food security had significantly worsened as a result of a hike in food prices. The Task Force on Food Security in 2009 estimated that poverty had increased to 36.1%, resulting in 62 million people living below the poverty line (State Bank of Pakistan, 2009).

Some of the most pressing economic problems facing Pakistan are inflation, low industrial productivity, and even lower agricultural outcomes. This is coupled with a large population and a high birth rate, gender inequality, low literacy rates, and poor human development indicators.

Pakistan has also faced political instability and conflict since it gained independence in 1947. Civilian governments have been overthrown or dismissed numerous times by presidents and generals, and the country has seen direct military rule for over half its existence. Pakistan has also experienced several wars with India, a civil war in which Bangladesh broke away from Pakistan, violent conflict with Islamist militants in tribal regions of Pakistan, and terrorist attacks throughout the country. This instability has had a profound effect on social institutions throughout Pakistan, including higher education.

When India and Pakistan gained independence in 1947, only the University of the Punjab existed on the Pakistani side of the partition. In the early 1970s, the Bhutto government nationalized education, and in 1979 the federal government centralized higher education funding. But, "In the mid-1980s, private educational institutions were again allowed to operate, on the condition that they uphold standards" (Coffman, 1997). In 2009–2010, there are 60 public universities and 42 private universities (HEC website, www.hec.gov.pk/Pages/main.aspx).

Pakistani higher education enrollment has increased dramatically over the past decade. Enrollment in both public and private universities and constituent colleges more than doubled from 2001–2008, while enrollment in distance learning (which is public) more than tripled in this period. In 2007–2008, students enrolled in universities, DAIs and Constituent Colleges were 53.7% male and 46.3% female. In addition, higher education funding has increased rapidly. In 2006, Pakistan spent about 0.29% of GDP on tertiary education, a major increase from the 0.09% spent in 2001 (World Bank, 2006c). Despite this tremendous growth in enrollment and funding, just 5% of Pakistanis aged 17–23 were enrolled in universities, constituent colleges, and affiliated colleges in 2008 (UNESCO Institute for Statistics, 2008).

The Higher Education Commission (HEC) is an autonomous body responsible for the allocation of government funds to universities and Degree Awarding Institutes (DAIs). Colleges are affiliated with universities and DAIs, but are funded and regulated by provincial governments and follow the curriculum of the universities and DAIs with which they are affiliated. In 2001, 51% of public HEI funds came from the government, while 49% were self-generated (Task Force on Improvement of Higher Education in Pakistan, 2002). A recent development has been the HEC's funding support for private universities for limited purposes such as research and infrastructure development (World Bank, 2006c). Otherwise, private universities are funded through tuition and other private sources of income.

The Higher Education Commission is also responsible for quality assurance, carried out through the Quality Assurance Agency (QAA), which works with universities to establish a Quality Enhancement Cell to "improve the quality of higher education in a systematic way with uniformity across the country" (HEC QAA, www.hec.gov.pk/InsideHEC/Divisions/QALI/Pages/QualityAssurance. aspx). By 2007–2008, Quality Enhancement Cells had been established at 30 public universities for the improvement of teaching and learning standards. The World Bank has assessed recent progress made by these efforts, but also notes several continuing challenges, including the acute shortage of qualified faculty, fragile evaluation systems of academic programs and faculties, and a generally low quality of education (World Bank, 2006c).

Especially relevant to our inquiry, community engagement is one of the aspects of universities' performance that is included in the QAA's Quality Assurance assessment process. The QAA explicitly states:

> The concept of integrated community participation in the whole process of learning and teaching is relatively a new concept but important to achieve the desired level of quality assurance. Therefore, more efforts are needed by the QECs to introduce the concept where it does not exist previously and to make it more effective where it exists in underlying way and is difficult to be practiced. The system of quality assurance ensures that a higher education institution, informed by its mission, makes a significant contribution to the community it belongs, to the society it serves and to the wider environment.
>
> *(Batool & Qureshi, 2006)*

Although only recently implemented as part of the quality assurance assessment process, the fact that civic engagement is imbedded in the higher education policy framework is an important development both for Pakistan and potentially as a model for higher education in other countries.

A Unique University with a Mandate for Social Development

Profile of Aga Khan University, Karachi (Pakistan)
By Susan E. Stroud (based on field visit,
December 15–16, 2009)

Background

The Aga Khan University (AKU) was chartered by the Pakistani government in 1983 as the country's first private university. Established by His Highness the Aga Khan, the 49th hereditary Imam (Spiritual Leader) of the Shia Ismaili Muslims, AKU is a non-denominational, autonomous not-for-profit university that "promotes human welfare through research, teaching and community service" (www.aku.edu). The University is international with campuses and programs in Pakistan, Kenya, Tanzania, Uganda, the UK, Afghanistan, Egypt, and Syria.

To understand the Aga Khan University, it is necessary to understand its relationship with the Aga Khan Development Network (AKDN), a group of private development agencies that works primarily in the developing countries of Asia, Africa, and Central Asia of which His Highness is the founder and chairman. In Islam's ethical tradition, religious leaders not only interpret the faith but also have a responsibility to help improve the quality of life in their community and in the societies among which they live. For His Highness the Aga Khan, this has meant a deep engagement with development for over 50 years through the agencies of the AKDN. The University operates as an academic center within the larger AKDN, and from that relationship, the University furthers its focus on community development and civic engagement. The University and the AKDN share a common goal "to create real and lasting improvements in the lives of the poor in ways that lead to self-reliance rather than dependence" (www.aku.edu). To this end, both institutions encourage and work with communities to identify and plan for their needs.

Management and Funding

His Highness the Aga Khan serves as the Chancellor and the University is overseen by an international Board of Trustees. The day-to-day academic and administrative operations of the University are the responsibility of the President and other key university officers. The Chancellor appoints the President and some members of the Board of Trustees.

Funding for the University comes from diverse sources. The Aga Khan provides funding for new programs and initiatives, as well as for some core activities. The Ismaili community makes significant contributions of time, professional services, and substantial financial resources to AKU and AKDN. Other funding sources include grants from governments, institutional and private sector partners, as well as donations from individuals around the world (www.aku.edu).

Vision, Mission, and Values of AKU

Civic engagement is core to the statement of the University's vision, mission, and values. The Charter of the university elucidates the vision to be an "international institution of distinction, primarily serving the developing world and Muslim societies in innovative and enduring ways" (University Charter, 1983). The University's mission includes being "committed to the development of human capacities through the discovery and dissemination of knowledge, and application through service. It seeks to prepare individuals for constructive and exemplary leadership roles, and shaping public and private policies, through strength in research and excellence in education, all dedicated to providing meaningful contributions to society." Among the strategies that the University has adopted in order to realize its mission which also highlight the importance of civic engagement are to:

- respond to identified needs in the countries and regions which it serves;
- prioritize teaching and research which will inform and underpin intellectual innovation and change;
- provide service that can both advance its educational and research mandate and support communities in resolving issues;
- promote access and equity by taking positive measures to make the University inclusive of all socioeconomic groups, addressing the particular needs and circumstances of the disadvantaged; promoting the welfare and advancement of women (www.aku.edu).

The questionnaire that was completed by University staff prior to my visit to AKU, states, "The institution's work in civic engagement is the fundamental *raison d'être* of the institution. As such, the work of each employee and faculty member is driven by the values and the commitment to civic engagement."

I visited the AKU campuses in central Karachi, Pakistan which, since its inception, have focused on the improvement of education and public health through the Institute for Educational Development (IED), the Medical College, School of Nursing and the University Hospital. In addition, IED has Professional Development Centers for teacher educators in Gilgit-Baltistan and Chitral in the northern part of the country. Civic engagement is a stated objective of AKU's growth plans (questionnaire) and since AKU plans to become a comprehensive university additional faculties are being developed on global sites including another Faculty of Health Sciences in Nairobi, Kenya. Faculties of Arts and Sciences are also being developed on a 1,000 acre site in Arusha, Tanzania and a 1,100 acre site in Karachi, Pakistan. In addition, eight graduate schools offering professional education are to being set up in East Africa and Pakistan.

The Immediate Context

AKU's Karachi campuses are focused on specific health and education needs of some of the most distressed communities in Pakistan's most populous city. Karachi is a sprawling city with a 2007 population of approximately 18 million and a 5% annual growth rate that is mostly due to rural–urban migration (City District Government Karachi, 2007). After Partition in 1947 and until 1958, Karachi was designated the capital of the new country with an initial population of 450,000. The population grew rapidly due primarily to the migration of Muslims from India and doubled in size within 3 years. Now Karachi is 40 times the size it was in 1947 and is the financial and commercial capital of Pakistan, accounting for approximately 20% of Pakistan's GDP (Asian Development Bank, 2009, www. adb.org). Major businesses include banking, IT, media, fishing and industrial production of various products.

The population is a diverse mix of different ethnic groups, including Mohajir (Urdu speaking), Sindhi, Pashtun, Punjabi, and Kashmiri. The religious make-up as of the 1998 Census was 96.5% Muslim, 2.35% Christian, .83% Hindu and other religious groups (Hasan & Mohib, 2002).

Academic Programs in Health Sciences

Over 27 years, AKU has become deeply engaged through its academic programs in several urban slums in Karachi, as well as developed strong ties with rural communities in many of the provinces. In its academic programs, AKU's pedagogical approach is problem-based and multidisciplinary, working closely with community members to identify needs and build capacity within those communities to implement solutions.

AKU was the first university in Pakistan to develop community-based medical education. The Medical College began in 1983 with the introduction of a five-year Bachelor of Medicine Bachelor of Surgery (MBBS) degree. There are now a variety of graduate and postgraduate programs as well as clinical postgraduate residencies. Partnerships with universities in Canada, the USA, and Sweden "enable higher training and research, specifically in areas where such opportunities are not available in Pakistan" (www.aku.edu).

Medical training begins by teaching students how to link work with community members in urban slums as well as in rural areas in order to identify their health needs. This training has evolved to helping communities mobilize themselves. Medical students and faculty conduct workshops with community members to develop their own community management teams that then operate as registered NGOs. First and second year students spend 20% of their time working directly with community members and carrying out research projects. As third year students, they engage directly in clinical work in the same communities as well as in the University Hospital.

"Brain drain" is a critical issue facing Pakistan and impacts AKU's aspirations to train young doctors to address the medical needs of the country and the region. Graduates of the Medical College represent the "cream-of-the-crop" of doctors in Pakistan, as AKU is ranked first in health sciences among all Pakistani universities (HEC website). Many graduates have opportunities to go abroad for further training. All of the medical students I interviewed in Pakistan plan to go abroad, and there was general agreement with the statement of one student that: "No one wants to be a general practitioner in a community health clinic in Pakistan. We applaud the doctors who go abroad for further training and then return to Pakistan, but we don't want to be them. You can't support a family and your parents (a strong cultural expectation) on the salaries a GP makes in a public health clinic." So there is an inherent dilemma between earning capacity in Pakistan and AKU's community service ethos. While the curriculum prepares doctors to work in community settings, they often do not engage in that work once they are qualified. Another student stated, "There are no financial incentives to return to Pakistan. The only incentives to return are to be with family/parents and to raise one's children in the culture we grew up in rather than in a western culture." The medical students believe strongly that there is an urgent need to change the financial dynamics of Pakistani healthcare to incentivize medical graduates to work in community medicine.

The Urban Health Program at AKU Pakistan began in 1983 with a mandate to address the needs of disadvantaged communities. Along with community-based organizations, the Urban Health Program currently manages primary healthcare programs in two squatter settlements in Karachi that provide health and development services to 60,000 people. The program has become the model for community health education in the region. Through the Community Health Services Program, AKU provided training for women members of the community to become "lady health visitors"—a model program that has been adopted by government and taken to scale by the Pakistani National Health Service.

The University Hospital is located on the main Karachi campus and has served over half a million patients in 2009; in the same year, off-campus health facilities served another 0.3 million, for a total of 0.88 million people. An active Patient Welfare Program provided 49,846 patients with financial assistance valued at $4.8M a reflection of AKU's commitment to providing health care regardless of one's ability to pay for services (questionnaire).

AKU offered the first university-based nursing degree in Pakistan; it was also the first academic program of AKU. Over time, the highly professional approach and community orientation to nursing education has changed the culture of nursing in Pakistan so that it is now an acceptable professional choice for women. The program has also gained regional and international recognition.

The degrees offered in the AKU School of Nursing Pakistan include RN, Post-RN BScN, BScN, and MScN. In the MScN program, community health nursing is mandatory. At a meeting with nursing students, several students stressed that the nursing program's emphasis on community-based learning was challenging, as "it is not easy to work in community because you need to invent solutions with limited resources." Asked if they would restructure the program to de-emphasize community engagement, there was unanimity in the students' responses that "knowledge is incomplete without experience in the community." Several students pointed to the faculty as role models. Ninety percent of faculty members in nursing are AKU graduates who were trained through a problem-based learning curriculum and in community nursing (author meeting with nursing students, December 15, 2009).

In addition to the health-related work being done in Pakistan, AKU has established health-related programs in several other countries. Advanced Nursing Studies programs were established in Nairobi, Kampala, and Dar es Salaam in response to requests from the governments of Kenya, Uganda, and Tanzania to improve the quality of patient care and the professional qualifications of nurses in East Africa; AKU also established a medical program along with a University Hospital in Nairobi, Kenya; postgraduate medical education programs are offered in Tanzania and Kenya; and nursing education programs are offered in Syria, Egypt and Afghanistan. Additionally, in Kabul, Afghanistan, AKU manages the French Medical Institute for Children through an innovative four-way partnership between the Governments of France and Afghanistan, AKDN and the French NGO, La Chaîne de l'Espoir; besides supporting postgraduate medical education, nursing education and the professional development of teacher educators in the country. In Syria, AKU supports nursing education, quality assurance in select government hospitals and the professional development of teacher educators also (www.aku.edu).

Academic Programs in Education

The Institute for Educational Development (IED) Pakistan was founded in 1993 and offers PhD and MEd programs, as well as advanced diploma and certificate programs, for practicing teachers, teacher educators and educational administrators. An Institute for Educational Development was also established in Tanzania to enhance teacher education in East Africa. IED Pakistan and East Africa students come from government and NGOs throughout the regions. There is a special focus on female teachers and designing programs that fit cultural norms. All programs emphasize a development perspective. In a conversation with IED Pakistan students, they emphasized that "outreach is not separate, but is part of the pedagogy," and "methodology is important, e.g., the use of case studies, community-based action research." The civic engagement component of their work at the IED reinforced their conviction that "our approach is not about charity, but about empowerment and social justice" (author meeting with IED students, AKU, December 16, 2009).

IED carries out extensive outreach efforts, including establishing and now supporting Professional Development Centers (PDC) in isolated locations of

Pakistan, most of which are led by AKU graduates. The PDCs provide professional development to teachers and teacher educators who otherwise would have little or no opportunity for professional development. IED also engages in extensive research, which focuses on the improvement of national education standards. The research results are used to engage policymakers around critical education issues. Previous research studies have had impacts such as convincing government to raise teacher salaries nationally (notes from interview of Director of IED, December 16, 2009).

AKU also operates programs to support the professional development of teachers in Afghanistan, Egypt, and Syria.

The Aga Khan University Examination Board (AKU-EB) is setting standards in national assessments, with the objective of improving the secondary and higher secondary school leaving certification system. In Pakistan, AKU-EB has introduced high quality examinations in both English and Urdu that emphasize the understanding and application of knowledge and, in the process, assess a wide range of abilities including comprehension, logical thinking, and problem-solving skills. In 2007, this examination model—of testing knowledge rather than rote learning—was adopted as national policy and will be followed by all government examination boards in the country.

Campus Resources

At the Karachi campus, the library health sciences collection is one of the best in South Asia and available to health professionals and medical researchers across the region. Sports and rehabilitation facilities are available to patients, and summer sport and youth camps are held in the sports facilities for youth from diverse backgrounds.

Engaging in the Civic and Social Responsibility Agenda

At AKU, community engagement and social responsibility are not only rhetoric; they are embedded in the culture of the institution and underlie all of the academic programs. Moreover, the faculty promotions committee is working with the Provost to re-examine the University's promotion policy to ensure that the value of civic engagement is clearly articulated as part of that policy (questionnaire). In addressing equity issues, the University's admission policy is needs-blind and based on merit, enabling the financially disadvantaged to attend. Regarding gender equity, 37% of AKU's workforce is female and the AKU faculty gender ratio is 1:1.

Going Forward

According to faculty and senior staff, the initial community perception of AKU was that it was an elitist institution, but it is now well-respected by the community, largely based on the community's interaction with the hospital and other community based programs. Faculty and senior staff also expressed the belief that the University has helped to influence national health and education policies due to the credibility established through its research and community work.

Given AKU's mandate of social development, almost all of its research activity is directed towards the needs of the communities in the areas where it works in the developing world, including East Africa, the Middle East, and South Asia, which all suffer from poor health and education indicators. Maternal and infant mortality rates are particularly high and several health-related research projects are directed towards finding affordable solutions to infant malnutrition, improved child delivery, and reduction and prevention of common infectious diseases. AKU is redeveloping its research strategy to focus on key areas where it aspires to develop global expertise in areas of significant potential impact for the developing world.

At AKU there are many examples of successful civic engagement activities, either in the design of entire academic programs such as the Urban Health Program or through a variety of short-term projects. One senior staff member mentioned another important aspect of civic engagement that is especially important in the long term, given civic engagement goals: "Community based work is participatory in nature and brings people into a democratic process with the goal of improving living conditions. Measurement of effectiveness does not mean only the immediate change in health status, etc. but in planting the seed for collective action for a better future. This is not easy" (questionnaire).

AKU has ambitious plans for expansion. As mentioned above there are plans to build two entirely new large campuses in Karachi and Arusha to house the Faculty of Arts and Sciences (FAS), a major step towards creating a comprehensive university. A focus of the new FAS will be on developing public leaders in government, business, and civil society who can drive economic and social change. The University's strategic plan calls for AKU to remain a relatively small university (2008: total full-time equivalent enrollment in Karachi was 2,475) with a large impact on development in the communities and countries where the University's programs are located. In regards to civic engagement and social responsibility, "civic engagement and work in the social development of the communities that surround AKU will be a central driving force in programs the University offers and the services it provides" (questionnaire).

Aga Khan University's approach to civic engagement, particularly with regards to public health and education, has had a significant impact on local communities. However, AKU remains a small private institution. Genuine social development and transformation will require similar efforts across the Pakistani higher education sector. AKU provides a successful global model for this type of work, and the Pakistani Higher Education Commission's recent emphasis on community engagement is a positive sign. The eight Pakistani universities that are also members of the Talloires Network demonstrate the increasing higher education commitment to engaging with the community. With a deepened commitment, Pakistani higher education could play a major role in confronting the social and economic challenges facing the country.

Peru and its Higher Education System

Peru has a population of 27 million, an average life expectancy for men of 69 and women of 74, and ranks 108th out of 173 in the Media Freedom Index. Its adult literacy rate is 90.5%; it has 1.2 doctors per 1,000 population; and an adult HIV/AIDS rate of 0.6% (*Guardian* "World Fact Files," 2009). Approximately 45% of Peru's population is Indigenous.

The higher education sector in Peru is regulated by the Constitution of 1980, the General Law of Education of 1982 and the University Law of 1983. Peru has 33 public universities, 46 private universities, and a number of well-regarded research institutions. Peru has several types of HEIs: University, Higher Postgraduate Centers, Technical Higher Institutes, Higher Pedagogical Institutes and Higher Schools (International Association of Universities, 2001). Peru's HE system has expanded rapidly since the 1960s. Peru had nine universities in 1960, and today has over 79 universities. HE in Peru has also become increasingly privatized. As of 2003, 61% of Peru's HEIs were private institutions (Butters et al., 2005).

University enrollment numbers in Peru have increased drastically over the past few decades. Between 1960 and 2003, enrollment increased by a factor of 9.6, which also corresponds to the increase in the number of universities over that time period, from 9 to 78 (Butters et al., 2005: 283). In 2005 there were 849,000 Peruvians enrolled in HEIs, 59% in public HEIs and 41% in private (Murakami & Blom, 2008: 11).

There are a number of social cohesion and access issues in Peruvian HE. First, access to higher education overall has increased over the last few decades, but still remains fairly low due to the prohibitive cost of private HEIs and the selectivity of public HEIs (due in part to limited public funding). Just 10% of Peruvians aged 19–22 are enrolled in higher education (Murakami & Blom, 2008: 39). Furthermore, low per-student expenditure on education has severely compromised the quality of higher education in Peru. Equality of access across socioeconomic lines is relatively high, but low compared to developed countries. Gender parity is also an issue, with more men than women enrolled in Peruvian HE, which is fairly rare, even in developing nations (Murakami & Blom, 2008: 40). Due to a number of factors, including a lack of HE instruction in Indigenous languages, access to HE among Indigenous peoples is also limited. Peru plans to open a new university catering specifically to Indigenous peoples, including with native language instruction, to try to reduce this inequality (International Association of Universities, 2001).

Public universities are funded partly by the government. Government spending on HEIs is quite low. While the United States invests about 2.3% of its GDP in higher education, Peru invests just 0.55% of its GDP in higher education, among the lowest rates in the region (Samoilovich, 2008). Public universities are forced to supplement their income by other means, including "offering paid courses for preparation for the university entrance exam." These non-public sources of funding provide about 34% of the finances of public universities (Samoilovich, 2008: 355). Private universities obtain most of their funding from tuition. Tuition rates for these universities can be quite prohibitive, as a World Bank study found that average private HEI yearly tuition rates are 98% of GDP per capita (Murakami & Blom, 2008: 28).

The Peruvian government's system for funding HE comes from the public treasury. Some of the funding comes from the petroleum levy.

> The income from the minerals levy enters as transfers made by regional governments to public universities, and by law should be used exclusively for programs of research and development. From 2002 to 2005, of the resources allocated by the state to public universities, this has been held at a constant percentage and is practically limited to current financial spending.
>
> *(Samoilovich, 2008: 355)*

Overall, quality of education is a major concern in Peruvian higher education. Due to the absence of tuition at public universities, as well as the greater prestige of public universities, the vast majority of students apply to public rather than private universities. Thus, private universities are much less selective, which compromises the quality of the student body. However, due to funding shortages, public universities also have serious quality control issues. Just 47% of university faculty in Peru have postgraduate degrees, and relatively few of them conduct research (Butters et al., 2005: 285).

A Regional Leader for Human and Economic Development

Profile of the Universidad Señor de Sipán (USS) (Peru)
By Elizabeth Babcock (based on field visit
November 11 and 12, 2009)

Origins and History

The Universidad Señor de Sipán (USS) is one of three Peruvian universities forming a consortium along with Universidad César Vallejo and Universidad Autónoma del Perú. The consortium was organized in 1997 and USS officially gained university status on July 5, 1999. Construction on the campus, located in the northern city of Chiclayo in the region of Lambayeque, began in October of 2000. The consortium of universities was founded by Dr César Acuña Peralta, a politician and businessman. He has been mayor of the city of Trujillo since 2007 and served in the national congress from 2001 to 2006.

USS is a private for-profit university that offers undergraduate degrees in administration, accounting, civil, industrial, mechanical, electrical and systems engineering, psychology, tourism and business, architecture and nursing. Dr Humberto Llempén Coronel has served as the Rector of the university since its founding. He has overseen the expansion of the university from several hundred to over 7,500 students in 2010.

A key goal for USS is to serve the higher education and development needs of the region. The city of Chiclayo, located over 770 kilometers north of Lima, is the fourth largest city in Peru and an important industrial capital. However, no higher education institutions served this city prior to 1994. The need for qualified engineers, nurses and business professionals has greatly increased in the last decade. At the same time, the region has extremely high levels of poverty and other social ills, including lack of access to health care, environmental degradation and crime. These persistent social problems exist against the backdrop of continued development and expansion of Chiclayo as an economic, cultural and tourism center.

Cultivating a Regional Identity

Universidad Señor de Sipán has worked to align its educational mission with both the needs and the identity of the region it serves. The university's name derives from one of the most important archeological discoveries in this region of the world in the last 30 years. The Lord of Sipán was a ruler of the Moche people and his tomb was found completely intact, with a multitude of jewelry, pottery, weapons, and mummies of family and servants. The Royal Tombs Museum of Sipán replicates the layers of the tomb and displays many of the most impressive artifacts from the site. It is one of the highest quality museums in South America.

Tourism is one of the most important economic drivers in Peru and USS recognizes the need to develop professionals who can work to identify and preserve important cultural and historical artifacts. USS also trains business leaders who will be able to respond to growing demands for tourist services in a city and region known chiefly in the recent past for agricultural production, including sugar cane and rice. The north of Peru, though rich in cultural heritage, lags far behind other regions in tourism.

Though the university's community engagement extends far beyond cultural and historical preservation, the unique identity that the university's name evokes further emphasizes the connection between place and purpose. This university is wholly of the region and exists to educate people from the region. Because almost all young people attending university live at home with their families, and many students from this region come from limited economic means, they will not seek admission at universities in other parts of the country. Most students studying in Peru today, particularly from lower socioeconomic backgrounds, will study at local universities. USS has aligned its identity with important cultural touchstones of the region and tailors its academic offerings to community development needs. Its 2008–2010 strategic plan specifically mentions "preserving cultural identity" as one of its objectives, along with "developing solutions to social problems" and "cultivating values, social commitment and a sense of solidarity" in its graduates.

Evolving Internal Structures

USS is a young institution and, as such, is still working to develop the structures and policies that will best implement its strategic goals. Its community engagement, extension and pre-professional practice programs are directed by the Vice-Rector of Student Affairs, and led by Susana Toso de Vera, through two offices: the Directorate of Extension and Community Outreach, led by Saúl Hernández Terán, and the Directorate of Well-being and Student Affairs, led by Edwin M. García Ramírez. All research and teaching are directly linked with local and regional economic and social problems. During my visit, the university was developing a campus-wide curriculum reform program that would add service-learning to every discipline. Staff are required to spend approximately eight hours per week on service or extension activities.

In one of the first meetings I had with university officials, we discussed the tension that sometimes exists in being recognized as a top-flight institution and being responsive to local needs. Luis R. Alarcón Llontop, Director of the School for Communication Sciences, stressed that "these two models of the university don't have to be in conflict." He emphasized how intellectual formation and personal development are complementary, saying, "Our students aren't just students. They are teachers and citizens, as well."

Despite a strong commitment to being an institution that is both academically excellent and socially responsive, USS faces several obstacles. We discussed whether their model is unique or innovative in Peru and how their academic preparation differs from other institutions. Several officials said that most of the educational system in Peru focuses on rote learning and is hierarchical. They struggle to train more experienced faculty to "change their perceptions about the curriculum." In order to assist in curriculum development and training, USS has brought in outside experts in the field to work with faculty and staff on service-learning and community engagement.

Being Present in the Community

One of the most notable features of USS is its far reaching presence in the community. This is achieved through a number of innovative community engagement programs combining teaching and service. The university is also able to draw on the knowledge of its students in serving the community, as the vast majority of the student body is from the region.

The first program that really demonstrates the university's commitment to being present in the community is CEDECOM. CEDECOM, which stands for Centros de Desarrollo Comunal or Community Development Centers, is a program that provides community services, like counseling, business plan development and tutoring to the community for free at university owned centers in urban and rural areas. Students, with guidance from faculty coordinators on site, engage in pre-professional practice or volunteer service with the community. I was able to visit two of the five centers. Cayaltí is a center located in a remote rural area approximately one hour from the university main campus. Distrito Jose Leonardo Ortiz is located in an urban area just outside the city of Chiclayo. Both centers operate with the same purpose and principles, but are serving very different community needs.

In Cayaltí, I met with center Coordinator Roberto Yep Burga and several students. Roberto told me he lives in Zaña, a remote village close to Cayaltí. He is very familiar with the needs of the community and, therefore, can more effectively recruit and direct students in their service and pre-professional training. He is trained as a psychologist and, in addition to coordinating the center, supervises the pre-professional work of the psychology students.

This center began by taking baseline assessments of community needs through surveys and focus groups with local people. One of the key concerns in this rural area is business development and increasing household income. The Cayaltí Center started a microenterprise program that surveys existing businesses and then creates a community wide economic development plan. This program also partners with local government to help build the capacity of the municipality to respond to community needs. Over 45 students come on a daily basis to volunteer. Roberto told me that they will continue to increase the services they offer as the community learns more about what they do. They advertise their services on radio, television, and in print, though word of mouth is the most crucial.

There are a number of challenges for the Cayaltí Center. Funding this work is difficult as the municipality itself is very poor and there are limited resources available from foundations. Students must provide their own transportation, so many students are unable to come. This particular center does not have internet, but they are working with the municipality to get the fiber optic cable laid. They aim to conduct impact evaluations of their work, but again require additional funding to support this activity. The multitude of challenges they face in reaching and serving very poor, rural communities underscores the commitment by the university to regional development and to a more dynamic and relevant educational experience for its students.

In Distrito Jose Leonardo Ortiz, the Center is able to draw on many more students to support its outreach and service programs due to its close proximity to the university and ease of transportation to the location. Here, the community needs and challenges are distinctly urban. This community has grown very rapidly, as people migrate from rural areas to the edges of the urban center of Chiclayo. One challenge the Center is addressing is the vast number of unregulated taxis that compete for limited business. By providing training in alternative microenterprise opportunities, and working to coordinate taxi drivers to create systems for fare collection and pickups, the Center is filling a gap in local government services. The coordinator of the Center, Gary Alarcón, said they are "not just identifying individual problems, but communal problems."

Psychology students at this Center are also highly engaged in a program trying to lessen domestic violence, called "Estoy Contigo" or "I Am with You." They train individuals as community leaders in violence prevention and conflict so they in turn can train their neighbors. Students also work with families in their homes and provide counseling and other services to women and children that have experienced abuse.

This Center also provides legal counsel for a wide variety of issues. Due to lack of public defenders and, at times, corruption in public services, law students represent community members so they are protected when they approach the local government or police. Community perception of this service, and many others, is very positive. The university built the Center in a highly visible location, so the community is very aware of their presence.

Gary emphasized the impact not just on the community, but on students as well. By directly tackling some of the most pressing social issues in their own region, students are exposed to real-world experience that helps them connect policy with practice. He said that he hopes "students will be the leaders of the future and use what they have learned to change government policy and create development." As future professionals, these students are already thinking about the quality of services available to the community and looking to address gaps through creative problem-solving.

Another critical community engagement program is PADEL, Local Development Assistance Program. PADEL promotes local development through the implementation of service-learning courses in every faculty. PADEL was formed in collaboration with the municipalities and civil society organizations and encompasses almost every community surrounding the university. Projects under the umbrella of PADEL include technical assistance for communities on the use of technology, training and management on the use of cultural resources for tourism and mentoring programs for children living in rural impoverished areas.

All projects have been established jointly with regional stakeholders to make them both effective and sustainable. One of the first projects was "Decreasing the Digital Divide," which works to provide underprivileged areas with greater access to information technology, with an emphasis on improving community members' digital literacy and awareness of the role IT can have in local development. The project won an award for regional development programs sponsored by the Inter-American Development Bank and the Andean Development Corporation, giving it increased recognition in the region. USS then decided to have each academic department create similar programs, and then began focusing on incorporating these projects into the curriculum as service-learning courses. Through connections with other service-learning practitioners in the region as well as its own experience, PADEL continues to improve its model and increase support among faculty and students. PADEL has become increasingly institutionalized at USS, with each academic school having at least one service-learning based solidarity project for community development.

Projects like this not only benefit the community, but also give the students valuable experience that supplements their standard academic work. Evelleyn Bazán Zuloeta, a student participant in the project "Decreasing the Digital Divide" stated, "I was able to test my knowledge in the real world and make a difference to people who were close to me." Juan Carlos Bautista Pérez, Coordinator of the "Coping with Family Violence" program, says, "Leadership is a constant practice and leaving the classroom and dealing with the community is the best way to learn. Students learn that academic research and practice go hand in hand. Now the students aspire to work much harder for the community." Students are so dedicated to the projects they have implemented that over 50% continue working with their community partners after the course ends.

Strengthening Civil Society and Local Government

A major challenge in many Latin American countries is public corruption. This is true in Peru and in the Lambayeque region. Many factors contribute to the problem, including poorly funded public servants and lack of public access to government information. USS is working to build the capacity of civil society to effectively engage leaders and with local government to improve its services and capacity.

The university has published several reports entitled "Transparency and Access to Public Information in Lambayeque." Luis Alarcón, Director of the School of Communication Sciences and a principle author of the publications, stressed how important transparency is to improving public services and combating corruption. This series of publications was funded by the Open Society Institute and contributes to a larger body of research being developed by a nationwide anti-corruption network that USS is a member of. The university is working with this network on a major initiative for 2010 that focuses on reducing government corruption.

Conclusion

As a relatively new institution, USS has been able to craft their identity around a new model of experiential education combined with service in the community.

Students and faculty come from the region and many of the poorest students receive need-based scholarships to attend USS. As a private university, USS does not receive much government support, so they must fund all university operations through fees, grants, and cooperative agreements. For this reason, the strength of their ties to the local community is even more critical as they must recruit new students and form new partnerships in order to thrive and grow as an institution.

The mission and vision of USS to serve the local community may be sound business practice, but there is also a real sense of solidarity with the community and recognition of the importance of education in regional and national development. The staff, students, and administrators I met were extremely dedicated and highly engaged. There was a strong culture of service that could be felt anywhere on campus and at the satellite community centers I visited. Antonio Sánchez Chacón, Director of International Relations, emphasized that USS is "trying to break the existing educational paradigm" where classroom education, professional development, service and extension are all separate activities. Engagement with the community is infused in the university experience at all levels for students and faculty.

A significant challenge of being so engaged in the community is the culture of "asistencialismo" or culture of dependency that pervades Peruvian society, and indeed many Latin American countries. USS is working to identify and cultivate community leaders to be advocates for social change and to improve the relationships between government and the people it serves. It is important when they work with the community to identify sustainable, long-term solutions so that communities don't become dependent on university services. Students are learning first-hand the difficulty in creating social change, rather than simply providing charity to those in need.

As this young institution expands its work, a key goal for them will be impact evaluation. They are looking at evaluating not only the effects of their interventions in the community, but also at the benefits of their educational model on the career path and civic behaviors of their students. At the time of my visit, they were still trying to obtain funding from private foundations to support these studies.

Despite the difficult environment in which USS is working, they have developed an extremely impressive number of service programs and are continuously engaged in refining their strategic plan to improve academic learning and community impact. It is heartening to see an entrepreneurial model of higher education in the developing world that is so responsive to local needs. With its continued growth and success, it is likely USS will influence other institutions in Peru to follow suit.

The Philippines and its Higher Education System

The Philippines has a population of 99.9 million, an average life expectancy for men of 69 and women of 74, and ranks 122 out of 175 in the Reporters without

Borders 2009 Press Freedom Index. Its adult literacy rate is 92.6%; it has 0.58 doctors per 1,000 population and an adult HIV/AIDS rate of 0.1%. Its infant mortality rate is 19.94 deaths per 1,000 live births, well below the world average of 55/1,000. As of 2006, approximately 32.9% of Filipinos lived below the poverty line (CIA, 2010).

The Philippine islands were a Spanish colony from the sixteenth to nineteenth centuries. The USA occupied the islands during the Spanish–American War in 1898. The Philippines became a commonwealth in 1935, was occupied by Japan during World War II and gained independence as the Republic of the Philippines in 1946. The Philippines has witnessed significant political turmoil, including the 20 year rule of President Ferdinand Marcos (1966–1986), which was ultimately toppled by the "people power" movement, another "people power" overthrow of President Joseph Estrada in 2001, and a Muslim insurgency on the southern island of Mindanao (where Notre Dame of Marbel University is located).

The higher education system in the Philippines is dominated by private institutions. Of 2,060 higher education institutions, 1,523 are private and 537 public (Commission on Higher Education, 2008). About 66% of total enrollment is served by the private institutions (Commission on Higher Education, Philippines, 2009). As a former US possession (1898–1946), the Philippines has been heavily influenced by the US higher education system. According to Philip Altbach, the structure of Filipino institutions, their curricula, and their relatively non-elitist nature (relative to other Asian higher education systems) are signs of America's traditional influence (Altbach, 2002).

Higher education enrollment has increased from 1.6 million in 1991 (UNESCO Institute for Statistics, 1991) to over 2.4 million in 2005 (Commission on Higher Education, Philippines, 2009). In 2008, the Gross Enrollment Ratio at the tertiary level was 29% (male, 26% and female, 32%) (UNESCO Institute for Statistics, 2006a), reflecting the country's relatively open access to higher education.

Higher education is overseen by the Commission on Higher Education, an independent body established by the Higher Education Act of 1994 as part of a series of educational reforms. CHED regulates the establishment of public and private institutions, their curricula and tuition fees, and accreditation/quality assurance. Public higher education institutions are subsidized by the government. State Universities and Colleges (SUCs) are funded by the national government while Local Universities and Colleges (LUCs) are funded by local governments. Public institutions supplement their government funding with relatively low tuition fees. Private institutions are funded through tuition fees and other private sources. Many of these private institutions are religious (mainly Roman Catholic) and run on a non-profit basis, while others are run by for-profit corporations. 35 exemplary private institutions have been granted autonomous/de-regulated status by CHED—including Notre Dame of Marbel University—giving them more independence from CHED (Commission on Higher Education, Philippines, 2009).

Public expenditure on education was just 2.5% of GDP in 2005—among the lowest rates in the region—just 13.3% of which was tertiary spending. With a combination of increased demand for higher education and limited government spending, relatively inexpensive public institutions are becoming crowded and quality is suffering. Many students are unable to afford more expensive and higher quality private education. Estimated annual cost of attending the average SUC in 2008 was $3,216, while more expensive private schools averaged $11,085 per student.

Higher education in the Philippines has long focused on being socially relevant through research and extension activities. The Commission on Higher Education speaks of the three pillars of higher education, "instruction, research, and extension," and has stated that HEIs should be "relevant to the needs of their clientele, stakeholders, and the communities they serve" (Commission on Higher Education, Philippines, 2009). In addition, CHED's current five-year plan states:

> Aside from manpower training, HEIs can extend various services to uplift the social environment in the community. Their research activities can address the employment and economic needs of the community. Industries and products in the community can be improved and expanded to enhance their competitive edge through application of research outputs of HEIs. Based on the outputs of various research activities, HEIs can serve as advocates for certain issues.
>
> *(Commission on Higher Education, Philippines, 2009)*

Volunteer Service to the Poor

Profile of Notre Dame of Marbel University (Philippines)
By Robert M. Hollister (based on field visit
January 11–12, 2010)

Origins and Context

As a non-sectarian, non-profit private university operated by the Marist Brothers, Notre Dame of Marbel University (NDMU) has a deep culture of service to the poor. Guided by the values of St Marcellin Champagnat, it is "dedicated to the spiritual, moral and academic formation of men and women who exemplify competence and social responsibility in the service of God and humanity." Core values of the institution include "preference for the least favored . . . those who are excluded from the mainstream of society, and those whose material poverty leads to deprivation in relation to health, family life, schooling, and educational values." Cultural sensitivity is another central value with strong implications for the University's community service activities. The University's mission statement emphasizes character, competence and culture in harmony. NDMU "offers an approach to education which stresses the development of the whole person who is animated by Christian values, who is competent and committed to render service through his chosen career, and who cherishes his rich cultural heritage."

NDMU is located in the agricultural southern province of Mindanao where there are substantial unmet community needs—economic, educational, and health. This is an agricultural region that raises rice, corn, coconut, pineapple, asparagus, papaya and banana; other major products are livestock, poultry and fish.

The second largest and southernmost island of the Philippines, Mindanao is a multicultural place—two-thirds of the population is Christian and one-third Muslim. It also is an area of considerable social and political unrest, although the immediate vicinity of the University is peaceful. Adjacent areas of conflict and threats of violence limit where the university can do community service work safely. The University's primary forms of civic engagement are student volunteer service and development assistance projects that are supported by international agencies.

The University is located in Koronadal, a city of 185,000 in the province of South Cotabato. 6,500 students, the vast majority of them undergraduates, study in a campus of one to four-story buildings. While it is owned and managed by the Marist Brothers, the University operates with lay personnel (there are only three Marist brothers on the staff, one of them the President). The tone on campus is friendly and energetic. NDMU is organized into five colleges— Health Sciences, Education, Business Administration, Engineering and Technology, Arts and Sciences—and the Graduate School, and in addition it manages a High School and the Elementary Levels of the Integrated Basic Education Department.

A Pervasive Ethic of Student Volunteer Service

At Notre Dame of Marbel University student volunteer service is a tangible part of the institution's culture and the focus of a wide range of programs, starting with participation of all entering students in the National Service Training Program and extending through the service projects of dozens of student clubs. The University has received multiple national awards from the national government for outstanding student volunteer service. In 2008, NDMU won the Best Student Service Award from the National Office of the Commission on Higher Education.

Volunteering is conducted with a dual commitment to service and also to empowerment of the poor. Student service leaders exude a respectful, authentic spirit of collaboration with community partners. As one student described her attitude toward her community partners, "We are not here just to serve you. We are here to learn from you; we benefit as well." Students consistently express a commitment to helping marginalized people to develop themselves by developing their communities. NDMU instills a thoroughgoing commitment to organizing volunteer service around and in response to community priorities. When discussing their service work, it is impressive that students universally emphasize this approach. Each student initiative starts by researching community needs. They then work with municipal officials to design specific projects.

All of the 60 to 70 student clubs, most of which are organized around students' career directions, are required to do community service. Administrative Vice-President Andres Magallanes annually evaluates the clubs' achievement in terms of their leadership development and the community services they provide. Students pay a 30 peso Community Extension Fee which is allocated among the various colleges to fund their community projects. Students in each college "adopt" a community where they focus their service work.

A central part of the university's approach to service is the National Service Training Program (NSTP) in which all first-year students in the Philippines institutions of higher education are required to participate. Students receive one academic credit for completing this year-long program (one-half day/week). The first semester is devoted to training, and then in the second term students work in teams doing community service. NSTP service projects fall into three categories: (1) Community Welfare Service (this option is chosen by 700–800 entering NDMU students each year); (2) Literacy Training (an average of 200 students per year); and (3) Service Officer Training (a small number). At NDMU the program is run by the Administrative Vice-President. He comments, "NSTP is a real eye-opener for many students; they become aware for the first time of community realities they previously did not see or understand." The Program aims to orient students to social issues and to their potential roles in addressing these challenges.

While 100% of entering students at Notre Dame of Marbel University participate in NSTP, much lower percentages participate in community outreach activities after their first year. In 2008–2009, 32% of NDMU employees were involved in outreach activities, but only 13% of students participated

Student volunteer projects range from tutoring to water supply improvement, from helping farmers' cooperatives to improve their marketing and financial management to building schools. Students in Engineering have helped their adopted community to develop its water system and trained public school teachers to use computers. Political science students have run workshops on political rights and biologists organized workshops on environmental protection. Students have built small schools in the Lake Sebu area, taught farmers to plant new crops and tutored students to help them prepare for the national achievement test.

In 2008–2009 several of the Colleges had as their Adopted Community the remote village of Sitio Tinoos, in the Lake Sebu area. After the standard process of needs assessment and co-planning with community representatives, working in partnership with governmental units and local schools, students from the College of Arts and Sciences donated school supplies and planted trees. Health Sciences students provided free medical checkups and led training workshops in family planning, maternal healthcare, immunization and proper hand-washing. Students led a nutrition program including distribution of vegetable seeds and instruction in planting backyard gardens.

Recently, the service activities of College of Engineering Technology students focused on their adopted community in Sitio Bangkal, Brgy. Tinago, Norala. They completed construction of a community center, distributed hygiene materials for community residents, tutored children, provided school supplies and used clothing. The College of Business Administration Student Council focused in 2009–2010 on developing sustainable income-generating activities and helping to support a successful, self-supporting cooperative. Students built cooperative members' knowledge of financial management skills, and provided training on packing, marketing and storage methods.

Students from across the University participated in relief efforts following destructive flooding of the Allah River. Working together with government agencies, and joined by 40 faculty members and staff, and President Wilfredo Lubrico, FMS, they distributed food and supplies, and assisted with reconstruction efforts.

Students are enthusiastic about the service that they provide and also pleased with the skills that they develop through their volunteering—skills in leadership, teamwork and communication. A student commented on her tutoring of younger poor children, "I learn to love them and to become more patient."

Organization and Leadership

NDMU's community engagement activities are a high personal priority for the President, Brother Wilfredo Lubrico, FMS. A community organizer for 17 years before he became a university president, Dr Lubrico wrote his doctoral dissertation on "A Conceptual Model for A Community Extension Program in an Educational Institution," an evaluation of community service at another Marist school in Mindanao. He states "when our students graduate, our goal is that they be community-oriented, that they be leaders in service." Brother Wilfredo deliberately has reserved for himself the role of Director of Special Programs, the organizational locus of Champagnat Community College and other community engagement programs at NDMU. Because the board of trustees of NDMU is very interested in community service, the University's service programs are part of the President's report at each board meeting.

The overall strong institutional commitment to service is reinforced by other top leaders of the University including the Administrative Vice-President Mr Andres S. Magallanes and the Academic Vice President Dr Noemi B. Silva. All of the college deans demonstrate strong support for the University's service work and believe that their units are substantially accomplishing the educational goal of preparing community-oriented leaders in service.

A Center that is Both a Community Extension Service and a Support System for Student Volunteer Service

Champagnat Community College (CCC) directed by Agnes Reyes plays a pivotal support and coordination role with respect to community outreach activities. "The community extension arm of NDMU," CCC is a combination of community extension service and volunteer service support system. Its outreach programs include community development, education, environmental protection, health service, and peace and development. CCC has had considerable success in garnering financial support from external aid agencies, including the US Agency for International Development; Child Fund Japan; and AusAID, the Australian aid agency.

In 2007–2008, a Community Extension Services (CES) Committee was organized "to systematize, monitor, implement, document and evaluate all community extension activities . . . The committee acts as a governing body to assure quality and relevance of proposed community extensions to the different colleges and departments." A faculty member is assigned as the CES coordinator in each college. Before implementing service projects, colleges, departments, clubs and organizations are required to submit their plans for review by the CES committee.

Earlier in its history NDMU ran what was called the "Farmers' College" which trained Indigenous farmers to improve their cultivation practices. Today the CCC operates several long-term extension programs that serve not only farmers, but also people seeking to earn their living in a wider range of occupations. Furthermore, the College's extension work addresses a broad spectrum of community and family development issues.

Some of the College's community extension programs are organized under Basic Education Assistance for Mindanao (BEAM). BEAM's goals are to improve the quality of, and the access to, basic education in South and Central Mindanao. BEAM has four components: Community Learning Centers, Early Children Education, Alternative Learning System, and Functional Literacy. It operates through an expanding network of 34 community learning centers.

CCC runs several programs to build the skills and employability of out-of-school youth (BEAM Alternative Learning System, and E-Skills and Technical Program) and adults. Job skills training includes metal arc welding, small engine repair, massage therapy, wiring installation, heavy equipment operation, and beauty care. Recent and current training programs for adults include acupressure and acupuncture, leadership and group dynamics, planning for sustainability, credit management, organic farming and vermin-culture.

An important element of its focus on child development and education is a program called CHILD, Community Help Integrated Lifelong Development, funded by Child Fund Japan. CHILD provides annual medical and dental checkups, and follow-up health services and nutritional interventions, and it teaches crafts and physical activities to children and their parents. CHILD aims to develop the skills of local leaders to run their projects following the support provided by the CCC.

Student service program leaders value greatly the guidance and support provided by CCC Director Reyes, Outreach Coordinator Danilo Fresco, and the entire Center staff. They comment that the working relationships of CCC staff with non-governmental organizations and government agencies in the area are invaluable when students plan and conduct service projects. In addition, Center staff provide training and ongoing advice to the leaders of student service initiatives. At the start of each school year the CCC leads workshops to teach social awareness to the leaders of students groups and to strengthen their community outreach skills.

In 2008, the College initiated an annual Community Extension Summit to showcase and recognize student projects. The theme of the summit was "The Young Leader as an Agent of Change." The annual Summit may mark a significant next stage in student service activities, one with increased focus on supporting students' planning initiatives and coordination among student groups. The Summit aims to "develop a network of young leaders of NDMU who will proactively work towards making positive change in the community after the summit."

Limited Implementation of Community Service Learning

NDMU administrators and faculty members have a mixed view of community service learning. This was the topic of a spirited discussion between the author and the deans of all of the colleges. While some favor expansion of service learning, many others are skeptical, or oppose it because they believe strongly in the higher value of voluntary action. The future of service learning at the University is uncertain because some of the academic programs that have used that pedagogic approach most extensively—Social Work, Library Science, and Community Development—are being phased out because of insufficient student enrollment.

Driving Factors

NDMU's civic engagement activities are shaped by the institution's religious values and traditions, its community context, its primary educational objectives, and the faculty rewards system. An ethos of service pervades the institution; it is consistently expressed by students, faculty, staff and administrators. It is a priority for NDMU to graduate students who are community-oriented leaders for service. Administrative Vice-President Magallanes attests, "A key role of the University is to provide access to education and development of the people. . . . We want to maximize the likelihood that our students will go back to their communities of origin and be agents for the development of their communities."

Community service and extension work is credited in annual faculty evaluations. Dr Noemi Silva, Academic Vice-President, credits NDMU's origins as a mission school as being a major influence on its enduring commitment to community service. She emphasizes also the extent and urgency of community needs as a primary influence.

NDMU's community service work is facilitated by an extensive network of working ties with local governmental agencies and non-governmental organizations. This infrastructure of community partnerships is reinforced by the fact that the vast majority of these units are staffed and directed by NDMU graduates. NDMU students come primarily from Mindanao and they tend to stay in the province after graduating. Further, NDMU administrators and professors are actively involved in local community affairs, and many sit on local governmental councils and committees. Administrative Vice-President Magallanes notes that in local governmental process, "NDMU is a consistent voice and proponent for action on human development and environmental sustainability." One example of an ongoing program to support local professionals is a Continuous Teacher Training Program that provides regular training to elementary and secondary school teachers across the region, which is overseen by Vice President Magallanes.

Challenges

A major limitation in the University's service experience is the dramatic decline in student volunteering after the required first year National Student Training Program. Student service groups have difficulty recruiting their peers to volunteer because students feel pressure to excel in their academic studies. Many of them feel that the time they would spend doing community service would detract from their studies. NDMU's ambivalence with respect to integrating service in academic courses closes off a potential strategy for overcoming this obstacle to volunteering. Service activities that are embedded in courses would mean that students would not have to choose to volunteer rather than to study.

President Lubrico and other administrators observe that in recent years, growing economic pressures make it much harder to secure external funds for development assistance projects, and that those development agencies that are willing to invest now are more demanding in the terms that they require. As was noted earlier, an additional challenge is that there are significant personal safety issues that make service activities impractical in certain geographic areas.

Future Directions and Reflections

NDMU is an impressive example of the powerful supportive impact of religious identity and traditions on a university's civic engagement and social responsibility. The University's experience demonstrates both the potential and the limitations of a primary focus on student volunteer service, accompanied by limited support for community service learning. As was discussed above, there is considerable interest in, and also significant reservations about, expanding the integration of service work in the academic curriculum. The future of this dimension of the University's community work is uncertain.

In the coming period NDMU'S civic engagement work is likely to look very similar to what it is today; "continue to respond to community needs and promote peace." President Lubrico is committed to continuing the institution's current service programs, and he would like to further increase coordination with government agencies and NGOs. Vice-President Magallanes states, "We will continue to respond to community needs and promote peace." Administrative and faculty leaders would like to increase documentation and research about the institution's service work and its impacts.

South Africa and its Higher Education System

South Africa has a population of 49 million, an average life expectancy for men of 50 and women of 48, and ranks 36th out of 173 in the Reporters without Borders 2008 Media Freedom Index. Its adult literacy rate is 86.4%, it has 0.8 doctors per 1,000 population, infant mortality of 43.78 deaths per 1,000 live births and an adult HIV/AIDS infection rate of 18.8% (*Guardian* "World Fact Files," 2009).

South Africa was colonized first by Dutch settlers (Boers/Afrikaaners) and later the British, who ultimately defeated opposition from the Boers during the Boer War (1899–1902). The Union of South Africa was established in 1910 and jointly ruled by the Afrikaaners and the British. From the earliest days of European settlement, racial conflict and oppression of native Africans by white settlers drove social, political, and economic developments in South Africa. This was accelerated when the National Party came to power in 1948 and instituted apartheid, the strict policy of racial segregation between the categories of white, Indian/Asian, black African, and coloured (mixed race). Decades of both non-violent and violent resistance to apartheid, led by the African National Congress, culminated in the end of apartheid and democratic elections in 1994. Since that time, South Africa has worked to overcome the apartheid legacy of poverty, poor housing, and poor health care especially among black and coloured South Africans.

Due to the creation of separate universities by the British and Afrikaaners, as well as schools segregated by race, South Africa developed a large number of universities; by the 1980s, South Africa had 36 universities and technikons (Subotzky, 2003). South African higher education has seen major reforms since the end of apartheid and the transition to inclusive democracy in 1994, guided heavily by the Education White Paper 3: A Program for the Transformation of Higher Education (1997) and the National Policy for Higher Education (2001). The various separate government departments governing educational institutions for different races were combined into one Department of Education, and a number of higher education institutions merged. Today, South African higher education is dominated by the country's 23 public universities. The number of private institutions has grown rapidly, but private tertiary enrollment in 2004 was approximately 85,000 (Van Harte et al., 2006). This compares with a student enrollment in public universities in 2008 of 799,387 (Department of Education, 2010). This represents a significant increase over the total enrollment of 473,000 in 1993 and 564,000 in 1999 (Subotzky, 2003). The gross enrollment ratio (GER) reached 16.3% in 2007 (South African Government Information, 2008), but major access and success gaps remain along racial lines. While GER of blacks in 2000 was 13%, this was significantly behind of GER of whites (47%) and Indians/Asians (39%) (Van Harte et al., 2006). In 2008, there were major gaps in the public university graduation rates among black Africans (74%), coloured students (77%), Indians/Asians (82%) and whites (86%) (Department of Education, 2010).

Higher Education is overseen by the Minister of Higher Education and Training within the Department of Education. In addition, "the South African Council on Higher Education (CHE), established under the Higher Education Act of 1997, is an independent statutory body responsible for advising the Minister of Higher Education and Training on all higher education policy issues, and for quality assurance in higher education and training" (Council on Higher Education, 2010). The CHE also oversees the accreditation of higher education programs through the Higher Education Quality Commission. The Department of Education funds programs accredited by the HEQC. Government funding is set to grow from approximately USD 2 billion in 2008–2009 to USD 2.8 billion in 2011–2012 (South African Government Information, 2008).

South Africa's reforms of higher education since the end of apartheid have focused considerable attention on promoting community engagement, especially to advance reconstruction and transformation in the post-apartheid democratic era. Community engagement and service-learning are embedded in South African documents such as the Green Paper on Higher Education Transformation (1996), the White Paper on Higher Education (1997), the National Plan for Higher Education (2001), the Founding Document of the Higher Education Quality Committee (HEQC) of the Council on Higher Education (2001), the HEQC Criteria for Institutional Audits (2004) and the HEQC Criteria for Program Accreditation (2004). The HEQC identifies "knowledge based community service" as one of three core functions of Higher Education—along with teaching and learning and research—as the basis for accreditation and quality assurance. As a result, South African HEIs as public institutions have to demonstrate greater responsibility and commitment to socioeconomic development of South African communities. Non-compliance could result in a cut in government subsidy (see questionnaire). In order to assist Higher Education Institutions to implement and assess service-learning, the HEQC and the Community-Higher Education Service Partnership (CHESP) project of the Joint Education Trust released *A Good Practice Guide and Self-evaluation Instruments for Managing the Quality of Service-Learning* in 2006. The Guide contains criteria for the good practice and self-assessment of service-learning at an institutional, faculty, program and module level (questionnaire). One of the goals listed in the 1997 White Paper was "To promote and develop social responsibility and awareness among students of the role of higher education in social and economic development through community service programs." To advance this goal, the HEQC has established "knowledge-based community service" as a criterion for accreditation and quality assurance and requires reporting on community engagement in institutional audits (Hall et al., 2010).

In response, South African universities have begun to establish community engagement offices and are in various stages of incorporating different community engagement methodologies into their activities and curricula. In November 2009, the South African Higher Education Community Engagement Forum (SAHECEF) was launched to represent university staff responsible for community engagement at each university. According to its constitution, SAHECEF is committed to:

- advocating, promoting, supporting, monitoring, and strengthening community engagement at South African Higher Education Institutions;
- furthering community engagement at Higher Education Institutions in partnership with all stakeholders with a sustainable social and economic impact on South African society;
- fostering an understanding of community engagement as integral to the core business of higher education.

Community Partnerships for Development and the Appropriation of New Knowledge

Profile of Cape Peninsula University of Technology (CPUT), South Africa
By Susan E. Stroud (based on field visit August 6–7, 2009)

Origins and History

The Cape Peninsula University of Technology (CPUT) was formed in January 2005 from the merger of the Cape Technikon and Peninsula Technikon. Cape Technikon began in 1920 as Cape Technical College to consolidate various technical courses offered in the greater Cape Town area and was open to white students only. Peninsula Technikon began in 1962 to provide technical education—under apartheid restrictions—to 'coloured' students. After the passage of the Technikons Act in 1976, both technical colleges were upgraded to technikons and were able to offer courses at the tertiary level, including Bachelors, Masters, and Doctorate degrees in Technology (CPUT, www.cput.ac.za/). With the collapse of apartheid and the election of a democratic government in 1994, the

Minister of Education sought a remedy for the structure of higher education that was based on official racial categories with accompanying disparities in resourcing. In 2001, the Minister announced a plan for mergers of higher education institutions as part of a national rationalization of the higher education system. At the same time, the Minister announced that technikons would be re-named as universities of technology. As part of that rationalization, Cape Technikon and Peninsula Technikon were merged in 2005 to create the Cape Peninsula University of Technology. Professor L. Vuyisa Tanga was appointed as the first Vice-Chancellor of the Cape Peninsula University of Technology in February 2006 (CPUT, www.cput.ac.za/).

In 2007 approximately 30,000 students were enrolled at CPUT, of which 85% were full-time students. About 2,000 were international students, including many from SADC countries. The University's academic offerings are organized in six faculties: Applied Sciences, Business, Education and Social Sciences, Engineering, Health and Wellness Sciences, and Informatics and Design. A special HIV/AIDS unit works to incorporate confronting the epidemic into all curricula, while at the same time doing research and community outreach on the pandemic (SARUA website).

Immediate Context

Cape Town is known as the "Mother City." The colonization of South Africa began in Cape Town with the Dutch establishment of a re-provisioning stop for trading vessels on their routes to the East. Cape Town is now the second most populous city in South Africa with approximately 3.5 million inhabitants (Community Survey, 2007). It is the location of the national Parliament and, consequently, the location of many government offices. Cape Town is historically and predominantly a city of coloured South Africans, the majority of whom are Afrikaans speaking. According to the 2001 Census, 48% of the population are coloured, 31% black Africans, 18.75% white and 1.43% Asian. Of the population, 46.6% are under 24; 38% have completed high school; 12.6% education beyond high school.

In the first decade of democracy, there were significant improvements in the quality of life for many South Africans. However, many challenges remain, including poverty, unemployment, HIV/AIDS, lack of housing, crime, and more recently there have been widespread acts of xenophobic violence. Poverty persists despite economic development and affluence in some sectors of the population. Economic progress has not been accompanied by social development to the same degree. In Cape Town, unemployment has risen from 13% in 1997 to 23% in 2004. Households living below or only marginally above the poverty line grew from 25% in 1996 to 38% in 2005. The city government of Cape Town acknowledges that development goals can only be achieved through "coordinated efforts of . . . government and the active involvement of civil society" (Haskins, 2006: 18).

CPUT and its Civic Engagement Agenda

CPUT defines its mission as "to develop and sustain an empowering environment where, through teaching, learning, research and scholarship our students and staff, in partnership with the community and industry, are able to create and apply knowledge that contributes to development" (CPUT, www.cput.ac.za/). The University defines its set of core values to include (among others) *ubuntu*, an African concept that defines the self as existing only in relation to others. How does CPUT actualize these mission and value statements in the context described above?

As described previously, government policy on higher education actively promotes community engagement as a core mission of public universities and a criterion for institutional assessment and quality assurance. In response to this national framework, CPUT has included responsiveness and community engagement as the third of six strategic directions for the institution after teaching and learning and research. This strategic direction is described as "Through sustained interaction, to determine national and regional priorities and transformation imperatives, as well as the academic and social development needs of all students and staff and enter into mutually beneficial partnerships for development, the appropriation of knowledge and life-long learning" (see questionnaire).

Further evidence of CPUT's commitment to community engagement is demonstrated by the creation in 2009 of a new senior level position of Director of Community Engagement and Work Integrated Learning. Joyce Nduna, who currently holds the new position, explained that as a former technikon, CPUT had incorporated work-based learning in its academic program, although most of the placements were in industry and focused largely on the development of students' technical skills. In 2005 when CPUT was created, a service learning unit was established, and in 2009 the Centre for Community Engagement and Work Integrated Learning was set up to serve as an institutional focal point for both work-based learning and community engagement. CPUT defines community engagement as "those activities and programs offered by CPUT which involve collaborative interaction with individuals, groups, and organizations external to CPUT at the local, regional, national and international levels to achieve economic and social objectives using volunteerism, community outreach and various forms of work-integrated learning, such as service learning and co-operative education" (see questionnaire). One of the shifts that have occurred is a shift to work-based learning assignments being made in community organizations as well as industry. Faculty with whom I met mentioned repeatedly that one of the goals of community engagement is the need to transfer knowledge to community organizations to improve their management and productivity to benefit the larger community.

Civic engagement and social responsibility objectives are also built into CPUT's performance management and promotion strategy. The policy on *Ad*

Hominem Promotion guides an annual staff promotion process and enables CPUT to reward staff who demonstrate commitment to the key strategic directions of teaching and learning, research and scholarship, and responsiveness and community engagement (questionnaire). Training is compulsory for all new faculty—including faculty teaching at honors and graduate levels—and service-learning is included as part of the training.

Academic Programs and Community Engagement

Three academic programs illustrate the variety of subjects in which community engagement has been successfully integrated. In the Textiles Department, senior students work with low income women in the townships to teach them how to design and produce clothing for specific occupations, e.g., producing construction workers' safety vests and lab coats for university students and staff—a business that is less volatile than the fashion industry. In several cases, these efforts have spun off into small businesses that generate much needed income and have also qualified the women owners of the business to apply for government subsidized machinery. Another senior student worked with unemployed fishermen on the west coast of the Western Cape who were taught to make cloth baskets to hold fish meal, which they are able to sell and generate income.

In the Department of Nursing and Radiography, students offer radiographic service delivery at community health clinics and produce posters dealing with the prevalent healthcare issues within communities. In addition students use their posters to educate communities on healthcare issues. This experience provides students with opportunities to integrate technical expertise with a caring approach in a primary healthcare setting and prepare them for their future careers.

The students from the Departments of Chemical Engineering and Chemistry provide support to predominantly disadvantaged secondary schools in the area of Mathematics and Science in order to engender an interest in these disciplines. The activities in which students are involved range from traditional mathematics and science tutoring to hands-on application of mathematics and science in the form of practicals, demonstrations and projects.

In a meeting I had with representatives of community organizations, several points were raised about how to strengthen their current partnerships with CPUT, including greater need for coordination, planning, and orientation. They mentioned that their organizations are already under-resourced and they need to realize the investment they make in the partnerships with CPUT. They also acknowledged the importance of the commitment of resources the University has made to establish the Centre for Work Integrated Learning and Community Engagement and expressed the belief that having staff to focus on university–community partnerships is a very positive development.

Challenges

The challenges to successful implementation of civic engagement programming at CPUT primarily fall into three categories: limited resources/competing priorities; the early stage of development of the field; and the challenges of partnering with communities.

Like many universities around the world, and particularly in developing countries, CPUT has limited financial resources. Professor Anthony Staak, Academic DVC, referred to community engagement in South African higher education as an "unfunded mandate." There are increasing expectations from government and society that universities will engage with their communities, but the resources needed for this additional work are not necessarily forthcoming. Furthermore, rising expectations in other areas are competing with community engagement for resources. The recent transition of CPUT from two technikons to a university has put pressure on the institution and its faculty to increase research output and publication.

In addition, the field of community engagement is still in an early and somewhat immature stage of development at CPUT. While there are excellent examples of community engagement being integrated into the curriculum, this has not yet occurred in a widespread way. Furthermore, the research base in the field is minimal. Only two Masters-level students at CPUT have focused on community engagement in their research. The limited research available has yet to translate into a truly engaged scholarship. As DVC Chris Nlapo said, "We have data, but not scholarship." To address these problems and produce high quality research, scholarship, and integration of community engagement into the curriculum, more faculty need to be trained and gain experience in the field. Given the resource limitations and competing priorities listed above, this will be a challenge.

Finally, building effective community partnerships is an ongoing challenge. Traditionally, technikons focused on partnerships with industry, so there is limited experience with the much different challenges of partnering with communities, schools, and NGOs. Both community members and CPUT staff with whom I met cited a need for community members and CPUT to work out clear expectations of each other in any partnership. Political dynamics in the community have also defeated several proposed community engagement projects, including a housing audit and an epidemiological study on the effects of toxins from a nearby plant.

Plans for the Future

CPUT plans future growth in its community engagement work through three main approaches: concrete steps to improve integration of community engagement with its other core functions; improved community collaboration; and building the field of community engagement through increased research and evaluation.

Several concrete proposals have been made to more effectively integrate community engagement into the university's activities. One proposal is to have a dedicated faculty community engagement coordinator in each department. This will ensure improved coordination and communication about community engagement and social responsibility activities. The university is also beginning to restructure its academic schedule to accommodate community engagement. For example, there are no classes in Entrepreneurship on Friday to give students time for community engagement activities, while students in Human Resources are encouraged to devote their Mondays to community engagement.

CPUT also plans increased collaboration outside the university community. The university hopes to form new partnerships at the local, regional, national, and international levels. The rise of Corporate Social Responsibility offices at many businesses is opening up a new set of potential collaborations for CPUT.

Finally, CPUT hopes to build the research base in community engagement. CPUT has discussed engaging in a wide-ranging review of its community engagement work, taking into account perspectives from all stakeholders, including faculty, students, community members, and government. CPUT also has plans for more impact studies on individual projects to determine what benefits they are having for the community. This will allow CPUT to improve its programming by learning what works and what does not.

Conclusion

The enabling policy environment has provided an important catalyst for all South African higher education institutions to rethink their role in contributing to community development and how their attention to community needs might reshape their approach to pedagogy and research. At the same time, as DVC Antony Staak pointed out, community engagement has been an unfunded mandate that universities are, nevertheless, held responsible for in terms of institutional assessment. CPUT has a special opportunity as a 'new' university to define its priorities, and community engagement has been a priority championed by Vice-Chancellor Tanga and, increasingly, by academic staff.

Sudan and its Higher Education System

Sudan is categorized according to the UN Human Development Index 2009 as a low-income, food deficient country and ranks 150 out of 182 countries and territories. Among Sudan's 39 million people (official government census results, 2009, which were widely disputed) life expectancy at birth is 53.5 for women and 51.6 for men. There are 0.3 doctors per 1,000 population, and an adult HIV/AIDS rate of 1.6% (*Guardian* "World Fact Files," 2009).

The adult literacy rate (above 15 years) is 60.9%, with illiteracy rates of women at 50% (UN HDR, 2009). The percentage of children under five years who are underweight is 41% (UN HDR, 2009). The nutrition status of Sudanese people is poor and malnutrition is widespread due to food shortages and imbalanced diet. Morbidity rates are high due to—among other reasons—the prevalence of communicable diseases, malaria and diarrhea. Sudan's ecosystem is fragile and deteriorating due to factors such as overgrazing, soil erosion, and desertification.

Sudan gained independence in 1956. Since then, the country has been engaged in a civil war that has continued for two decades in the south and the conflict in Darfur since 2003. These conflicts have resulted—by some estimates—in 200,000 deaths and more than 3.5 million displaced people, depleted human and natural resources, and destroyed the infrastructure that previously existed.

The political situation in Sudan remains highly volatile, creating unstable conditions for higher education in the country. In the April 2010 election Omar al-Bashir was re-elected after winning two-thirds of the vote, amid accusations of vote-rigging and intimidation (Rice, 2010). In terms of transparency, Sudan is ranked 173 out of 178 countries (Transparency International, 2008). According to Reporters without Borders' Press Freedom Index, Sudan was 148 out of 175 countries in 2008.

Sudan is rich in many natural resources, mainly oil in the South, uranium and gold in the West, metals and minerals in the East, and agricultural and animal wealth in the central and Northern regions. However, political instability, mismanagement, a poorly-trained workforce, and inadequate infrastructure and technology are considered the main factors in the underdevelopment of Sudan and create a vicious circle of poverty for the majority of the population.

Higher education in Sudan consists of universities, higher education institutes, and colleges that offer degree and diploma courses in a variety of fields. The last two decades saw a sustained expansion of higher education. In 1989 when Omar al-Bashir came to power during a coup, there were only five public universities and two private universities in Sudan. By 2006, there were 27 public universities, five private universities, nine public technical colleges and 46 private colleges—a dramatic expansion of higher education in a relatively short period of time. According to the IAU World Higher Education Database, student intake also increased dramatically in the 1990s from 6,080 in 1989 to 38,623 in 1999/2000, which represented an increase of 535% (2006). Total tertiary enrollment in 2000 was 204,114 students; 47% of students were female (UN Data, 2007). The development of higher education in Sudan was significantly advanced by the Conference on Higher Education in 1990 in Khartoum, followed by the enactment of the 1990 Higher Education Act.

According to the International Bureau of Education, "Higher education remains the responsibility of the central government through the Federal Ministry of Higher Education and Scientific Research. The National Council for Higher Education is responsible for the implementation of the government's higher education policies. The Council is headed by the Federal Minister of Higher Education, assisted by the Vice-Chancellors of universities and other prominent educators" (International Bureau of Education, 2006). Several committees of the National Council for Higher Education are responsible for assessing the performance of both governmental and private higher education and scientific research institutions.

The government recently announced plans for several initiatives to enhance science and technology and higher education. Among these initiatives are a science and technology "city" (500 hectares at a site 20 kilometers from Khartoum) that will build strong ties with universities and research institutes and will focus on technology commercialization and knowledge transfer in areas such as biotechnology, nanotechnology, health, energy, agricultural and medical research (*University World News*, June 2010). This knowledge transfer is geared towards countering Sudan's severe developmental challenges. In fact, among the goals for higher education spelled out in the 1990 Higher Education Act are several that directly address the application of knowledge to the development needs of the country (UNESCO 2006d).

Empowering Women as Agents of Change through Education

Profile of Ahfad University for Women (Sudan)
By Susan E. Stroud (based on field visit on 27 &28 January, 2010)

Origins and History

Ahfad University for Women (AUW) is located in Omdurman, which is adjacent to Khartoum, the capital of Sudan and the seat of government. AUW's origin was in the first school for girls in Sudan founded in 1907 by Sheikh Babiker Badri (the current president's grandfather). At the time the school represented a radical idea of providing secular education to girls and the empowerment of women through education. Sheik Babiker saw that educated women were essential to achieving improvements in nutrition, health, child care, and community development—all of which were essential for Sudan's development.

From that first school, Yusuf Badri (Babiker's son and the current president's father) established Ahfad University College for Women in 1966 to provide access to higher education opportunities for women. AUW was the first non-government secular university established in Sudan. Yusuf had a strong commitment to serving rural communities and poor people, which was reflected in the curriculum established at the College. The first two faculties created at the new College were Family Sciences (with an emphasis on nutrition education) and Psychology and Preschool Education.

The School of Management opened in 1976; the School of Rural Education, Extension and Development in 1987; the School of Medicine with community and problem-based orientation in 1990; and the School of Pharmacy in 2001.

AUW was granted full university status in 1995. Under the leadership of the current president, Gasim Badri, the university has an ambitious plan to expand academic programs.

Currently AUW serves approximately 6,500 students who come from all regions of Sudan and several neighboring countries. Students are enrolled in one of six schools—which are organized along practical professional lines—rather than the traditional academic fields. The six schools are Health Sciences; Psychology and Preschool Education; Management Studies; Rural Extension, Education and Development; Medicine; and Pharmacy. In addition, AUW offers seven graduate programs in Human Nutrition; Gender and Development; Gender and Peace Studies; Business Administration; Microfinance and Development; Psychology and Counseling; Sustainable Rural Development and two high diplomas in Family Sciences Education, and Teaching of English as a Foreign Language.

AUW's Vision, Mission, and Goals

As stated in the 1995 legislation granting full university status to Ahfad, AUW's vision is "to create proactive women change agents and leaders from all parts of Sudan who can participate actively in the development of their families and communities." AUW's mission is "to provide quality education for women to strengthen their roles in national development, and in seeking equity for themselves and other fellow women in all facets of Sudanese society."

It is worth listing verbatim several of the goals set out in the 1995 legislation, because they explicitly state AUW's aspirations for civic engagement and social responsibility as the underlying principles of the university and its academic program:

* Develop appropriate curriculum that would promote the students' analytical and critical skills in order to contribute effectively for the improvement and enhancement of the Sudanese communities and people.
* Develop outreach programs that are directly related to serve the outside communities, particularly in rural areas. These could be various programs of comprehensive nature for continual education, distant education, training, advocacy or awareness raising activities in a way to make the university an effective tool and seat for civic engagement with a special focus on reaching the rural communities.
* Create networking and close partnerships with the civil society, public and private sectors whether nationally, regionally or internationally. These partnerships could be in areas of joint curriculum development to serve the needs of the society, state and the market as well as contribute to the promotion of technology for services and production purposes.
* Establish good cooperation with other universities and academic or research institutes nationally, regionally and internationally in different spheres of

knowledge promotion particularly as pertaining to develop appropriate and relevant curriculum and technology that serves the ever changing needs of Sudan.

• Empower women to best serve their families to achieve harmony and a consolidated satisfaction emotionally, spiritually and materially. Further, to enable them to effectively serve their communities and society in urban and rural settings particularly through undertaking relevant research and other capacity building programs and interventions.

As a women's university with an explicit mandate for outreach, civic engagement, and promoting national development, AUW presents a unique model, particularly given its national context.

Curriculum Design and University Policies Aligned with Civic Engagement and Social Responsibility

There is a high level of congruence between AUW's mission statement, curriculum design, and the institutional policies that support civic engagement. Strong emphasis is placed on a curriculum that is community-oriented, academically sound in reference to international standards, and relevant to the Sudanese context. Courses are regularly evaluated and updated to be responsive to current and changing community and national needs. There are eleven university courses that are required of all undergraduate students, including rural extension, population studies, reproductive health, environmental studies, women and gender studies, career development, research methodology, talent development skills, introduction to behavioral sciences, and English and Arabic languages. All students are required to participate in community-based learning and research projects regardless of academic major, including residence in rural communities for 4–6 weeks during the summer vacation for either two or three periods, depending on the student's academic major.

All new faculty hires are expected to sign a contract that includes a statement acknowledging and agreeing to adhere to the university's philosophy of civic engagement and social responsibility. As of 2001, all faculties—regardless of their specialization—agree to be involved in the rural extension program for at least four successive years. Thereafter, all faculty members are expected to spend 6–10 hours/week in civic activities, which can be in relation to a university project, research, training, or consultancies that contribute to the university's overall civic engagement mission. In 2001 an evaluation system was adopted for faculty promotion in which civic engagement is considered one of the criteria for promotion. Civic engagement activities can be counted for as much as 30% of promotion criteria, although according to the Amna Badri, the Vice-President for Academic Affairs, "no specific measurement has been created as yet."

President Badri estimates that 20% of the university's budget is allocated to support academic and extra-curricular civic engagement activities. These funds come from donations, sponsored research, and the university's own resources.

The university demonstrates a strong commitment to providing financial aid to enable students from all regions of the country and all financial backgrounds to attend. A total of 33% of students receive scholarships for full tuition; 40% of students receive reduced and/or waived fees. Special consideration is given to students who are the first females in their families to attend university and to students from less developed states. The university makes 50 places available each year to students from the south and 50 places each year for students from Darfur. Ahfad also encourages the use of the university's facilities by staff, students, alumni and the neighborhood or catchment areas within the university radius.

Academic Programs with Strong Civic Engagement Orientation

The majority of academic programs within the university's six schools integrate community-based teaching and research with a strong emphasis on civic engagement.

The Rural Extension program is designed to assist the training of rural development professionals and to mobilize the students to become better change agents through field work in rural areas. The program has two parts. The first is for the students in the School of Rural Extension, Education and Development where they spend one month in rural communities for two consecutive years (after 4th and 6th semesters), and during which they enroll in a rural developmental project and produce a report afterwards. The second has been established in 1974 as a compulsory course for all students regardless of academic major. Students go to rural areas in teams of mixed specializations and spend two weeks in rural villages. They are trained to design simple educational messages and deliver them to people in rural communities. They also carry out surveys, collect baseline data, and conduct workshop for local residents. As a result, more than 300 village leaders have been trained. Since 1999, 200 villages in 10 localities of northern Sudan were mobilized and organized into 400 community-based organizations (CBOs), and each organization has developed action plans to provide service for education, health, water and sanitation for the villages. More than 800 CBOs have been established over time and 50 literacy classes have opened in different rural areas, especially Kordufan and River Nile State.

In the School of Medicine, students in the Family Attachment Program are attached to families in poor urban areas with whom they meet once a month for four years to educate families about child, maternal, and family health and to assist them with accessing health services.

Students in the School of Health Sciences are attached to health and feeding centers at the community level for a month to carry nutrition educational and child growth monitoring activities as well as community awareness raising in family health. School of Psychology and Preschool Education students are attached to prisons, psycho-health centers, psychiatric wards at hospitals, kindergartens, special handicapped centers, and to primary and secondary schools in poor communities for practical work that is central to students' academic and professional preparation.

In Management Studies, faculty and students help build capacity of women in small enterprises and operate a microfinance revolving fund for women small business entrepreneurs.

In addition to the six schools of the university mentioned above, there are a number of specialized units, the majority of which address specific community needs or serve as research institutes focused on the role of women as change agents. Among these specialized units are the Institute for Women, Gender and Development Studies; Nutrition Center for Training and Research; Ahfad Center for Science and Technology; Documentation for Women Studies; Teacher Training Resource Unit; Ahfad Institute of Languages; Ahfad Family Health Center; *Ahfad Journal: Women and Change* (academic peer reviewed journal that publishes scientific and social science articles and book reviews that reflect on women's issues in Sudan and other developing countries); Early Childhood Development Center; Ombadda Teaching Hospital (provides service to 1.5 million people in the Ombadda community and in the camps for displaced people); and University Teaching Farm (student training unit situated adjacent to camp for displaced people) and primary and high schools that serve as training units for students as well as providing services to the community and AUW staff and students.

AUW's academic programs cover a wide range of disciplines that raise the awareness of civic engagement. However, there are other effective programs that strive to achieve this goal.

Extracurricular Civic Engagement Programs

In addition to the academic program, Ahfad encourages participation in extracurricular civic engagement programs. The university has fostered the development of several development NGOs that started as university projects led by students, and which the university continues to house and otherwise provide significant support, for example, by seconding a full-time staff person to work directly with them. Examples of two such NGOs include the Babiker Badri Scientific Association for Women Studies (BBSAWS) and CAFA Sudanese Community Development Association

The Babiker Badri Scientific Association for Women Studies (BBSAWS) was established in 1979 by AUW faculty and partner women activists and operates projects in many parts of Sudan that focus on women's empowerment. Approaches include research and publications, training and capacity building of local organizations, media awareness, advocacy, and production of documentary films. Outcomes have included development of women to run their own organizations, increased awareness regarding gender, changes in women and family law, and advocacy for women's rights.

CAFA was founded in 1998 by a group of committed students and graduates and became an independent NGO in 2001. CAFA focuses on providing HIV/AIDS and human rights awareness, education about reproductive rights, efforts at poverty reduction for women and youth, providing after-school programs, and a microfinance program for women.

There is a broad array of other student organizations supported by the university. *Ana Sudan* [I am Sudan], is a national student organization involving 200,000 volunteers in all states and strong participation from Ahfad students. Nationally, students have built 105 schools and maintain 500 more. Students in AMSA, the Ahfad Medical Students Association, work under World Health Organization supervision to organize free health clinics in which they typically treat 200–300 people/day for endemic diseases. Some 125 Ahfad medical students actively participate in weekly projects. The Nuba Mountains Student Society—AUW's affiliation with the Nuba Mountains Students and Scholars Coalition, a national NGO—engages students who receive scholarships and must pledge to work in their villages or similar locations for five years post-graduation, especially with organizations that address women's empowerment issues. *Tanweer* students association also provides awareness-raising for communities around Khartoum State in HIV/AIDS. *The Promising Half* magazine is produced by students to reflect on their community experiences and the work of Ahfad graduates.

Challenges

There are a number of important challenges facing AUW in its efforts to continue to emphasize civic engagement as a priority of the university. First among the issues is the shortage of funds for provision of services and engagement in long-term projects. Sudan does not have robust corporate or philanthropic sectors and many of its graduates work in community and public sector positions. The university has been successful at developing strong relations with international donors, including bilateral donors DFID, USAID, GTZ, CIDA, the Dutch government, NORAD, DAAD, as well as the EU, UN agencies, WHO, Population Council, and others. These donor organizations have helped to sustain much of the community development work of the university and are a key resource to assist in the sustainability of the civic activities.

Amna Badri, the Vice-President for Academic Affairs, observed that continual improvement is a challenge, despite the emphasis the university has placed on developing monitoring and evaluation systems. In 2000 a quality assurance program was conducted to improve the administration and management system and academic structure of the university. Many changes resulted from this process, including improvements in curriculum content and activities of the civic engagement related courses. Training manuals and practical guides were designed for students, including teaching guides for junior faculty and practical materials for the rural extension work all students participate in. One of Amna Badri's goals is to establish a university office of monitoring and evaluation to provide better documentation of civic engagement activities and results. She also plans to increase both qualitative and quantitative research to improve practice and curriculum.

Several faculty members mentioned that finding the time to do the kind of community-based civic engagement work to which they are committed is a constant challenge. The university leadership acknowledges that the community-based research and teaching on which the university is built requires time commitments from faculty and staff that exceed the expectations on their counterparts at other universities in Sudan.

Ahfad staff and faculty have been actively involved in working with government ministries concerned with planning and development in efforts to reform national policies and improve the provision of services in both urban areas, remote rural regions of the countries, and in the many camps established for displaced people. Given the political environment in Sudan, these relationships are often challenging.

Vision for the Future

President Badri has expressed the aspiration for Ahfad to be one of the top 25 universities in Africa. In order to achieve this, he knows that faculty must increase research and publication. He commented that Ahfad is oriented more towards Africa than the Middle East, and that the community-based, problem-based curriculum developed at Ahfad is both unique and serves as an academic model that is well suited to the African context—perhaps "better suited than those of other African universities that aspire to be like European and North American universities."

President Badri expressed an interest in making greater use of technology to promote the results of Ahfad's civic work. Internet use has increased exponentially since it first became available in Sudan in 2000 and is now available as a means of connecting students and faculty to community organizations in a way that was not possible a few years ago. He acknowledges the significant effect that access to the internet has also had on the faculty's access to information and their ability to contribute new knowledge to national and international conversations about a range of development issues.

President Badri also plans to organize Ahfad graduates in the different states of Sudan to reflect on how Ahfad's civic engagement agenda might develop and to solicit their assistance in brokering connections to local communities. He is eager to increase international and regional knowledge exchange through a variety of associations and would like to create a network of Sudanese universities to focus on civically engaged teaching and research, including Khartoum University, University of Gezira, University of Juba, the University of the Red Sea and others.

Conclusion

AUW is a remarkable university in many ways. Given the radical departure that a secular university for women represents in Sudan, it is all the more impressive that it has maintained a strong focus on educating women for roles as change agents in their communities. It is also noteworthy that three generations of men in the same family have served as president of the university and each successive generation has continued to expand the university's commitment to women's empowerment, social justice, gender equality, and community development—and in a context that is amongst the most challenging anywhere in the world.

This may not have been possible without the clearly articulated alignment of the university's mission, rhetoric leadership, policies, and commitment of resources to support civic engagement.

In challenging circumstances, with fairly limited resources, Ahfad University for Women runs high-quality civic engagement programs that have a major impact on the community, particularly on vulnerable populations. Given the tremendous growth in Sudanese higher education over the past two decades, there is a unique opportunity for other institutions to follow Ahfad's lead. In one of the poorest and most conflict-wracked countries in the world, there is an acute need for engaged and socially responsible higher education institutions to overcome the challenges facing Sudanese society.

Tanzania and its Higher Education System

Tanzania has a population of 41 million, an average life expectancy for men of 50 and women of 54, and ranks 70th out of 173 in the Reporters without Borders 2008 Media Freedom Index. Its adult literacy rate is 69.4% (men, 77.5%; women, 62.2%). It has 1.2 doctors per 1,000 population, and an adult HIV/AIDS rate of 6.2%. The infant mortality rate is 68.1 deaths per thousand live births (*Guardian* "World Fact Files," 2009).

Tanzania was established in 1964 when the recently independent British colonies of Tanganyika and Zanzibar merged. Conflict between the semi-autonomous Zanzibar and the rest of Tanzania has played an important and contentious role in the country's politics. Tanzania lived under one-party rule until elections in 1995. Since then, Tanzania has continued to hold democratic elections, though there have been voting irregularities. Among the other challenges facing Tanzania are high rates of poverty, low economic development, and the presence of more refugees than in any other country in Africa—over 0.5 million (CIA, 2010).

Tanzania's first higher education institution was established in 1961 as a college of the University of London. It then became a constituent college of the University of East Africa, and finally the independent University of Dar es Salaam in 1970 (Mkude & Cooksey, 2003: 22). Today, Tanzania's higher education sector remains underdeveloped, and access to higher education is limited. In 2008, there were 11 public universities and colleges and 19 private universities and colleges. There is also a non-university sector "comprised of institutes and colleges offering a multitude of technical, vocational, and professional courses in accounting, computer science, business administration, journalism and mass communication, engineering, teacher education, clinical medicine, agriculture, community development and social welfare" ("Higher Education Finance and Cost-Sharing in Tanzania"). Except for one Catholic university, the private institutions are all relatively new. According to the Ministry of Science and Technology and Higher Education, enrollment has increased tremendously; total higher education enrollment increased from 18,355 in 1998 to 48,236 in 2005, and enrollment at the University of Dar es Salaam increased from 4,131 to 10,394 over the same period (2005). However, this remains a very low figure in a country of over 40 million; the gross enrollment ratio in 2008 was just 1.5% (World Bank, 2008b). There is also a significant gender gap in higher education. In 2000 women accounted for just 24% of tertiary enrollment (Mkude et al., 2003). As a result of national policy, efforts to increase female enrollment brought this figure to 33% in 2006 (Graduate School of Education, 2007).

Tanzania's higher education system is overseen by the Ministry of Science, Technology, and Higher Education. Public institutions are funded primarily by the government. Traditionally public higher education—including room/board and other expenses—was free, placing a large burden on the government. Starting in 1992, the government has gradually shifted financial burdens to students and their families (Graduate School of Education, 2007). Private institutions rely on student fees, donations, endowments, and self-generated income and their students come mainly from the wealthiest sectors of society (Mkude & Cooksey, 2003). According to Tanzania's National Higher Education Policy (1999), accreditation and quality assurance is overseen by the Higher Education Accreditation Council, established in 1995.

The government has traditionally viewed universities as having an important role in social and economic development. This view found expression particularly at UDSM, Tanzania's first university and the model for the Tanzanian higher education system. In the 1970s, a course in Development Studies was introduced and made mandatory for students. Field attachment programs were also introduced in each faculty with several goals (Mkude, et al., 2003), to:

- enable students to apply theory to solving real-life problems;
- give students an opportunity to acquire appropriate work experience to complement their academic training;
- establish close contact between employers and the faculties for mutual benefit.

Overall, Tanzania has traditionally sought to connect higher education with national development needs. However, limited resources, relatively low access to higher education, and gaps in educational attainment based on income and gender remain a challenge.

Knowledge for Development

Profile of University of Dar es Salaam (Tanzania)
By Susan E. Stroud (based on field visit July 27–28, 2009)

Origins and Context

The history of the University of Dar es Salaam (UDSM) and the history of higher education in Tanzania are closely intertwined. The University of Dar es Salaam began in 1961 (the same year it gained independence from Britain, ending its colonial rule) as University College, a constituent college of the University of London. In 1963, University College became one of three affiliated colleges that comprised the University of East Africa, together with Makerere University College in Uganda and Nairobi University College in Kenya. In 1970, the independent University of Dar es Salaam was established by Tanzania's Parliament and became the first independent public university in East Africa. The University of Dar es Salaam has changed significantly since it admitted its first 14 students to study law in 1961. In the 2009–2010 academic year there were approximately 16,500 students; 38% of undergraduates were women. The university has five campuses located around the city of Dar es Salaam (UDSM, www.udsm.ac.tz/).

With 2.8 million people, Dar es Salaam is the largest and wealthiest city in Tanzania and one of the largest cities in Africa. With a population growth of 4.39% annually, the city has become the third fastest growing in Africa (ninth fastest in the world). Dar es Salaam is Tanzania's most important city for both business and government. It is also the educational center of the country with multiple higher education institutions and elite secondary schools. Although no longer the capital of Tanzania, it remains the center of the permanent government bureaucracy. Dar es Salaam's economy is heavily dependent on manufacturing, accounting for about one half of all manufacturing jobs in Tanzania. Employment opportunities have attracted migrants from interior rural areas where 80% of the population lives. This migration has resulted in the development of squatter communities and has created a strain on the city's social services, housing, water supply, and transportation. There is a relatively high degree of social integration of a population that is predominantly Swahili and incorporates migrants from the African interior as well as from the shores of the western Indian Ocean (Brennan et al., 2007).

Community Engagement as an Institutional Priority

Higher education in Tanzania was heavily influenced by Julius Nyerere, Tanzania's first president and one of modern Africa's early public intellectuals. In the

1950s when he began organizing for an independent Tanzania, he was a school teacher and one of only two Tanzanians to have attended university. After the establishment of UDSM, he was also the University's first Chancellor. He had a strong influence on educational philosophy at both the school and higher education levels in the newly independent country. In 1963, shortly after the founding of the University's predecessor institution as part of the University of East Africa, Nyerere warned against the prevailing view of universities as isolated and elitist:

> For let us be clear; the University has not been established purely for prestige purposes. It has a very definite role to play in development in this area, and to do so effectively it must be in, and of, the community it has been established to serve, The University of East Africa has to draw upon experience and ideas from East Africa as well as the rest of the world. And it must direct its energies particularly towards the needs of East Africa.
>
> *(questionnaire)*

And he further challenged students—and others who had benefited from the rare opportunity for higher education:

> [Students] are like the man who has been given all the food available in a starving village in order that he might have the strength to bring supplies back from a distant place. If he takes this food and does not bring help to his brothers, he is a traitor. Similarly, if any of the young men and women who are given an education by the people of this Republic adopt attitudes of superiority, or fail to use their knowledge to help the development of this country, then they are betraying our Union.
>
> *(questionnaire)*

Some 47 years later, Nyerere's influence is still felt in Tanzania and at the University of Dar es Salaam. The mandate to engage with community development continues to be central to the University's institutional strategic plan, although there have been other significant developments in that time that have resulted in other priorities for the University as well.

Beginning in the mid-1980s the political situation changed with the end of the socialist-liberal 'experiment' that had characterized Tanzania since independence. The government shifted from a centralized to a more open market economy. Two new public universities were established and private universities were permitted. In light of these developments, the University of Dar es Salaam engaged in a comprehensive review of its mission, goals, and objectives. "Since 1994, the University has been deeply involved in the process of building a new identity with its own distinctive characteristics in an effort to achieve and maintain a reputable regional and international position in terms of the relevance and quality of its prime outputs" (questionnaire). UDSM has adopted a Corporate

Strategic Plan for 2005–2013 which incorporates five-year rolling strategic plans from all academic and non-academic units of the university. Public service aimed at the attainment of "equitable and socio-economic development of Tanzania and the rest of Africa" remains a priority of the University, but "the improved volume and quality of research publications, and . . . improved number and quality of consultancy and services" (UDSM questionnaire) would seem to be given increased weight in the current strategic plan.

According to a recent institutional self-assessment, 84.2% of the academic units have research agendas. University leadership has emphasized the development of multidisciplinary research agendas in the belief that multidisciplinary approaches are more likely to be responsive to national development concerns and be more effective at informing policy and proposing solutions to socioeconomic problems (questionnaire).

The current institutional strategic plan puts a strong emphasis on consultancy services. In my meetings with various faculty across a range of disciplines, many stressed the consultancies they were involved in on behalf of various government ministries and other local clients and foreign donors—40% and 60%, respectively across the University (questionnaire)—to illustrate their commitment to community engagement. These consultancies provide a source of income for the University and support for individual faculty research programs, as well as material for publication. I was struck, however, at how few graduate and undergraduate students were involved in the consultancy projects that various faculty described, all of which seemed to have potential for student involvement. Given the enthusiasm for direct involvement with community groups that I heard from the students with whom I met, and given how extensive faculty consultancies appear to be, I suspect there is a missed opportunity to develop many more community-based learning experiences for both graduate and undergraduate students. The concept of experiential learning does not appear to be well developed at UDSM.

Community Engagement Projects

Many faculties have significant community connections—Engineering and Technology, Education, Journalism and Mass Communications, Entrepreneurship Center, Molecular Biology and Biotechnology, Law, Geology—to name a few with whom I held meetings. Two projects were identified by a university committee as exemplary to be included in UDSM's self-assessment of civic engagement for the Talloires Network—REDET and TUSEME—primarily because of their scale and documented impact.

Research and Education for Democracy in Tanzania (REDET)

According to Professor Benson Bana, the Coordinator of REDET, the program was begun as a project of the Department of Political Science and Public

Administration in 1992 at the time when Tanzania moved from a one-party to a multi-party democratic government to provide public education on democratic governance and civic rights for 'fuller and equitable participation in national affairs" (questionnaire). The first step in the project was to design and conduct a national survey to capture the civic competence of the public. Interventions were then designed based on the research from the national study. Various interventions included holding public meetings on participation at the grassroots level and involving local governments. Other strategies involved working with public sector groups such as the police to promote the idea of "public servants", facilitating programs targeting poor women and youth, producing materials for use by teachers in primary and secondary schools and teachers colleges, holding programs for leaders of university student unions, and working with leaders of political parties. REDET staff organized a School for Democracy on Zanzibar following a serious outbreak of violence between young people associated with different political factions on the island.

Unlike many of the projects that were described to me during my visit to UDSM, REDET involves graduate students to help run the programs, and undergraduate students (from multiple disciplines) are involved in research, organizing of events in local communities, and in election monitoring. In 2007, discussion forums were held nationwide in 256 villages, 64 wards, and 16 districts. To date REDET has produced 28 books and monographs, conducted opinion polling related to political issues and elections, produced weekly television and radio programs, and organizes an annual State of Politics conference that focuses on a specific issue.

TUSEME (in Swahili Meaning "Let Us Speak Out")

Professor Herbert Makoye, the Coordinator of TUSEME in the Department of Fine and Performing Arts (FPA), was an undergraduate in FPA at UDSM in 1989 when he became involved in organizing weekend programs that brought children, teenagers, and adults to campus for arts activities such as dance, drums, painting, and children's theater projects. The popularity of the programs grew quickly, and the Canadian International Development Agency provided support to expand the program off the campus and into Dar es Salaam and two other regions of the country. In 1996 the TUSEME program was founded to specifically address the need for intervention in secondary schools to boost the academic achievement and social development of girls. Initially the program was offered in seven secondary schools, and in 2009 the program was mainstreamed in all 1,890 secondary schools as a result of adoption as a national strategy by the Ministry of Education to address the gender gap in retention and achievement. Since 2004 the program has been replicated in other countries on the continent. In traditional African culture, theater has long been used as a way of transmitting information and for mobilizing people to take action. Girls who participate in the program learn to identify, analyze, and design action to address problems that impede their social and academic development. Professor Makoye described the involvement of FPA in the TUSEME project as being consistent with UDSM's Transformational Program (strategic plan) to act as a catalyst for social change in society.

Student-Run Projects

The Joint Environmental Management Association (JEMA) was started in 1996 by students to mobilize the university community to work with the local community to address environmental problems. In 2009 approximately 600 student members and graduates from all disciplines were involved in university and community-based JEMA projects, including organizing a 'campus greening' awareness program, starting a solid waste management project within the university, organizing debates and other events, and training program for students on environmental management. JEMA also raises 10,000 trees on campus each year, which they distribute to community groups.

The student leadership with whom I met—a student from engineering and another from law—expressed strong views about the role of the university vis-à-vis the community as part of the university's transformation agenda and the importance of civic engagement as a part of the training in their professional fields. They confirmed the University is supportive of JEMA in several ways—providing materials, a facility for their organization, limited financial support, cooperating on activities and events, consulting on projects related to the environment, and including exposure of all first year students during orientation. They also expressed a strong desire to be of service to the community by putting their learning to the test in practical problem-solving applications. The law student mentioned the transformative effect his work with the community around environmental issues has had on his ideas about the legal profession. He explained that he now views the legal notion of 'right to life' as an expansive idea that includes the right to protection against environmental degradation.

Although JEMA has strong student involvement across the campus, it also appears to be unique as a student-run organization with a civic engagement focus.

University Policies Related to Civic Engagement and Social Responsibility

The University's faculty performance and promotion policy is based on teaching and research. Several faculty members with whom I spoke about the incentive structure for engaging in community outreach expressed some frustration that, regardless of the stated policy, the only thing that matters for promotion is peer reviewed publications. Unofficially, there is a tacit understanding: "Though it is not spelt out in the contractual terms that staff should undertake civic and social responsibilities, all staff are nevertheless encouraged to perform such assignments as a matter of demonstrating relevancy and usefulness to the civil society" (questionnaire).

To further emphasize the importance of consultancies, the University recently established a Directorate of Public Service to respond to tenders and broker faculty expertise. Most consultancies support faculty research and are conducted for foreign agencies (60%) and local clients (40%)—primarily government ministries and local government. The Directorate also markets continuing education to government, the private sector, and non-profit and international organizations. Dr Lihamba, the director, stated that the directorate will also eventually serve as the university-wide focal point for outreach, which is now organized by individual faculty and academic units.

UDSM provides services to the local community through access to the health center, ICT training, and the university gymnasium. Recently the University contracted with a developer to build a shopping center on University land and also plans to build a conference center—both of which serve the public and also provide sources of revenue to the University.

In terms of human resource development policy, the University has signed agreements with other East African and SADC countries regarding postgraduate study at UDSM. Graduate students from countries encompassed by the agreement are required to return to their countries to contribute to development efforts. It is not clear how or if this policy is enforced, but it illustrates a commitment to "education for development" by the signatories.

Conclusion

USDM has had a proud tradition since its founding of responding to national development needs through teaching, research, and public service. As the University has continued to define its role in the changing context of higher education in Tanzania, more emphasis has been put on defining itself as a research institution, thereby distinguishing itself from other tertiary institutions in Tanzania and continuing its prominence in the region. The focus on research—and on consultancies as a means of supporting research activities—has resulted in much of the community engagement undertaken by individual faculty and departments to be carried out in the context of research. At UDSM this has resulted in few students participating in the various community-based research projects. In speaking with faculty across many disciplines, I repeatedly asked the question about student involvement in their work. Most faculty responded that no undergraduates participate and only occasionally graduate students were involved in data collection. I have noted several exceptions of greater student involvement in this chapter, but the potential for engaging much larger numbers of students in community-based research projects is largely untapped.

Based on interviews with students associated with the JEMA project, there appears to be a strong interest on the part of students for community-based work that is both academically based as well as activity not associated with academic work. Recently, students have started forming a number of NGOs "to act as a bridge to support the general community" (questionnaire). But there appear to be relatively few opportunities for undergraduates in projects that are academically based. One exception is the practical field sessions in which students participate during August and September. Students are attached to relevant work places for 6–8 weeks under the supervision of the persons in charge of training at the respective work places. During their placements, students are assessed at least twice by university staff. Each student must produce a report on his/her experience. A grade is assigned based on the student's work supervisor, university staff who provided the assessment, and the quality of the student's report. The grade counts towards the classification of the student's degree at graduation. Government provides stipends to cover students' living expenses during the practical field experience course (questionnaire).

The University is responsive to market demand and stakeholder feedback. Information is obtained from annual stakeholder meetings and tracer studies of graduates and is factored into curriculum reviews at least every five years. New developmental programs might be formed at any time that respond to identified need and for which resourcing is identified.

As UDSM approaches the 50th anniversary of its founding, VC Mukandala has made an effort to revive the volunteering spirit that was an established tradition in the early years of the university. Actions taken to date include addressing staff and student groups about the need for greater involvement with the community and sending some of the education students to remote areas to complete their teaching practice. The Directorate of Public Service has been assigned the task of working out other means for members of the University community to be involved in meaningful voluntary work. The Vice-Chancellor's statements and support of community engagement is an assertion of the University's long history, and especially its beginnings, of providing education and research for the benefit of society.

Ukraine and its Higher Education System

Ukraine has a population of 46 million, an average life expectancy for men of 62 and women of 73, and ranks 87th out of 173 in the Media Freedom Index. Its adult literacy rate is 99.7%; it has 3.1 doctors per 1,000 population; and an adult HIV/AIDS rate of 1.4% (*Guardian* "World Fact Files," 2009).

Public expenditure on Higher Education per student in 2005 was approximately $2,400 (World Bank, 2007).

Through its higher education system Ukraine exhibits all of the key dilemmas of a former Soviet state adapting to the realities of a new Europe (not least the "enlargement" of the European Community to now touch its western border). There are resulting tensions around language, around cross-border political allegiances, and around such academic matters as the structure of qualifications.

The 2002 Ukrainian Law on Higher Education "provides for the decentralization of the decision-making process." Higher education institutions hold certain rights of self-organization. In 2009 there were approximately 900 different institutions of higher education, and government policy is looking to reduce their number.

Autonomy is apparently guaranteed. "Each higher education institution, as a community of scientists, teaching staff, and students, accepts corporate responsibility for the activities of its administration and governance. Higher education institutions may also establish their own organizational forms of instruction and research, both within the institution as a whole and in the subordinate structures (institutes, colleges, technical schools, departments, etc.)" (Kremen & Nikolajenko, 2006: 19).

But it has limits. A European Commission report concludes, "New education legislation adopted in 1991 granted higher education institutions a considerable degree of autonomy. However, the Ministry of Education and Science is still responsible for the planning of curricula and (troubled) financing of higher education" (European Commission, 2005: 2).

There is considerable tension between Russian-speaking Ukrainians (concentrated in south-east Ukraine and the Autonomous Republic of Crimea) and the Ukrainian-speaking majority, which has tended to be suspicious of Russia and has recently become more western-oriented. These tensions are particularly clear in electoral politics since the "Orange Revolution" of 2004. Mykolayiv Oblast (home to Petro Mohyla Black Sea University, profiled here) has a relatively low proportion of Russian-speakers (14.1%), but the province voted for the pro-Russian presidential candidate Viktor Yanukovych in the 2004 election. In the most recent election (2010) Yanukovich won the Presidency defeating the Prime Minister Yulia Tymoshenko, and commentators have subsequently observed a series of policy shifts in favor of *rapprochement* with Russia.

According to an assessment in the *World University News*, following the election:

> Ukraine's higher education system will not undergo any radical reform following the recent election of a new president and government. But some changes are likely to be implemented, including modification of a controversial testing system.
>
> Dmitriy Tabachnik, the new Minister of Education, said the government would tighten admission requirements for national universities and the principles for studying in them.
>
> At the same time, the authorities are planning to retain a controversial system of external testing for applicants. This has acted as an alternative to

entrance examinations in Ukrainian universities over the past few years but has been unpopular with the heads of several major universities.

The independent system is based on applicants taking special tests to determine whether they should be accepted or not by the universities.

In 2009, the government even imposed a ban on independent examinations conducted by the universities unless they required special skills, such as drawing for architects and designers.

One main reason for introducing the system was the authorities' desire to end corruption in the admissions processes. But this aim has been only partially achieved.

In addition, most university presidents have said the current admission requirements are too formalized and do not evaluate applicants' skill levels.

Despite weaknesses in the current admission system, the government is planning to keep it, although Vice Prime Minister Volodymyr Seminozhenko said the system would be significantly improved during the next few years. Seminozhenko believes such changes will help avoid corruption and make Ukrainian universities more competitive in Europe.

Meanwhile, as part of the country's higher education reform, local authorities have not ruled out the possibility of cutting the number of higher education institutions by 30%, as is planned in neighboring Russia.

(Vorotnikov, 2010)

Mykolayiv Oblast also has high levels of poverty and unemployment. PMBSU's Institutional Assessment states, "Among the chief economic and social needs [of Mykolayiv] are low wages, bad incomes of senior citizens, low level of medical service, poor conditions of orphanages, a high level of drug addiction and other problems of the transition period" (PMBSU, 2007). It is a particularly interesting case, as an institution in a formerly highly Soviet-oriented part of the nation seeking to strengthen civil society through various forms of partnership: local; national; and international.

Building Civil Society

Profile of Petro Mohyla Black Sea State University (Ukraine)
By David Watson (based on field visit 11 September 2009)

Origins and History

Petro Mohyla Black Sea State University (PMU) is an institution in a city (Mykolayiv) in a state (Ukraine), each of which has been though recent and massive change.

The University was founded in 1996 as a branch of the historic National University, the Kyiv-Mohyla Academy. It has since gone through two significant changes of status: in 2002 it won its independence as the Petro-Mohyla University of the Humanities; in 2008 it was re-formed as the Petro Mohyla Black Sea State University. Within the Ukrainian system of university accreditation it is part of the fourth (or top) level, with the potential to offer a full range of subjects and awards (including Master's and PhD programs). Its work is divided among seven faculties and five research centers, and it currently serves about 4,500 full-time and about 700 part-time students.

For 220 years Mykolayiv/Nikolayev has been one of the great hubs of ship-building (especially military) of the world. As such it formed a critical part of the Soviet Union's economy and diplomatic strategy. Until the independence of the Ukraine in 1991 it was a closed city. While ship-building went through a severe slump thereafter, it has recovered somewhat, and the city has developed other lead roles within the Southern Ukraine, notably in the creative industries. Nonetheless, it remains a large city (approximately 520,000) with significant pockets of deprivation and social tension.

Ukraine itself has an iconic history within Eastern Europe, as the center of the first eastern Slavic state, as a route to the Black Sea for the Russian Empire, and from 1922 for the Soviet Union; as a source of agricultural wealth, brutally collectivized during the early 1930s; and as a leading newly-independent nation from 1991. Among the challenges of independence have been the drives to eliminate corruption from public life, including in some aspects of the leadership and management of universities. PMBSU itself refers in its constitution to the "transition from communism to a free market economy and democratic life." The latest major turn of events was the "Orange Revolution" of 2004, after which a new sense of national leadership has emerged. That said, it has always been a linguistically, ethnically and culturally diverse society.

Building Civil Society

As suggested, the constitution of the University contains some strong commitments, including to developing "responsible leadership" among "Ukrainian elites," to the "democratization of university management," to "involvement in community service," to the "internationalization of university education," and to "developing civil society in Ukraine."

The founding Rector, Professor Leonid Klymenko, explained how it was his intention to "use all of the faculties of the university to serve the local community." The first Vice-Rector, with responsibility for education, Professor Olexander Trunov, emphasized how this worked through into the content and style of the curriculum, guaranteeing access to "both the wider world and to local values." One example cited by the Rector was the Masters program designed to "change the human consciousness" of state employees, and running for the past four years.

These are followed through in PMBSU's leadership of the emergent Association of Ukrainian Universities. Professor Klymenko is President of the Association (founded following a conference at Yalta in June 2009) and a strong advocate of its founding charter with its emphasis on "education for sustainable development of society," leading to "key roles in economic and social development, improvement of living standards, and in building national and international harmony and peace based on human rights, democracy, tolerance and respect" (The "Charter of Ukrainian Universities," Mykolayiv 2009: 6). A total of 26 universities have signed the Charter to date.

Governance and Funding

These priorities are not followed through at the level of national policy or funding. The Rector explained that while this civic and community engagement mission does not enjoy such official endorsement, it was significant that the powers that be "haven't stopped us." He also referred to support of the academic Senate (formally the University's governing body) who were emphatically committed to this idea: it is "part of the general spirit of the University," and now plays a part in individual performance review and promotion. Professor Oleksandr Meschaninov, Vice-Rector for Research and International Affairs, stressed, however, the constraints under which formally autonomous universities felt themselves to be operating, and the legal uncertainty which surrounds Ministry directives for the use of funds. In his view the institutional strategy is more one of "taking opportunities than asserting rights."

The City, which is home to four public universities (the other three more specialized), provides considerable support to the PMBSU mission, through planning and accommodation, if not through direct funding.

Professor Yuriy Verlanov, Dean of the Faculty of Economics, described, however, an uphill struggle with what he called the "post-Soviet tradition" and continued low levels of trust in "the state and officials." His department has tried, in particular to improve the level of understanding of modern economics, in schools as well as the wider community, including through their sponsorship of a student-led Youth Economic Academy, now in its third year.

International Support

It is no accident that much of the pace (and the atmosphere, or "weather") is made for the University's civic engagement by the Faculty of Modern Languages (Foreign Philology). The Dean, Professor Oleksandr Pronkevych (also the Talloires contact) described a similar relationship to the Rectorate as the Rector described between his team and the government. "They have never said no." In his case, however, this is more than mere moral support: university funding has been forthcoming for a wide series of relevant initiatives. In this sense, strategic understanding of the issues—and the possibilities—at the top of the University is allied with trust that the Faculties will deliver sensibly.

Notably through the Faculty's efforts, the University has built a number of important overseas alliances, elsewhere in Europe and with the United States. Reference was made during my visit to links with Hungary, Germany, Sweden, Poland, Bulgaria, Georgia, and the UK, as well as the USA. A relatively high proportion of students have been on international exchange programs. These are organized by the International Relations Office, led by Volodymyr Romakin, whose view of civic engagement is "while the country doesn't have it as a priority, our university does." As a "new and young university," in his words, the goal is to provide an "alternative vision" to the region of what the future might hold.

On the one hand, these involve PMBSU students in travel and experience overseas. Natalia Babkova, the Camp America Coordinator, described a six-year period of PMBSU students involved in a wide variety of North American experiences related directly to their academic study and professional development. Three lecturers in German—Olha Teteryatnikova, Anna Visko, and Valeria Muratova—described a range of interdisciplinary projects, involving students working internationally and presenting both at home and overseas, including on hot political issues such as the morality of war, communities' experiences of World War II and European identity. Dmytro Say—a PMBSU graduate, now working in the State Employees Institute following a Fulbright scholarship—has written an account of the University's leadership of the International Outreach Coalition (IOC) in hosting summer camps in Armenia and the Ukraine, and in supporting a host of Youth Engaging Society (YES) projects by student volunteers in their home villages, towns or cities. Two themes run through all of this activity: languages and leadership.

On the other hand, they involve institutional partnerships—across Europe, with Asia and with North America. Three Peace Corps volunteers—Brittany McLean, Chuck McConnell and Louise Barber—talked about their experience in very different fields: Brittany using film to instill media and English skills, but also to raise key social issues; Chuck in "professional writing in English"; and Louise in building local and international partnerships with NGOs (notably on the art therapy initiative referred to below).

An important consideration is the extent to which these interactions will influence the speed of development towards a system of awards that integrates more smoothly with the rest of Europe. Ukraine is a signatory to the various "Bologna" declarations on the structure and mutual recognition of qualifications. Among the intentions of this process are greater articulation of standards and freer movement of qualified persons. However, as Professor Pronkevych has pointed out at international meetings, a five level Soviet-inherited system of wards sits uneasily alongside the three cycle Bologna framework. A key test will be the intended introduction of an internationally calibrated PhD in 2010. PMBSU is well set to be a pioneer in assessing the implications of this type of change.

A City (and a Generation) on the Move

Until 1991, Mykolayiv was a closed Soviet city. I visited on the eve of the celebration of the 220th anniversary of its founding, and the main square and thor-
oughfare (Sovietskaya) gave palpable evidence of how much has changed, as a
richly cosmopolitan community prepared to party. In the words of my host,
Oleksandr Pronkevych, "this is my city now" (he also has a local TV program).
Maryna Vashenko (introduced below) talked about the role of the university in
"opening the city to the world."

There is a strong sense of generational movement within the University, with
many students and younger members of staff adept in more than one European
language other than Ukrainian and Russian (including frequently English) and
very conscious of worldwide issues and discussions mediated by the new technology. The older University leadership is, however, well aware of this and the
positive opportunities as well as the tensions it could case. Professor Trunov
pointed to student leadership of the communications networks across the university, including a successful newspaper and many special web pages. Tetiana
Solodaeva, a teacher of creative writing, described how literary festivals got the
community and the university students working together. One of her classes had
been defining democracy, and one of her students wrote as follows: "if we will let
it in, democracy will penetrate our essence and unite us." Chuck McConnell had
meanwhile been working with his students in professional English on a Ukrainian
version of the "Beloit College mindset" exercise (the world-view of the class of
2009). Alongside "they think St Petersburg and Leningrad are separate cities" is
the statement: "their parents have always voted in parliamentary and presidential
elections."

Representatives of community groups endorsed many of these effects.
Olha Anikina described how, as a recent graduate, she was able to continue
to rely on support from the University for community-based projects. Andriy
Lopakov—a former student dean—similarly referred to the links between
university student affairs and the interests of community groups. Yuriy Zhepalo,
Head of the "Mykolayiv Humanitarian Project," talked about taking skills learned
at the university into informational media projects about challenges facing the
city.

"Creating the Atmosphere"

The efforts of students—supported by staff—are evident across the city, notably
in work with orphanages, young people and the elderly. Volunteering is high
profile, as are summer camps and support for schools. The University is deliberately flexible in adjusting personal and group timetables to take account of
these opportunities. The enthusiasm of the students I met in small groups was
humbling.

Oksana Stopchenko, Yuliya Shetuhina, Yuliya Khurchakova, Evheniya Dulko, Kseniya Vakulenko, Fatima Agaeva, Yuliya Shevchenko, Slava Vlasov, Christina Agrilova, Sasha Topchij, Lyuba Semenenko, Olena Mikhaylova, and Yana Cherednychenko described a kaleidoscope of activities of which the following are only examples:

- funding-raising for social projects;
- designing and delivering summer camps;
- direct volunteering with NGOs including orphanages, old peoples' centers and community groups;
- work with schools;
- sports activities (including organizing "street-ball" and "ultra-sport";
- excursions, exhibitions, debates, and cultural festivals;
- "awareness" programs around HIV/AIDS and other social and medical issues; and
- participation in the European Youth Parliament (including sessions in Mykolayiv).

Many of them had made conscious decisions about the optimum balance between academic and community work, and were aware of both the personal development and future employability implications of their choices.

Professor Lyudmyla Liapina, Dean of the Faculty of Social Work and Sociology, described how such activity not only cashes out in improved student academic performance (reflected in grades) but also builds employment opportunities with the non-governmental organizations (NGOs) on which the emerging field of social work in the Ukraine characteristically depends. I was able to explore in some detail two examples of highly innovative approaches. The first was the University's organization of an international conference on art therapy in May 2009: a pioneering initiative for the country, which has yet to recognize the professional fields of both art and music therapy. Yanina Kovalchuk, CEO of the lead NGO "Dialog," explained the push this gave to professional psychology within the health service, as well as the initial spin-offs in professional workshops, but also how much more development was needed. The second was a program involving trained volunteers, designed to offer emotional and affective support to orphans, led by Maryna Vashenko—a PMBSU graduate, who did her doctoral work at Tufts University—called "Big Sisters." I discussed with her and Olena Yatsiuk, the PMBSU coordinator, how this not only mitigates a historically strong "medical" mode of treatment, but has opened up personal and professional opportunities for a wide range of volunteers (who receive a small stipend).

Meanwhile, the University is clear that its cultural and concrete assets—its library, gallery, sports facilities, and meeting rooms—are freely available to the community.

Conclusions

PMBSU represents the only case in our sample of a university from the "new" Central and Eastern Europe. In this context, it is significant that it has taken a self-consciously "leadership" role within the national high education system in support of civic and community engagement, with (as suggested above) only tacit support and no special funding from the Ministry of Education or from national policy. In the words of Professor Pronkevych, "it has helped to establish the name of the university."

PMU is thus an example of a leading-edge "open" institution, in a society and an economy striving for openness more generally. On some levels it has to step cautiously, and to establish a "progressive engagement" with the issues its leaders, its staff and its students wish to focus on. On others it can be (and clearly has been) bolder. In the words of Michael Daxner, former President of Oldenburg University and post-war EU Education Commissioner in Kosovo: "East of Vienna," he has said, "the role of universities is in society-making, not state-making." Universities are needed, he says "because of our dangerous knowledge" (quoted in Watson, 2007: 41). Not least through its leadership position among Ukrainian universities—with the focus of their declaration on "academic freedom, university autonomy and education"—but also in its immediate impact on its city, its region and its nation, PMU is attempting to restore this fundamental purpose of university life.

The United Kingdom and its Higher Education System

The United Kingdom of Great Britain (England, Wales and Scotland and Northern Ireland) has a population of 61 million, an average life expectancy for men of 77 and women of 81, and ranks 23rd out of 173 in the Media Freedom Index. Its adult literacy rate is 99%; it has 2.3 doctors per 1,000 population, and an adult HIV/AIDS rate of 0.2% (*Guardian* "World Fact Files," 2009).

It has 166 recognized (i.e. at least part publicly funded) higher education institutions, of which 116 are universities (Universities UK, 2009). In 2005, the UK spent $11,822 per student, compared with the OECD average of $10,655 per student and WEI average of $4,451 per student (OECD/UNESCO WEI, 2005).

The UK has a large and diverse higher education. Historically, it offers a more or less complete exemplification of the pattern of university foundations set out in Part I.

The system operates on a highly distinctive pattern of advanced autonomy (UK HEIs own assets, employ their staff, and can set their "character and mission" independently) and centralization (secured mostly by public contracts for teaching and research). Degree awarding powers, university title and sector-wide arrangements for quality and standards are regulated by the Quality Assurance Agency for Higher Education (QAA), which is "owned" by the institutions.

Centralization is also seen in the tendency of government regularly to reform and to micro-manage the system. It has, however, been somewhat mitigated by political devolution (to a Scottish Parliament, a Welsh Assembly and the power-sharing administration of Northern Ireland at Stormont). To demonstrate the regularity of government intervention in the system as a whole, the main landmarks of reform since the early 1960s are set out below:

GOVERNMENT HE INITIATIVES 1963–2009

1. The Robbins Report (1963): creation of "new" universities, plus the "ability to benefit" criterion.
2. The "Woolwich speech" and the creation of the Polytechnics (1965).
3. The James Report (1972): reorganization of teacher-education and "diversification."
4. Withdrawal of the overseas student subsidy (1980), public expenditure cuts (1981) and White Paper proposing a smaller and rationalized system (1985).
5. Creation of the National Advisory Body for Public Sector HE (NAB) centralizing the former local authority responsibility for higher education outside the universities (1985).
6. White Paper endorsing expansion and incorporation of the Polytechnics, Central Institutions and large Colleges (1987) achieved in the Education Reform Act (1988).
7. White Paper on the ending of the binary line (1991), achieved in the Further and Higher Education Act (1992) along with Funding Councils for the devolved administrations; creation of the "new new" universities.
8. The Dearing Report (1997) opens the way for undergraduate fees legislated for in the Teaching and Higher Education Act (1998).
9. White Paper (2003) leads to "variable" fees, establishment of the "new new new" universities (without research-degree awarding powers), and potential foundation-degree awarding powers for further education institutions in the Higher Education Act (2004).
10. White Paper, *Higher Ambitions: the future of universities in a knowledge economy* (2009).

Since the General Election of May 2010, a coalition government is in power (between Conservatives and Liberal Democrats), which will have to receive and respond to a review of fees for undergraduate students in the context of severe restrictions on public expenditure. Early indications of coalition policy are that higher education will have to bear considerable cuts in public funding (perhaps up to 25%) but with some protection for so-called STEM subjects (Science, Technology, Engineering and Mathematics) and for research. This is likely to be accomplished by restricting publicly-funded places (a policy of "consolidation") and (as set out in Part I here) further encouragement of the private sector.

In terms of regional systems the country is within, but in some respects on the edge of the European Union (e.g. the UK is the only powerful first or second wave member not to be in the single currency Euro-zone). A practical example is a somewhat ambiguous relationship to the Bologna reforms on the structure and mutual recognition of academic qualifications.

UK higher education experienced a very rapid expansion of undergraduate places between the mid-1980s and the turn of the century. This process has now stalled—not least as a consequence of the economic downturn—although it remains a government objective to get participation of the young age group (18–30) above 50%. The age participation rate in HE is 45% in England, against this national target (already achieved in Scotland). A total of 51% of young women and 40% of young men go to university (BBC News Online, 31 March 2010). Concerns have been expressed about the equity of access for those from poorer backgrounds and some ethnic minorities. Compared with the rest of Europe, the UK had a high number of international students (351,000 in 2007–2008, 33% of which came from other EU countries) and a very varied pattern of recruitment by level and mode (a minority of all students are on full-time first degrees, and there has been rapid expansion recently of taught postgraduate students).

The two institutions profiled in this chapter come from very different parts of the sector. The Open University is arguably the UK's most distinctive and well-regarded "curriculum innovation" university. It pioneered open access and supported distance learning, and has become an international reference point for such activities. It is the largest single institution in our sample. The University of Winchester has drawn upon its foundation as a denominational teacher-education institution to develop a modern variety of engaged "liberal" higher education.

Open Access for Social Justice

Profile of the Open University (UK)
By David Watson (based on field visit on 26 and 27 May 2009
and telephone interviews on 1 June 2009)

Origins and History

The Open University (OU) was founded in 1965 as "the university of the air." Its charter (awarded in 1969) prescribed not only a special duty of "promoting the educational well-being of the community generally" but also pedagogical innovation: "the advancement and dissemination of knowledge by teaching and research by a diversity of means such as broadcasting and technological devices appropriate to higher education, by correspondence tuition, residential courses and seminars and in other relevant ways." Critically, it revolutionized the British system by requiring no prior qualifications for entry.

The goal of this innovation was clearly social justice. Over time, the founders' confidence in the abilities of "new" types of student—without traditional qualifications, without family or surrounding community experience of higher education, and significantly with disabilities—that would make conventional study patterns difficult or impossible—has been amply justified. Kathryn Dunn, who is charged with reporting and facilitating aspects of the University's "third" (or service) mission, pointed out that since 1996/1997 people who were not qualified to study at other universities have gained over 34,000 graduate and postgraduate degrees, and over 75,000 undergraduate and postgraduate certificates and diplomas from the OU; this is about one-quarter of the national awards from the Open University in this period.

Members of the UK higher education community today acknowledge the OU as one of their proudest achievements. At the time—as recorded in the papers and biography of its founding minister, Jennie Lee—they fought its establishment tooth and nail.

What is more, this change of heart is matched by general public approbation. Levels of public confidence in the OU are extremely high (in contrast to the rest of the UK system). It is also highly significant in scale and reach: cumulatively it has served over 2 million students since 1971 and produced over 0.5 million qualified alumni (graduates and holders of certificates and diplomas). Roz Allison, Deputy Director of Development and Head of Alumni Relations, pointed out to me that the University is in regular e-mail contact with over 100,000 graduates and postal contact with over 300,000. It is no accident that on the first day of my field visit, the Leader of the Opposition (and future Prime Minister), David Cameron MP, chose the OU as the site on which to deliver his major speech on reform of the UK parliamentary system. Student satisfaction is also remarkably high, with the University regularly appearing at the top of tables generated by the National Student Survey (NSS), not least because of its necessarily highly structured and disciplined approach to feedback.

A Changed Environment

The Open University has had to reinvent itself in order to continue to fulfill its mission. It now plays its part in a system of mass higher education. As a result, it has moved from being a creative and almost unique option for "second chance" students to a distinctive competitor (among a host of others) for "first choice" students. Over 20 years the median age of students has dropped from 47 to 32. The founding Chancellor (Lord Crowther) famously committed the University to be "open as to people, places, methods and ideas." There is a dynamic element in this vision, which has enabled the University progressively to reinvent itself.

In doing so, it has to hold on to its distinctive founding concept—that of "supported distance learning"—and its pivotal position as a provider of research-informed part-time higher education, at a time when many other institutions of higher education—traditional and new—have moved on to this territory. It still has one-third of all of the of the UK's part-time undergraduates, who are themselves 42% of all registrations at this level.

The Open University Today

Among the changes reflected in the self-assessment, and discussed during my visit were the following:

- an increased sensitivity to the need to support learners in their own communities;
- a heightened interest in higher education for employability;
- radical changes in the ICT (information and communication technology) environment in which all universities operate;
- political developments, including devolution of powers to Scotland, Wales and Northern Ireland, as well as a regional framework for economic development in England;
- funding policies for HE including the movement from a central grant to treatment alongside other English HEIs and the recent removal of funding for students with equivalent or lower qualifications (ELQ).

In response, the University has both adjusted its strategy and modified its structures.

Each of these elements is reflected here.

The OU and the World of Work

Kathryn Dunn mused with me on how it has not been until relatively recently that the University has had to use the concept of "employability" in structuring its relationship with business and industry. What traditionally is a highly personalized support service for individual learners, who use their graduate status as a platform for the next stage in their individual life-courses, has been supplemented and in some areas replaced by more specific professional and vocational courses in which "license to practice" is a clear objective. This often involves a dynamic three-way relationship between employers, university and student/employee. Dr Basiro Davey of the Faculty of Science and Dr Caroline Holland of Health and Social Care showed me how this plays out in their own fields, notably through the development of Foundation degrees. The value of the "transparent curriculum" as well as a strong focus on "practitioner research" that are at the heart of a distance-learning institution is readily apparent.

Citizenship

Also in the context of graduate attributes, I was made aware of a serious strategic discussion of the concept of modern citizenship. The Vice-Chancellor (VC), Brenda Gourley, finds in the concept of "global citizenship" one of the most powerful validations of the thrust of the Talloires Declaration.

Professor Engin Isin, Director of the Centre for Citizenship, Identities and Governance, described a European Union (EU) project on "enacting European citizenship" across six countries, which he declared would, in his view, have been "impossible" to lead from any base other than the Open University. The research process involves analyzing, playing back and then reflecting on "acts of citizenship" in very varied and complex contexts. The essential OU elements are the strength and flexibility of its web-based systems as well as the commitment fully to merge the research and teaching agendas in a new Masters course. John Oates, a well-known developmental psychologist, made similar points about his pioneering work with English and Hungarian national programs establishing scalable techniques for supporting people who work in nurseries and kindergartens and parents of young children with disabilities.

. . . and Technology

The V-C sees the University's key role as being played out in the "digital space." She spoke about the need for the University to move beyond its historical (or "industrial") model of curriculum and teaching materials) to embrace today's (and tomorrow's) dynamic and fluid technological environment. Her successor (from October 2009) is Martin Bean, who currently leads worldwide educational projects for Microsoft, and is well-placed to take this theme forward. Pro-Vice-Chancellor Brigid Heywood was clear about her own goal: "no student should leave the University without having participated fully in the digital world." She pointed to the remarkable success of "Orange RockCorps" as a new model of community volunteering "at scale" whereby over 40,000 participants—linked by mobile texts—gave four or more hours of service in return for concert tickets (www.orangerockcorps.co.uk). This is a model the Open University is seeking to develop in the context of climate change and in support of adult literacy.

The evolution of the University's founding partnership with the British Broadcasting Corporation (BBC) also captures this theme of responsiveness to the digital environment. Sally Crompton and Bernard Coen of the Open Broadcasting Unit (OBU) described "a learning journey" as both the OU and the BBC have moved from co-production of course-focused learning material to a much more fluid, risk-sharing approach of internet-based services and online resources. OpenLearn—an initiative providing free access to online learning coupled with facilities to share material—is both a symbolic and a highly practical example of this. It is supported by a wide range of state-of-the-art approaches, including pod-casting and iTunes.

The power of the University in this field is palpable. Its role within "Darwin year" (the celebration of the 200th anniversary of *The Origin of Species*) is a good example. Among many activities, the creation of an information chart on "the tree of life" led to 450,000 copies being distributed on demand. I discussed with Jonathan Silvertown (Professor of Ecology) how this links to student recruitment, to interactive ecological projects, and to the development of what he calls "citizen science." Professor Phil Potts (Dean of Science) pointed to the power of open access in drawing students into the so-called "strategic and vulnerable subjects" of science and technology, as well as of "a global online university."

National and Local

Understandably, the University struggles with its sense of location, or "place."

There is a national dimension to this, with the separate brands of OU Scotland, Wales and Northern Ireland.

There is also an English regional dimension, with the status of the 10 regional divisions, each now branded as "the OU in (London, East Midlands, North West, etc.)." I spoke to three of the regional directors (Lynda Brady, Gordon Lammie and Mike Rookes). They have a sense that the regions are now more "tightly controlled" (in support of university-wide priorities); at the same time their sensitivity to local conditions, access to emerging markets and to the priorities of key partners such as the Regional Development Agencies (RDA) loom ever larger. In terms of the higher education landscape, the OU's regional offices are seen as important elements in local partnerships with other HEIs, partly because of the special skills and knowledge they bring, and partly because of their independence from the inevitable turf wars of institutions whose physical locations are close to each other.

There are special issues surrounding the OU's headquarters, in Milton Keynes (MK), where several respondents reported on its "invisibility" until very recently. This particular issue has intensified as MK is experiencing a national recession for the first time in its history as a "new town." The University has recently taken over (from Cranfield University) the accountability for the Milton Keynes Enterprise Hub, whose work I discussed with Chris Dunkley (the Director). It is co-located with the Open University Business School and provides support for high growth potential start-ups (including 24 "incubation" workstations); a service for international small and medium-sized enterprises (SMEs) wishing to explore developing a base in the UK/Europe and support for graduate entrepreneurs. Through the new Buckinghamshire and Milton Keynes Innovation Growth Team initiative from 2009 business support is being extended to established companies: assisting their growth through innovation across their operations.

In terms of that part of social justice which is summarized as "widening participation" (WP), the professionals in the regions see what works as being, in the words of Margaret Hart (Head of WP and Student Services) "long-haul, sustained partnerships with community groups." The OU is a powerful leader in a number of locally-designed and targeted WP initiatives across the country prioritizing areas recognized by government as being the most "multiply-deprived."

Alumni donors support the OU's widening participation mission with fee support for students in need not qualifying for support from UK government and improving the facilities available for students with disabilities (e.g. developing digital talking books).

Indeed, partnership working is present across the full-range of the University's teaching and research work. I discussed with Gill Perry (Professor of Art History) and Natalie Walton (the Director of Education at the MK Gallery) the development of a web-site called the "Open Arts Archive" that will provide structured access to a wealth of material generated by both the University and network of galleries and museums across the UK. In a similar vein, Professor Rob Paton spoke about the Business School's pioneering work in supporting the so-called "third sector" and social enterprise, which has now become part of mainstream provision.

This activity is strongly supplemented by a focus on volunteering by staff and students, and by impressive initiatives such as the "student ambassadors" (current and recent students employed on a part-time basis to work in and with communities like those from which they came). The University's "supporters' fund" makes a major contribution to activities like this. Several witnesses (including Peter Taylor, Professor of Organic Chemistry and Stephanie O'Halloran, Coordinator of the Active Community Program, ACP) stressed the steps taken to ensure that public engagement activities are conducted with the same degree of professionalism as teaching, research and administration.

. . . and International

The University also has a significant global reach. This is partly through its validation and accreditation services, for example in association with the seven-country "Arab OU," through direct recruitment and through highly targeted collaborative projects. Two examples of the latter, both in Africa, are HEAT (Health Education and Training—directed at the training of distributed health professionals) and TESSA (Teacher Education in Sub-Saharan Africa—supplying resources to primary teachers; and soon also to the secondary sector). The OU Africa Office links to a wide range of individual research, teaching and service projects. Fundraising activities are highly-tuned towards securing substantial philanthropic gifts to support these. Meanwhile in the new Europe, James Fleck (Professor of Innovation Dynamics and Dean of the Business School) pointed to the substantial contribution made to the creation of a civil society and entrepreneurship in the post-Berlin-Wall states of East and Central Europe where the OU, working in partnership, has over 3,500 students.

Several of these initiatives have raised important issues around cultural sensitivity. Kate Clarke (Director of the OU's Validation Services) and Jane Gill (of OU Worldwide) explained how open access has meant new opportunities for groups throughout the world, like the Arab OU's services for the Bedoon (a stateless population living in Kuwait), for women, and for guest workers.

Part-Time Study and Credit

As the UK sector faces up to economic restrictions at the same time as significantly increased demand for higher education these two features of its provision would seem to be especially important. Part-time study enables especially younger students to "learn and earn" at the same time; it assists those establishing or established in careers sensibly to claim for employer co-funding; and above all it brings flexibility to the learning life-course. At the same time, the OU, almost uniquely in the UK system seems to have made credit accumulation and transfer (CATS) as well as Accreditation of Prior Experiential Learning (APEL) work well. Individual course credits (of 10, 30 or 60) points are valued and stored to be built upon. A recent initiative called "Openings" has been an extraordinary success. It is just one of a number of devices the University has pioneered for helping people to turn informal into formal learning.

In contrast, the rest of the system is highly reluctant to give credit for such progress, and students who start and then stop on more conventional courses seem unable to benefit from their elements of achievement. In this sense there is a much more North American "feel" about the OU processes. Since my visit (on 26 June), the Prime Minister has announced a HEFCE-funded initiative ("Shared Returns") to assist students who have been unable—for economic and other reasons—to complete their degrees at other institutions including the OU.

It is also important that such educational experiences are not seen as simply "alternative" or "deficit" models. Among the suite of opportunities the OU has led in picking up has been the Young Associate Students in Schools (or YASS initiative), which enables successful children to begin their higher education at school.

Who or What is the OU's "Community"?

All of this raises the complex question of who (or what) the OU's "community" is. As in most (perhaps almost all) cases, the answer has to be multiple, but there is a special resonance here. If the trends outlined above continue, it will increasingly be in cyber-space; which poses unique challenges for civic and community engagement.

Meanwhile, the University's success in touching the lives of those outside the mainstream has been remarkable. To take one dramatic example, since

2000–2001 over 5,000 people have started study with the OU while in prison. I discussed with both Bobby Cummines (a former student and now head of the charity "Unlock") and Mike Rookes (Regional Director of the West Midlands) the longer-term effects of this engagement: of the 500 who continued studying with the OU after leaving prison only 3% have returned to prison.

Conclusions

There are several themes arising from the OU profile of immediate interest to our wider project.

First, the OU demonstrates at large scale the higher education institution's tension between altruism and self-interest. Many of its activities are high visibility, extremely effective, open access contributions to social and personal development. These include its open source resources, its partnerships with governments and the third sector, and its investment in community projects. At the same time it has to finance its activities from the core sources of public and private funding for teaching, research and service, and in direct competition with other institutions now offering far more than before in the fields of distance learning and part-time courses.

This relates to the position of the OU as a major player within British civil society. This is partly about politics, but more significantly as a "touchstone" institution in public life. It is—in former Vice-Chancellor John Daniels' term—Britain's only "mega-university."

Finally, there are the special opportunities and constraints that arise from sustaining a position as a worldwide pioneer in distance learning. The OU is, literally, everywhere and nowhere. Many more people know about it (and approve of it) than use it. Many others who could use it do not do so yet. As a result it has to balance making use of its power as a national institution with its commitment to carefully chosen specific projects.

Personal Declaration

I have had a number of professional and personal contacts with the OU. I have carried out consultancy projects for the university, mentored senior staff, served on the Open University Validation Board (and chaired accreditation visits in New Zealand and Singapore), and contributed to university conferences. In 2002, I was awarded an Honorary Doctorate of the University. I have also offered some informal advice to the Development Board of the University Centre Milton Keynes (UCMK) in which the OU is a key partner. I would like to express my special gratitude to Catherine Colohan, Assistant Head of the V-C's office for her invaluable help in planning and coordinating my visit.

Reinventing Liberal Higher Education

Profile of the University of Winchester (UK)
By David Watson (based on field visit 18 and 19 June 2009)

Origins and History

The University of Winchester's history is rooted in teacher education under the auspices of the Church of England. It was founded in 1840 as the Winchester Diocesan Training College, and renamed in 1928 as King Alfred's College. In 2004 it achieved its own degree awarding powers as University College Winchester and in 2005 its current title as the University of Winchester. The Anglican Church remains central to its governance (nominating eight members of the 25 member Board of Governors, while the Bishop of Winchester is a member *ex officio*). The University is an active member of the Council of Church Colleges and Universities.

Faith and Spirituality

In all of its official publications, the University lays great stress on its agreed core values. Alongside "intellectual freedom," "social justice," "diversity," "individuals matter," and "creativity," is "spirituality," defined as follows: "we celebrate our Christian foundation encouraging those living within the Christian faith, whilst also welcoming those who live within other faiths and those who have no faith." Christianity generally—more particularly the Anglican Church, the Diocese of Winchester, and Winchester Cathedral—remain powerful presences in the life of the University.

However, this is anything but an exclusive or an uncritical influence. The Vice-Chancellor, Professor Joy Carter, speaks of "an inclusive Christianity," and the evidence is strong of theological, religious and ethical concerns being pursued by the University across a very wide spectrum. The V-C described how the University's mission has developed "with the grain of its constitution" in an open and imaginative way. Particularly important has been the evolution of the "Foundation Committee" (a body representing the major internal and external stakeholders reporting to her and the Governors on strategic options) towards an inquiring and away from a defensive posture.

Professor Lisa Isherwood, Director of Theological Partnerships, spoke about "an Anglican tradition that is not stuck." She leads an initiative called "Theological Partnerships," which has used the University's independent role as the creator of a space in which an unlikely range of denominations have been able to talk to each other. More broadly, Professor Liz Stuart (Pro-Vice-Chancellor for Academic Affairs) talked about the University's interest in "producing people who want to change the world." Dean of the Faculty of Business, Law and Sport,

Professor Neil Marriott, said "the values give us an edge" (he also pointed to the University's signature of the "Principles for Responsible Management Education" of the UN Global Compact).

The student body at Winchester is diversifying, although at a slower rate than the UK system as a whole: 4% of its students are from outside the UK compared to 12% nationally. Several recent intakes have been surveyed about their religious affiliations. In 2007, 55% of responding students (n.776) identified as Christian and 39% as of no faith. The equivalent numbers for staff (n.122) were 70% and 24%.

I saw the University's careful integration of the values of "intellectual freedom" and "spirituality" worked out in the extended process of approving a new Masters course in Islamic Studies to support a diaspora of teachers emanating from Syria.

A University on a Human Scale

Historically, UK higher education has expressed pride in its intimate scale and a close pedagogical relationship between teachers and students. As the system has expanded rapidly, and especially in large institutions, these priorities are felt to be under threat. Winchester is acutely aware that it is relatively small, and has a relatively limited but cohesive subject and professional curriculum offering. It builds on this by emphasizing the quality of relationships with students and between staff of various kinds.

Size (or the lack of it) does matter. Community representatives spoke of how accessible the University was, particularly the senior team, and how willing to discuss their programmes and priorities. Staff spoke with pride about initiatives led by the colleagues, often in entirely different parts of the institution. Students regarded themselves as not just benefiting, but also being responsible for an ethos of care.

A Pillar of the Community

Winchester is a historic but relatively small city. Until the eleventh century it was arguably England's most important city. Other than a small campus of the University of Southampton (based on its acquisition of the Winchester School of Art), the University of Winchester is the only higher education provider in the city and in the county of Hampshire. It takes its place alongside a number of pillars of the community. These include: Winchester Cathedral; the headquarters of both the Hampshire County Council and the Winchester City Council; Winchester College (one of the UK's most exclusive independent schools for boys); the Hampshire Constabulary; Winchester Hospital; the Theatre Royal; Her Majesty's Prison Winchester; the Chamber of Commerce; and the army. The University relates to all of these, and many of their subsidiary operations.

Examples of the latter include the Discovery Centre (a Cultural Centre based on the former Winchester Lending Library and now supporting an extensive range of activities from art exhibitions through literature to film), the Winchester Sport Stadium (a new joint facility of the University and the local authorities, the arrival of which was marked by a Sports Festival) and Café Culture (a network of over 300 practitioners in the creative industries). Representatives of each of these enterprises described the key role of both University staff and students in supporting their on-going activities.

Powerful vehicles for such engagement include a strong emphasis on joint projects, and on student and staff volunteering. Students receive (when compared with other UK HEIs) regular and structured course credit (although they would like more). They spoke in a mature way about the balance between altruism and self-interest in this context. Staff volunteering is similarly well-structured. Members of staff are entitled to one day's paid leave to undertake community-based voluntary action, and an extension to this scheme whereby the University would "match" holiday leave used for this purpose is under discussion.

Community representatives acknowledged not only the drive and enthusiasm of the students with whom they had engaged, but also the "sharing and proactive approach of the faculty members." One said that "community engagement is so clearly part of the culture." Terri Sandison (Director of Lifelong Learning and Staff Development) also referred to the degree of autonomy she felt when representing the University in the partnership projects across her patch. Compared to many of her peers (representatives from other HEIs) she felt "empowered to make suggestions and respond quickly to proposed initiatives from partners which might commit the institution."

In the spirit of the times, employers are also seen as vital partners, in the private as well as the public and voluntary sectors. The University has recently invested in a post of Employer Engagement Manager. For some time it has had a Business Advisory Group. Sue Dovey, Chief Executive of Community Action Hampshire, described how her organization and the University had used funds from the Higher Education Funding Council for England (HEFCE)'s "Economic Challenge" initiative to devise an "internship" program for graduates from the University in business working in regionally-based voluntary and charitable organizations. Since 2005, the University has also run a Business Start-Up scheme, selecting two enterprises a year, emanating from the University, to support through their essential incubation phase.

In the words of Dean of the Faculty of Arts, Professor Anthony Dean, "the body language of this university is that it should engage." I found strong evidence that this is the case, not just in relation to collaborative projects and activities but also across the core fields of teaching and research.

In teaching, the University has (for the UK) a very strong presence of "service learning" (not that it uses this term) through accredited modules of practice, volunteer support and work placement. The examples are legion: a "social legacy" module in the degree in event and leisure management; the careful training and marshalling of community volunteers to develop materials for the University's contribution to the New Victorian County History of Hampshire; the community empowerment themes ("participation, democracy and sustainability") that inform the MA in Theatre and Media for Development; the annual productions in Winchester Prison produced and directed by the student-based company "Playing for Time" an "Enterprise Network" (now with 200 members) sponsored by the new Business School, and many more.

On research, Yvon Bonenfant, Director of Research and Knowledge Exchange, described a strategic choice of "scholarly engagement with wider communities." What is more, these developments have apparently caught the wave of several current priorities in national policy and funding priorities. This include: a recognition of the importance of the creative and cultural industries; a search for measures of "impact" that will include social and community dimensions; and a commitment to develop indicators for the new Research Excellence Framework (REF, which will succeed the UK's Research Assessment Exercise, RAE) that acknowledge the role of "knowledge exchange" (the term of art chosen by the University to characterize much of its work). These more recent initiatives all build on the University's traditional strengths in the humanities and education, notably archaeology, history and theology. "Suddenly" says Bonenfant, "we seem to be ahead of many other institutions."

Beyond Winchester

Winchester has also moved to take up key roles in partnership working on a regional basis. Director of Regional Partnerships, Paul Chamberlain, described the challenge of the project to develop a "university centre" in Basingstoke (where the University already has a small campus) as not just devising an attractive set of course but "embedding it into the university community." Terri Sandison similarly described the University's leadership role in Andover (another notorious "cold spot" in the county for progression) as being on behalf of the community and the sector as a whole (because of the University's focused subject range, many of the successful participants would obviously go on to study elsewhere). Morag Currie from Hampshire Children's Services described the University's contribution to a "compact" designed to assist the progress into and through higher education of "children in care" (at which the UK system as a whole is scandalously bad), the success of which was confirmed for me by students who had both benefited from and worked as volunteers within the program.

At the other end of the geographical scale, the University has a selective set of international partnerships and projects, notably in Africa. There is an interesting contrast between the individual institutional tie-up with the Kintampo Rural Health School in Ghana (supported by the British Council and designed not only to improve mental health services but also to assist with the School's development towards University status) and the link with the South-west region of Uganda (through the charity Education Uganda), and intended in due to course to promote shared learning and teacher exchange between the University, Hampshire Schools and the participating schools and training institutes in Uganda.

Reinventing Liberal Higher Education

One of the newest of the University's undergraduate programmes (to begin in 2010) has the title "liberal arts." Its development has a wider significance than for the small group of students who will graduate under this title. The declared goal of fostering a "higher education that embraces ways of thinking that change how we think about ourselves, others and the world in general" comes close to encapsulating the University's overall educational philosophy. Breadth as well as depth of study is an overt goal, and was acknowledged as such by the students I met.

As a relatively young University-level institution, there is significant energy and iconoclasm about. This is partly represented by a broad range of specific groups and programs: "Real World Learning" (designed to demonstrate that "learning is a learnable craft" led by Professors Bill Lucas and Guy Claxton), the "English Project" (launched in 2008 to "deepen peoples' understanding of the richness of the English language") and "eco-theology" (led by Professor Lisa Isherwood) are examples. The latter has inspired a permanent installation on the campus; the "cosmic walk." Canon Roly Riem from Winchester Cathedral spoke about "a young institution saying yes to a lot of things." He was, however, simultaneously confident in the way in which the University used the structure of its value statement to sift through the possibilities.

Professor June Boyce-Tillman summed this up as the role of the university in "enabling the wider society to understand itself more fully." She has made a number of major contributions in this direction over 20 years in the institution, notably the development of "Foundation Music." This remarkable project emerged from the University's decision some time ago to cease formal instruction in music. Today it is a substantial network of staff and students who "who meet regularly during term time to rehearse and perform. Open to all staff and students of the University, there are no auditions and it is all free." They carry its work well beyond the University's walls, as in the local, regional and national projects inspired by Professor Boyce-Tillman, such as "Space for Peace" (January 2009) which attracted more than 200 participants from local schools, the University, community and church choirs to the Cathedral to "explore the merging of sounds from Jewish, Christian and secular sources."

Sustainability and succession planning are clearly vital in areas which have depended on strong individual or small group leadership. "Foundation Music" is a good example of this in practice, as it has been incorporated for management purposes into Student Services, with key roles distributed to four people and appropriate business (and commercial) arrangements made for its external activities.

Understanding Performance

The university makes significant efforts to both understand and measure its impact on society. Its self-reflection about civic and community engagement is palpable. Much of this is formal and systematic. The University led on a project for the Council of University Chairs (CUC) on developing relevant key performance indicators (KPI). The chosen measures were around student volunteering and external attendance at University events, and have seen a combined growth of approximately 250% over the past three years. It has also recently conducted a "Community Leaders' Perception Survey" (February 2009), with over 100 completed responses from senior stakeholders of various kinds.

Meanwhile, Winchester is one of the few Talloires signatories who attempted (in response to the self-assessment questionnaire) to break down the proportion of its activities directly focused on civic engagement (for research the result was 34%).

Conclusions

For the project, the University of Winchester shows the opportunities and the constraints experienced by a relatively small but flexible institution in acknowledging, appreciating and adapting its historical mission in contemporary circumstances. The opportunities include agility, quick response and short decision cycles. The constraints include individual and small-group dependencies and related questions of sustainability. "We are riding on the coat-tails of our own success" says Yvon Bonenfant; "we now need to take some hard decisions about how we hone our focus for the future."

It also demonstrates the power of a chief executive (the Vice-Chancellor) taking direct responsibility for the civic and community aspects of the institutional mission. Professor Carter described her initially uncomfortable reaction to the self-description of the University she had been invited to lead as "permeable." "Now, I know exactly what they meant" she said, and "we *are* permeable" (as a geologist this was not going to be a term she would use uncritically).

Finally, there is the set of questions about a faith foundation making its way in a diverse and widely-networked modern world. The choice of liberal higher education as means of doing so is a brave and confident solution.

Personal Declaration

I have had a number of professional and personal contacts with the University of Winchester. I took part in several "validation" visits to King Alfred's College as a member of the Council for National Academic Awards, and have led research seminars. I have contributed regularly since 1979 to the journal *Literature and History*, which is edited at the University, and published a monograph in the series *Winchester Research Papers in the Humanities*. I was an external member of the panel which appointed the present Vice-Chancellor. In 2005, I was awarded an Honorary Doctorate of the University.

The United States of America and its Higher Education System

The USA has a population of 307 million (the third largest in the world), an average life expectancy for men of 75 and women of 80 and ranks 20th out of 175 in the Reporters without Borders 2009 Press Freedom Index (Media Freedom Index, 2009). Its adult literacy rate is 99%, it has 2.56 doctors per 1,000 population, and its adult HIV/AIDS rate is 0.6% (*Guardian* "World Fact Files," 2009).

In 2005, there were 4,216 accredited higher education institutions (public and private). These included 2,533 four-year colleges and universities and 1,683 two-year colleges (UNESCO International Bureau of Education, 2006f). Higher education in the United States is incredibly diverse and decentralized.

Total enrollment increased rapidly during the 1970s, from 8.58 million in 1970 to 12 million in 1980. Enrollment has increased more slowly but steadily since then, reaching 15.3 million in 2000 and 18.25 million in 2007 (Institution of Education Sciences, US Department of Education, 2010). There is fairly widespread access to higher education. The 2008 tertiary Gross Enrollment Ratio was 83% (male, 69%; female, 97%) (UNESCO Institute for Statistics, 2010). While educational attainment gaps remain between whites and minority students, these have gradually decreased. For example, blacks went from 9.9% in 1998 of tertiary degrees to 12.8% in 2008, and Hispanics went from 8.2% to 12.2% in the same period (Institution of Education Sciences, US Department of Education, 2010).

US higher education does not receive significant federal oversight. The federal Department of Education's main involvement with higher education is to provide grants to institutions, oversee a major federal student loan program and enforce non-discrimination laws. There is no centralized quality assurance or accreditation authority. There are a number of regional, national and specialized accrediting agencies. Public higher education institutions are funded by the states, or—in the case of community colleges—by local jurisdictions. State authorities thus have greater oversight over these institutions, but institutional autonomy is still fairly strong.

Most higher education institutions receive some state and federal financial support, although public institutions receive a much higher proportion of their budgets from public sources. All institutions, including public HEIs, also rely on student tuition and fees, endowments, and support from foundations and individuals (UNESCO International Bureau of Education, 2006f). Federal support for higher education has increased significantly in recent, rising 49% between 2001 and 2009, reaching $19.3 billion in 2009 (United States, Department of Education, 2008). Overall, America spends more on higher education per student than any other nation. In 2008, the United States spent $24,370 per student in tertiary education, far more than the OECD average of $11,512 (OECD, 2008b).

United States higher education has long been focused on community engagement and social relevance. This has strong roots in the development of public education. The Morrill Act of 1862 created federal incentives—including grants of federally-controlled land—for the establishment of HEIs with an emphasis on agriculture and other vocational training in addition to classical studies. The Smith–Lever Act (1914) then established a Cooperative Extension Service at each land-grant university, providing ongoing federal matching support for extension activities such as continuing education and public dissemination of information and resources, particularly in practical fields such as agriculture (West Virginia University Extension Service, 2010). These extension services continue today in every state.

Many colleges and universities, both public and private, also began to develop a culture of volunteerism in the twentieth century. This was accelerated with the founding of Campus Compact, a national coalition that seeks to help colleges and universities institutionalize community engagement and develop support structures for students who want to engage in service, such as civic engagement offices, service learning courses, and community-based research approaches (Campus Compact, 2010).

Today, civic engagement is increasingly recognized as an important component of higher education. For example, a 2009 study found that "The majority of [US] college faculty (55.5%) . . . now consider it 'very important' or 'essential' to 'instill in students a commitment to community service,' an increase of 19.1 percentage points since the survey was last conducted in 2004–05" (Higher Education Research Institute, UCLA , 2009). There are also a wide variety of major recognitions of higher education community engagement. For example, the Carnegie Commission on Higher Education, which created a Classification system for higher education institutions in 1970, adopted an elective classification on community engagement in 2006 (Carnegie Foundation for the Advancement of Teaching, 2010). Also in 2006, the Corporation for National and Community Service, which oversees federal service programs like AmeriCorps, launched the President's Higher Education Community Service Honor Roll (Learn and Serve America, 2010).

Knowledge to Serve the City

Profile of Portland State University (USA)
By Robert M. Hollister (based on field visit
December 7 and 8, 2009)

Overview

A public urban university with a student enrollment of 28,000, Portland State University is well-recognized nationally, and internationally as a leader in university civic engagement. Its civic engagement programs have garnered multiple awards and have influenced the policies of many other institutions of higher education. The University's community engagement commitment lies at the heart of its institutional mission and shows a close connection to the metropolitan area in which it is located. Thus it seems natural and fitting that PSU's motto "Let Knowledge Serve the City" is emblazoned in large bronze letters on an elevated skyway above a main downtown street that bisects the campus, reminding the university and the community at large that the community engagement is a central focus of the university. "Let Knowledge Serve the City" is an accurate, broadly understood and supported statement of PSU's identity and community role, both within and outside the institution.

The University has implemented extensive integration of service-learning in the curriculum—including a capstone interdisciplinary course that is required of nearly all students graduating with a degree from Portland State University. In addition to having this important and high profile graduation requirement, Portland State supports several research centers that conduct applied research which informs and contributes directly to public policy decision-making of local, regional and state bodies. PSU is successful in its community engagement because it combines unusually strong leadership and participation by the president and other top administrative leadership, civic engagement program staff, faculty members across the disciplines, and a network of engaged and committed community partners.

PSU's civic engagement policies and programs are well-established and comparatively mature, which makes its experience especially relevant to the large number of institutions of higher education that are at earlier stages in the development of their civic activities, and whose subsequent stages of development could move in the direction of the path that PSU has charted. Embedding service-learning in the curriculum is a key part of this University's model and has been of particular interest and relevance to the broader higher education community who seeks to engage students in community-based work. PSU's commitment to community engagement is evidenced by the participation annually of 8,000 students, faculty and staff in formal community partnerships through courses, research, and other service efforts. Students, faculty and staff contribute over 1.3 million hours of service in the community through their work in classes, research and service.

Engaging all Students Through a Required Senior Community-Based Learning Capstone Course

Over 400 undergraduate courses in diverse disciplines incorporate community-based learning, making it a defining feature of the curriculum. This six-credit, interdisciplinary capstone course engages a team of students and a faculty member with a community partner to address a community-identified concern. In order to implement this requirement, Portland State each year offers 240 capstone courses, taught by faculty members and experienced community practitioners. These courses are designed to be a culminating experience for the general education dimension of students' college experience—an opportunity to integrate and to apply what they have learned earlier in their college years. Capstones "build cooperative learning communities by taking students out of the classroom and into the field." What this requirement means is that nearly all 3,000 graduating seniors have an integrative service-learning experience. In addition to the educational impact of the requirement on individual students, the large scale of this part of the curriculum has a profound effect on the academic culture and also on the local community outside of the University.

Recent capstone course titles include: Creating Livable Communities for an Aging Society, Women and Development, Poverty and Homelessness in Old Town, and Social Justice Education Theory, Grantswriting for Environmental Advocacy, and Ending Global Poverty. The students in these courses come from a variety of disciplines. Their disciplinary backgrounds are used to inform how they respond to the complex concerns of their community partner. The faculty who offer these courses are from traditional academic disciplines, yet the applied nature of these courses requires them to facilitate and manage student application of knowledge. Often applied researchers and practitioners are who are most drawn to teaching these interdisciplinary applied courses. In the author's discussion with capstone faculty members, one said, "Some students move from cynicism to hope that change is possible, change both in themselves and in communities." Another commented, "The multidisciplinary experience helps students to understand how their different lenses are important to solving community problems." The program operates a comprehensive, highly effective system for selecting and supporting these courses. Because the courses are such an important part of students' educational experience, they require that students partner with a community organization to address a real community-identified need, and challenge students to work interdisciplinarily.

In addition to Capstone courses, students (both undergraduate and graduate) have opportunities to work in community settings as a part of their degree programs. A wide range of academic programs—Child and Family Studies, Urban

Studies and Planning, Public Administration, Environmental Sciences, Administration of Justice, Applied Linguistics, and Speech and Hearing Sciences—require students to complete practicums or internships with local non-profits and government agencies. In most departments faculty teach courses that engage their students in projects in the community. Applied Linguistics uses service-learning as a major focus, with several faculty members involving their students in community projects with local organizations who serve English language learners. In the School of Education a team of 6–8 professors teach Introduction to Education and Society, a course that all students who seek admission to the pre-service teacher education program must take. Each year more than 500 PSU students work with the Portland Public Schools Migrant Education Program, providing formal tutoring and classroom support for children from migrant families. A model for integration of theory and practice, service and learning, the course "dispels myths and stereotypes regarding poor children and children of color" and allows students who think they want to be teachers an opportunity to spend some time working with kids in a classroom setting.

Dilafruz Williams, Professor in the Graduate School of Education, exemplifies PSU's support for the role of teacher-scholar-public citizen. Highly accomplished in her fields of academic specialization, she is also a leader in service-learning. Recipient of the Ehrlich Award for Faculty Service-Learning, the highest award for a US faculty leader in this field, she says, "I don't teach a single course in which my students aren't in the community." Her scholarship, teaching and service are inextricably intertwined with community work. Dr Williams was an innovator and advisor in the initial development of Portland State's community engagement programs. Since 2003 she has served as an elected official on the Portland Public School board. She co-founded Sunnyside Environmental School, a K-8 school within the Portland Public School system that utilizes service-learning and social justice as a school-wide educational practice. Today she is active in the trend toward faculty-led service trips abroad, leading students on trips to India.

Although there are several student volunteer service groups, in comparison with other colleges and universities around the world, volunteer service is a smaller portion of PSU's overall civic engagement record. This situation results because there are substantial service-learning opportunities in the curriculum of many departments and schools.

A Defining Focus on University–Community Partnerships

For the past 15 years community partnerships has been a key strategy in PSU's civic work, and more recently community partnerships have become an increasingly distinctive focus of the University's approach. Office of University–Community Partnerships Director Kevin Kecskes and Assistant Director Amy Spring and their colleagues have staked out a significant leadership role on this dimension of the higher education civic engagement movement. At PSU partnerships are now a topic of research and for convening and capacity-building, both internally and with other higher education institutions. To that end Portland State has established the International Partnership Initiative, which sponsors a biannual global institute and provides research grants for faculty and their community partners to study the ingredients and impacts of strong partnerships. The University is contributing to the collective knowledge base about university–community partnerships and is building a network of exchange and joint action on this topic.

Research Institutes Contribute to Local and State Public Policy

Many universities host research institutes that directly inform public policy-making. PSU supports an unusually large number of such institutes and these units attract unusually high levels of public participation and support. The University's policy research centers play significant agenda-setting and cross-sector convening roles in addition to providing a great deal of basic research service. A common approach of these institutes is to involve community leaders in setting research agenda and also in actively using the research results. Research institutes such as Portland State Business Accelerator, Survey Research Lab, Institute on Aging, Population Research Center, the Institute for Metropolitan Studies and Regional Research Institute for Human Services collect data and perform analyses for governmental agencies.

The College of Urban and Public Affairs is the home to several research institutes that inform and guide regional policy development. (1) The Social Equity Forum developed a Regional Equity Atlas and is promoting a Regional Equity Action Agenda. The Forum is developing a process for assessing the social sustainability impacts of development. The Equity Atlas, produced in collaboration with the University's Institute of Portland Metropolitan Studies, examines the distribution of benefits and burdens of growth in the region and provides a framework for understanding whether populations are receiving their fair share of investment in the physical and social infrastructures. (2) Institute of Portland Metropolitan Studies, directed by Professor Sheila Martin, is conducting research about regional policy challenges. Institute projects include Greater Portland–Vancouver Indicators, Food System Sustainability, and Community Geography (using Geographic Information Systems technology to help citizens and K-12 students to address community issues more strategically). Professor Martin states, "My primary objective as Director is to ensure that the Institute, the College of Urban and Public Affairs and the University are serving the city by providing independent information about the key issues facing our region and a venue for discussing those issues in a productive, thoughtful way." (3) The School of Urban Studies and Planning regularly hosts projects through which faculty and student conduct applied research and develop proposed policies on regional housing, transportation, waste management, and other environmental issues.

Visionary Leadership

PSU's civic engagement has been shaped by presidents who are innovative leaders in this dimension of higher education. Dynamic leadership from the top has been accompanied by similarly effective mid-level administrative and faculty leadership. Portland State's civic engagement experience really is a story of collective leadership throughout the institution.

In the mid-1990s, former president Judith Ramaley led a major reform of undergraduate general education requirements to emphasize interdisciplinary, service-learning that takes advantage of the urban setting available to Portland State. Her successor Daniel Bernstine once stated, "My vision is of a university so thoroughly engaged with its community . . . that people throughout the region refer to it as 'our university.'" An institutional vision statement developed during Bernstine's tenure advocated that PSU become "an internationally recognized urban university known for excellence in student learning, innovative research, and community engagement that contributes to the economic vitality, environmental sustainability, and quality of life in the Portland region and beyond."

Current president Wim Wiewel, an internationally recognized specialist in the economic impacts of colleges and universities, is extending the vision of his predecessors. He is author of *Global Universities and Urban Development* (2008), *The University as Urban Developer* (2005), and *Partnerships for Smart Growth: University Community Collaboration for Better Public Places* (2005). He embraces earlier Presidents' commitment to focusing research and teaching around community needs and opportunity. Wiewel comments that at most institutions of higher education, curricular integration of service work is a major challenge, but "here you don't have to struggle with it." He adds, "Intellectually and politically, we have to advance research through deep engagement with the problems around us . . . We need to take our problem sets from the world around us."

In the coming period, Wiewel advocates that PSU "even more thoroughly integrate partnership approaches as we grow our stature as a research university." He is expanding the partnership approach to encompass collaborations with the private sector, as well as with government and the non-profit sector.

Provost Roy Koch observes, "Service-learning is fundamental to undergraduate education . . . it is more and more part of our culture." The university uses service-learning enrollments as a performance measure with the state. The Provost is a staunch advocate of service-learning because experiential learning enhances students' learning. He notes financial advantages as well: "Financial pressures make it increasingly difficult to support civic engagement as a separate activity, therefore these pressures are an additional reason to integrate service activities with instructional and research activities."

The Office of Community–University Partnerships is formally responsible for facilitating community partnerships that contribute to PSU's extensive community-based learning activities. Over time, this unit has taken on much broader and encompassing civic engagement coordination responsibilities. The Office supports working relationships with community organizations that serve as service-learning sites for faculty and students. The Office also functions as a university-wide catalyst and as a resource to faculty members working to strengthen community–university partnerships. An effective strategy employed by CUP is its Engaged Department Initiative that provides mini-grants to build its civic engagement capabilities within academic programs. This step represents an innovative stage beyond the more common approach of supporting the work of individual faculty members.

Driving Factors

Key determinants of PSU's civic engagement approach are top leadership and leadership throughout the institution, and qualities of the university's metropolitan setting. As was noted above, the University has a central commitment to improving the metropolitan area in which it is located. PSU's vision is "to enhance recognition of the value of higher education by continually strengthening the metropolitan environment and utilizing that strength for its own growth toward standards of excellence in accessible high quality research, teaching and outreach programs." The environmental qualities and the civic culture and infrastructure of Portland, Oregon, are a major asset to the University's civic engagement efforts. PSU has capitalized effectively on its location and contributes substantially to it. The region is a learning and research laboratory for the University: "The University's urban setting and many community partnerships act as a 'living laboratory' that provides diverse opportunities to live, learn, and gain the real world experience that students need to succeed."

Portland hosts a dense concentration of community-based non-profit organizations. These groups and the staff who lead them are natural allies of PSU's civic work. Non-profit organizations and the staff that work in them host student placements, are the clients for student field projects and are at times alumni of Portland State. President Wiewel notes that the 70,000 PSU alumni in the region are a major asset for the institution's community engagement activities. These alumni understand the community engagement aspects of the PSU curriculum and often are able to envision ways to further their work through connections with the university. Given their knowledge of the institution they are often able to negotiate partnerships with their former faculty members.

Faculty Rewards and Institutional Accountability

Part of the Oregon University System, PSU is deeply committed to strengthening the metropolitan environment. Its mission "is to enhance the intellectual, social, cultural and economic qualities of urban life by providing access throughout the life span to a quality liberal education for undergraduates and an appropriate array of professional and graduate programs especially relevant to metropolitan areas." As a public university, PSU is accountable to the Chancellor of the Oregon University System which is governed by a Governor-appointed State Board of Higher Education. The University is acutely conscious of its responsibility to its metropolitan region and to citizens of the State.

Does PSU reward faculty members for their community engaged teaching and research? Yes, more so than do most other US college and universities, but with limitations. Provost Koch explains that civic engagement does not receive special credit or separate recognition in the University's faculty tenure and promotion policies. But he is quick to point out that community-based research can be a route to high quality research and that community-based teaching can be high quality teaching, and mentions many PSU professors who exemplify both paths. He notes, "With respect to the role of civic engagement in assessing faculty performance, we're an educational institution so we would expect evidence and scholarly outputs to demonstrate of high quality education and research. Community-based teaching and research is teaching and research done in partnership with a community organization and produces a scholarly output. Mere engagement with a community organization is not sufficient evidence of high quality performance." The Provost acknowledges that doing community-based research does pose a special challenge in those instances when the policies of peer-reviewed academic publications do not fully recognize a professor's scholarly achievement.

Challenges and Future Directions

Portland State has been doing this work for more than 15 years. There are many arenas where the university has had successes. Yet there are still areas where its work can be improved and expanded.

1. A primary future priority for administrative and faculty leaders is to continue to increase the number of faculty who teach and do research in partnership with community organizations. An obstacle to achieving this goal cited by President Wiewel is the additional time required to effectively collaborate, in a context where faculty carry heavy teaching loads, plus the financial pressures on the University's community partners, which similarly constrain their ability to invest staff time in collaboration.
2. A second priority is that community partnerships move in the direction of larger group efforts—contributing to increased visibility and larger scale impacts. Most recent illustrations of this kind of more focused partnership effort can we seen in PSU's community-wide initiative on sustainability and its comprehensive collaboration with the Portland Public Schools—that can achieve greatest strategic impacts in the community. Sustainability is an area of increasing strategic emphasis at PSU, which translates into a growing

number of instances where programs focused on community-based teaching and research contribute to that major effort.

3. PSU is putting a priority on elevating the international dimensions of its education, research and service, and on bringing together its civic engagement and its international program development goals. The socioeconomic status of its student body means that few students can afford to do a full semester of study abroad. As a result the University is organizing an increasing number of faculty-led short study and service trips for students. Gil Latz, Vice-Provost for International Affairs, reports, "We are incorporating service-learning into our study abroad programs." He adds that a growing number of PSU faculty members are leading short-term service-oriented trips abroad, expanding PSUs engagement activities from the local/regional engagement to the global. Also contributing to PSU's growth of global engagement is the co-location of the International Partnership for Service Learning & Leadership in Portland with a strong affiliation with PSU. The Partnership operates study abroad programs that include volunteer service.

4. The university increasingly is developing more sophisticated strategies to assess student learning and faculty performance in community based teaching and research. Staff and faculty across the institution are seeking to expand assessment activities and to develop new ones that will more fully measure what student learn and the effectiveness of faculty members' community-based work.

Social Justice Education and Research and Service

Profile of Georgetown University (USA)
By Robert M. Hollister (based on field visit March 16 and 18, 2010)

At Georgetown University, civic engagement and social responsibility are a pervasive part of the culture and programs of the institution, where an overriding theme is social justice. Georgetown has well-developed, extensive programs of volunteer service, community-based learning integrated in academic courses, and community-based research and the application of research to public policy-making. These elements reinforce one another in the work and experience of both faculty and students, and have a cumulative effect in building and sustaining a university-wide culture of service.

The University's civic work embraces the conceptual vocabulary of service, but faculty and administrative leaders consciously eschew this perspective out of concern for its one-directional and *noblesse oblige* connotations, preferring "community-based learning" rather than "community service learning," and talking of social justice as well as service.

At both the undergraduate level, and in major graduate professional schools as well, social justice and public service are prominent dimensions of the academic curriculum and also of a broad range of extracurricular programs. On the Main Campus a well-staffed Center for Social Justice runs myriad volunteer service programs, encourages and assists faculty members to practice community-based learning in their courses, and plays a robust advocacy and coordinating role.

Georgetown's service work is profoundly shaped by its Jesuit identity and also by its location in the US Capitol, a city of dramatic inequities in the wellbeing and living conditions of its residents, as well as the site of public service functions of the federal government. University President Jack DeGioia's personal commitment to service and social justice is felt deeply by faculty members and students alike. As a prominent research university with a strong institutional commitment to service, a fundamental dynamic at the University is managing the inevitable tensions between these major goals.

Two departments offer undergraduate concentrations in community engagement. Undergraduates in all fields have a "4th credit option"—they can earn an additional fourth credit in selected courses by doing an additional social action project.

Faculty Leadership in Community-Based Learning

A hallmark of Georgetown's approach to civic engagement is its focus on promoting community-based learning in the curriculum. About two dozen faculty members regularly teach community-based learning course. In 2008, after a persistent initiative, community-based learning (CBL) was approved as a formal course designation and notation on the transcript. This designation contributes to students' course selection process and recognizes faculty participation. In 2008–2009, 57 CBL courses were offered in 19 departments or schools, and involved 70 faculty. The combined enrollment in these courses was approximately 1,200. Examples included: The Church and the Poor, in Theology; Project DC: Research Internship on Urban Issues, in Sociology; and Civic Engagement in Public Education, in Philosophy.

Heidi Elmendorf, Associate Professor of Biology, a specialist in cellular and molecular biology, offers a year-long course entitled Teaching Biology, through which 10–12 students design and teach curriculum modules in DC public middle and high schools, critically reflect on the experience, and research what the high school students learn as a result of this intervention. A key satisfaction for Elmendorf is seeing first-hand the powerful impact of the experience on these students and their growth.

Sam Marullo, Professor and former Chair of the Department of Sociology, is a leading advocate and practitioner of community-based learning within Georgetown and nationally as well. Marullo co-created the interuniversity Community Research and Learning Network in DC, which he directed from 2000 to 2006. His department offers a track for its majors in Social Justice Analysis, and four of the core faculty in Sociology teach community-based learning courses. Marullo sees impressive impacts of community-based learning on students' development and community benefits as well. He observes that CBL courses tend to operate in the same geographic areas and with many of the same community partners as are the focus of student volunteer programs. Thus these curricular and the co-curricular efforts reinforce one another.

Another faculty proponent of community-based learning is Robert Bies, Professor of Management and Founder of the Executive Master's in Leadership Program at the McDonough School of Business. He uses this pedagogic approach in all of his undergraduate classes. Bies states, "I'm of the belief that all courses could be community-based learning. I have a social justice agenda, but I embrace community-based learning because in it I see a powerful pedagogy." In his course on Management and Organizational Behavior Bies helps students to understand their moral purpose as global business leaders "and how such a purpose can make a difference in the lives of others." One-third of each student's course grade is based on a "making a difference project," a team service project that the students design together with community partners.

While they are enthusiastic about community-based learning and its impacts on their students, faculty advocates of this approach feel that it is not rewarded by the university. There is universal agreement that the faculty reward system values research achievement most highly, and that the additional effort required, and the accomplishments generated, by CBL courses are much less valued. Kathleen Maas Weigert, founding director of the Center for Social Justice, observes, "Our social justice work relies extensively on the good will of many mid-level faculty members and adjuncts, and a small number of tenured professors." Acknowledging that the tenure and promotion criteria are constraining, President DeGioia says, "I would not encourage non-tenured faculty to do this work." The same lack of incentives for community service work that is felt by faculty members is perceived by graduate students as well. This situation steers the service energies of graduate students toward co-curricular opportunities. Community service is seen by graduate students as "the thing that happens outside the classroom."

Its adherents aspire, over time, to elevate institutional support for CBL. States Professor Elmendorf, "Our opportunity is to embrace community-based learning not as frosting on the cake but as the cake itself." She adds, "We need to validate community-based learning as a central part of what it means to be an educator and to be educated . . . This is scholarly work . . . it's more than 'doing good.'" In the context of limited incentives, it is not surprising that faculty participation in community-based learning at Georgetown is growing very slowly.

A Focus on Improving Public K-12 Education

A large portion of the University's social justice and service activities concentrate on strengthening the education of students in the DC public schools.

Georgetown has a long history of sponsoring after-school programs for local public school students. A previous Superintendant of Schools invited the University to focus its public school improvement efforts in Ward Seven. As a result
Georgetown organized the Ward Seven Initiative, an intensive effort to mobilize
University resources to support students, families and schools in that part of the
city. Component programs include a weekend and summer college preparatory
program that serves about 50 high school students each year. An ardent champion
of this program, President DeGioia notes, "In a city where only 30% of students
graduate from high school, and just 8% from college, 98% of the participants in
the program have graduated from high school and 75% from college."

The Center for Social Justice runs the DC Reads Program through which each
year over 100 students tutor students in five local public schools. In addition it
operates the DC Schools Program, annually training and supervising university
students to help 175 K-12 students and 100 adult English as a Second Language
students.

A Tradition of Service in Graduate and Professional Schools

Public service and social justice are distinctive strengths of Georgetown's large
graduate schools in law and in medicine. Both schools have developed well-staffed
infrastructures that support both curricular and co-curricular service opportunities
for their students.

"Public service is the soul of the Law Center (school)," states Barbara Moulton,
Assistant Dean and Director of the Office of Public Interest and Community Service. Many faculty members are oriented to public interest law, and the Center
attracts many students who plan a career in public service law. The concentration
of federal agencies in Washington, DC, is of course a powerful reinforcing factor. Programmatically this distinctive focus includes legal services clinics and pro
bono projects, a loan repayment assistance program for alumni practicing public
service law, summer public service placements, and externships with non-profits
and government agencies. Students have many different kinds of service opportunities—ranging from work with the federal government to local community-
based organizations. The Law Center's service functions are handled by two offices,
Clinical Programs (three full-time staff and a faculty director) and Public Interest
and Community Service with a staff of six. Three faculty committees oversee public
interest dimensions of the school—the Public Interest Committee guides policies
and programs of the Office of Public Interest and Community Service, and the
Public Interest Law Scholars Program. The Committee on Clinics, Externships and
Experiential Learning advises on those aspects of the curriculum. The Financial Aid
Committee oversees administration of a Loan Repayment Assistance Program.

The Law Center offers an externship course through which students work
in local non-profit or government agency for 10 hours per week. Students who
take an externship are required to take a related course either at the same time

or beforehand and also to prepare a reflection paper on the experience. In addition the Center provides extensive financial support for summer public service placements. Dean Moulton notes that many students find that an obstacle to pursuing their public service passions as a career is the considerable debt that they accumulate in order to complete their degree, combined with the comparatively low salaries that they can earn in public service law jobs. The Loan Repayment Assistance Program helps students who are practicing public service law to pay off their educational loans.

All first-year students at the School of Medicine take a required course, Introduction to Health Care, which incorporates service learning. In 2008 the School instituted a Health Justice Scholars track, through which students take seminars on social justice in healthcare, learn advocacy skills for underserved groups and complete a month-long policy advocacy experience. The Medical School maintains a Service-Learning Program office and sponsors multiple health service initiatives. With a staff of two, the Service-Learning Program provides support, curriculum and technical assistance to assure the quality of experience of medical student, faculty and community partners. This office coordinates the community partnerships that are an essential part of the year-long Introduction to Health Care course.

Strong Organizational Structure and Leadership

The Center for Social Justice was established in 2001 to coordinate and support community-based work across the University. Twelve full-time staff operate three direct service programs, run a student leadership program, maintain working ties with community organizations and broker community-based research projects, and assist faculty in developing and strengthening community-based learning courses. The Center also coordinates a 4th Credit Option for Social Action program, which for the past twenty years has enabled students to earn an additional credit for completing social action projects as part of a course. The Center's Advisory Board for Student Organizations oversees more than 40 student social justice organizations. They provide training for the leaders of these groups and foster coordination among them. Reporting to the Provost, the Center is a robust resource to multiple constituencies in Georgetown's service and social justice activities—students, faculty members and community partners.

The Center operates three large volunteer service programs—DC Reads (in which over 150 students tutor students in five local schools), DC Schools Project (individual and group tutoring, and an adult education program on Saturdays) and the After School Kids Program (tutoring and mentoring for adjudicated youth). Efforts to strengthen K-12 education are a major focus because this is such a high community priority.

Research Director Deanna Cooke states that the Center encourages faculty and students to channel their service work into long-term partnerships, in order to maximize community impacts and also to elevate research and learning outcomes. She cites as an example, the University's continuing collaboration with groups like DC. Voice, an education advocacy group with which different classes have worked. Cooke adds that the Center is placing additional emphasis on evaluating impacts on both community and students.

Driving Factors: Jesuit Identity, Location in a City of Extreme Inequities, and Dynamic Presidential Leadership

Georgetown's Jesuit identity is a driving force for both faculty and students. It is a moral imperative that is felt deeply by both. One professor comments, "This was a surprise for me in coming here and it is big reason that will keep me at Georgetown."

The University's stated mission is a forceful commitment to civic engagement and social responsibility:

> Georgetown is a Catholic and Jesuit student-centered research university, founded on the principle that serious and sustained discourse among people of different faiths, cultures and beliefs promotes intellectual, ethical and spiritual understanding. We embody this principle in our commitment to justice and the common good. An academic community dedicated to creating and communicating knowledge, Georgetown provides excellent education in the Jesuit tradition, for the glory of God and the well-being of humankind. Georgetown educates women and men to be reflective life-long learners, to be responsible and active participants in civic life, and to live generously in service to others.

A recent reaffirmation of this strong institutional commitment was a recommendation by the Intellectual Life Committee appointed by the Provost that "efforts to encourage engagement with Washington, D.C. and to participate in community service, especially in the Center for Social Justice, be integrated into the Undergraduate Learning Initiative component of the capital campaign."

President DeGioia reflects, "Our service and social justice work is very informed by our Catholic and Jesuit identity." He explains how Jesuit leader Father Pedro Arupe's seminal statement "Women and Men for Others" called upon all Jesuit schools to come to terms with their responsibility for justice in the world. DeGioia adds, "We have an obligation to keep engaging that question." His view is that there is not a single or a stable answer, but the institution has a responsibility to pose the issue and to continually wrestle with it.

Washington, DC is a city of haves and have-nots, areas of privilege adjacent to horrendous public health and educational deficits. This context translates into high expectations from local government and non-profit organizations that the university help to address critical local priorities. States President DeGioia, "I don't care how much we're doing, in light of the extreme unmet needs of our neighbors, it's not enough."

The fact that Georgetown is a very student-focused institution is a powerful facilitating factor because the University attracts many students who expect service to be part of their college experience and their lives after they graduate. One professor notes, "We tend to follow a lot the interests and passions of students. The President and the faculty really listen to students."

Future Directions, Challenges, and Reflections

There is every reason to be confident that service and social justice will continue to be a defining focus at Georgetown. Georgetown is an impressive example of the enduring impact of strong religious identity and founding values. In addition to sustaining and strengthening its current programs, the University seeks to augment the international aspects of its service work and to increase support for the "public scholarship" of its faculty.

In recent years, Georgetown has increased its international social justice and service partnerships and expects to extend this dimension of activity. Current programs include an annual two-week study tour to Kenya by a different group each year of 8–12 faculty and staff members; alumni are supporting student service trips to several countries; and the Medical School has a long history of service partnerships in Haiti, which are the focus of intense current expansion due to the 2010 earthquake.

President DeGioia is encouraging additional attention to the impacts of globalization. He asks, "What is the university's role in this era of globalization? What is our responsibility to people who are being marginalized by the forces of globalization? What are our best opportunities to make a difference with respect to these impacts?"

A new Presidential initiative, Reflective Engagement in the Public Interest, has funded several faculty members to extend and complement their research by applying it public policy decision-making. For example, distinguished ethicist Professor Henry Richardson was supported to develop clinical trial research protocols in developing countries. A growing Public Policy Institute at Georgetown also represents new opportunities for growing the university's civic engagement work.

Georgetown will continue to face challenges in its service and social justice endeavors. University personnel consistently cite financial constraints as a limiting factor. Students feel tension between their volunteer service motivations and the pressure to focus on preparation for employment. As is the case at other institutions of higher education, the academic calendar is an obstacle to university–community partnerships. President DeGioia notes, "Of necessity we have to organize around the capacity of student volunteers vs. being guided entirely by community needs."

The institution illustrates the profound tensions between the research aspirations of a private research university and its ambitious social justice and public service commitments. Faculty leaders teaching community-based learning courses uniformly note that these cross-pressures constrain the public service efforts of their colleagues. The faculty reward structure recognizes research accomplishments far more than public service achievements.

Venezuela and its Higher Education System

Venezuela has a population of 28 million, an average life expectancy for men of 71 and women of 78 and ranks 113th out of 173 in the Media Freedom Index. Its adult literacy rate is 93%; it has 1.94 doctors per 1,000 population, and an adult HIV/AIDS rate of 0.7% (*Guardian* "World Fact Files," 2009).

Venezuelan HEIs consist of both universities (72% of enrollment) and non-universities (28% of enrollment) (Holm-Nielsen et al., 2005). These are further divided into private HEIs and public HEIs. Public HEIs are further divided into autonomous universities founded before 1958, and the universities founded since 1958. Called *universidades experimentales*, these institutions are under more government control and their authorities are appointed by the government (Albornoz, 2003).

In 1999, private HEIs accounted for 43.9% of enrollment, but this number has declined through deliberate government efforts to increase the public sector's share of higher education, such as through the foundation of new HEIs like the massive *Universidad Bolivariana de Venezuela* (Muhr & Verger, 2006). Since Hugo Chávez's rise to power in 1998, the Venezuelan government has greatly increased its involvement in education, including higher education, as a key to transforming Venezuela's society. On May 18, 2010, Chavez announced the nationalization of the Santa Inés University, the first private university to come under government control in Venezuela. This follows a trend by the current government to exert more control over all facets of the education system.

The 1999 Constitution does guarantee some autonomy for public and private institutions. It states that they may "adopt their own rules for their governance and operation and the efficient management of their property, under such control and vigilance as may be established by law to this end. Autonomy of universities is established in the planning, organization, preparation and updating of research, teaching and extension programs" (Constitution of the Bolivarian Republic of Venezuela, 1999). However, institutional leaders increasingly recognize the need to be careful politically when making any institutional decisions in the current hostile political climate.

Professor Orlando Albornoz of the Universidad Central de Venezuela argues, "If current trends continue, Venezuela's complex and diverse higher education system may come to resemble the centralized Cuban system" (Albornoz,

2003). Albornoz and his co-author Elsi Jiménez, Professor at Universidad Central de Venezuela, also state, "There is in fact a new methodology being used in Venezuela in order to control the higher education system, which goes away from direct confrontation and prefers intimidation, threats and the creation of an atmosphere of fear in which members of the divided academic community choose silence and conform to the situation as much as they can" (Albornoz & Jimenez: 7).

Chávez apologists such as Professor Thomas Muhr of the University of Bristol and Professor Antoni Verger of the Universitat Autònoma de Barcelona also admit that Venezuela's government is rejecting HEI autonomy as a capitalist concept (Muhr & Verger, 2006).

Under Chávez, spending on education overall, including HE, has increased. In 2002, Venezuela spent 2% of its GDP on HE, well above most of Latin America (Holm-Nielsen et al, 2005: 47). Public HEIs are funded primarily by the central government, and Chávez has deliberately sought to increase public finance in higher education, bucking the global trend toward private financing (Hahn, 2007: 10). Private HEIs are funded mainly by tuition fees as well as private contributions and receive no direct government financial support (Talloires Network, 2009: 2). Public education in Venezuela is free.

Data indicates that university enrollment has increased greatly since the 1999 Constitution guaranteed free HE as a right and the government massively expanded the public university system. Venezuela abolished university entrance exams in 2007.

A major social cohesion issue for HE, closely linked to the political conflict, is class inequality. Between 1981 and 2002 the gap in higher education attendance between the richest and poorest social groups increased significantly, with 54.7% of the wealthiest 20–24 year-olds attending college, while only 20.8% of the poorest attended (Muhr &Verger, 2006).

Although university enrollment has increased across the board under Chávez, the economic gap has actually widened despite official efforts to increase equity.

TABLE 5.4 Higher Education Attendance of 20–24-Year-Olds According to Social Class (%)

	1981	*1997*	*2002*
Quintile 1 (poorest)	28.5	16.4	20.8
Quintile 2	23.7	20.0	27.8
Quintile 3	23.9	24.5	29.7
Quintile 4	25.9	31.1	39.3
Quintile 5 (richest)	33.3	43.8	54.7

Muhr & Verger (2006).

From Education for National Development to Community Solidarity

Profile of the Universidad Metropolitana en Caracas (UNIMET)
By Elizabeth Babcock (based on field visit
May 11 and 12, 2009)

Origins and History

Universidad Metropolitana (UNIMET) was founded as a private non-profit university on October 22, 1970 following six years of preliminary work by a group of businessmen and professionals led by Don Eugenio Mendoza Goiticoa. The founders envisioned a college to train young people, forming "qualified future professionals to influence decision making in the country's development."

UNIMET began operating with 203 pupils and 29 teachers divided into five fields of study: Mechanical Engineering, Electrical Engineering, Chemical Engineering, Administrative Sciences, and Industrial Mathematics. Today UNIMET has over 7,000 students, 600 faculty and both undergraduate and graduate degree programs. Its graduates are some of the most highly sought after professionals for large national and multinational corporations. They have a reputation as being one of the best private universities in Venezuela.

The budget structure relies mainly on tuition fees and the institution does not receive financial support from government offices. The institution centers its academic process on student learning, research and extension and community activities in different areas of knowledge within the context of a scientific-social and human approach, always aimed at serving society at large. Learning processes as well as management of the institution are based on a strong spirit of democracy, social justice and human solidarity.

Engagement and Isolation

Though the university's founding principles adhere to a strong sense of social responsibility and a "spirit of democracy, social justice and human solidarity," the university also has a reputation for exclusivity as a result of its location (abutting a national park and divided from Petare, the largest slum in Latin America, by a large highway) and its elite status as a private institution.

Venezuelan society and Caracas in particular face enumerable social and economic challenges. The university has identified some of the key social problems to help guide their community engagement work. These include low levels of economic development for a significant percentage of population, high inflation rates, crime and violence, inadequate housing and services, such as electricity, water, education, and health, pollution, high dropout rates, and political polarization. The university strives to respond to these issues through various outreach, education and research programs.

Internal and external policy developments have pushed UNIMET to respond to social needs. On September 14, 2005 Venezuela passed a national law requiring all university graduates complete 120 hours of service prior to graduation (Ley del Servicio Comunitario del Estudiante de Educación Superior). Though the university had a similar program in place prior to the law being passed, this change marked the moment when community service activities encountered more political pressure than before. The University assists students in finding community service opportunities, but must also delicately manage relationships in the highly politicized landscape, carefully choosing community partners, while attempting to remain true to their founding principles and values.

The founder of UNIMET, Eugenio Mendoza (December 3, 1974), laid out his vision for the role of the university in Venezuelan society:

> It is not enough to create industries and employment, it is also necessary to create and support programs of social responsibility and give and share our experiences and our resources with other institutions of higher education.

It is important to note that the concept of social responsibility in Latin American universities has a strong history and has continued to grow in importance and focus in the last 10 years. The "social responsibility" concept, which emerged in the business sector, recognizes the need of important institutions in society to contribute to human and social development, through the fostering of civic values and behaviors. Universities in Latin America that recognize social responsibility as part of their mission understand that higher education is uniquely placed to build civil society through the personal and professional development of students and through its own policies and programs.

This is a particularly important concept for this institution of higher education, situated in the most economically unequal region of the world in one of the most unequal countries in the region. Indeed, the university is trying to expose its students to conditions beyond the boundaries of their campus. It runs several educational, volunteer and research programs in Petare, the largest slum in Latin America, as well as other communities in Caracas and in more remote locations outside the city.

Despite the mission focused on civic and community engagement, UNIMET faculty acknowledge that it is difficult to change the campus culture, where many students do not yet see the value of engaging in community outreach or service. There are faculty members who also resist incorporating service or engagement work into their courses. As a result, the university is defining strategies and a new program directed mainly to faculty in order to emphasize the teaching of civic skills, attitudes and behaviors in the classroom alongside service work.

Community Perception and Leadership

The university strives to fulfill its mission in the face of some negative community perceptions of the institution. Indeed, in Latin America many public universities, while seen as prestigious, are also seen as more accessible and are more trusted. Private institutions like UNIMET must manage the tension between a mission with social relevance and the community perception of elitism. This has become even more crucial due to the political pressure to reorient many public and private institutions to the priorities of the state in achieving greater social equality.

The current Rector of the university, José Ignacio Moreno León, is a member of the Talloires Network Steering Committee and has taken on a leadership role in Latin America to promote civic engagement and social responsibility in higher education. He attended the 2005 conference that launched the network and shortly thereafter published an Op-Ed in *El Universal* promoting university–community engagement to solve issues of poverty and social exclusion. He has sought to bring his voice as an institutional leader to the public square and influence the way universities are engaging with their community and society.

William Requejo Orobio, who directs the Center for Community Service "Pablo Rivera Cardona" read the Op-Ed and was angered at the time because he didn't think UNIMET was doing enough to promote engagement with the community, particularly the poorest and most marginalized. He wrote a letter to Rector Moreno León in response, challenging the university to do more to reach out to marginalized communities. As a result of his letter, the university opened spaces for Requejo to develop new community engagement programs. He helped launch the UNIMET summer camp for marginalized children and their families and also made way for students to volunteer in the communities of Libertador, Petare, Los Teques, and Catia, among others. Some, though not all, of these projects are faculty-led, with support from students who participate as part of the curriculum of their courses, while others participate in purely voluntary extra-curricular programs.

Strategic Planning: Shaping Community Engagement for the Future

In 2003, the university introduced a strategic planning process based on a three-year cycle. For the first time, social responsibility was incorporated as one of the main institutional objectives. This process recognizes that the university must take into account the effects of its own processes and actions in the following four areas: (1) Within the organization, internally; (2) in teaching and learning; (3) in knowledge production and research; and (4) in the community.

Mercedes de la Oliva, the Secretary General of UNIMET, directs the coordinating committee for strategic planning on social responsibility. Dr de la Oliva spoke of the challenges of this strategic planning process: "The first challenge is internal. We need to build our internal community. We have over 1,000 employees. As we build a new concept of the engaged university that includes staff, students and professors, we are also doing this in parallel with community work."

The first step was to engage in an assessment phase to map all the social responsibility projects within the university community as well as in the external community. The social responsibility coordinating committee was preparing in May 2009 the first of several public presentations on this self-evaluation exercise and strategic plans going forward.

Though the university is striving to include community representatives in the process, de la Oliva acknowledges that they need to "build more bridges." She stated that, "The perception of the university in the community is not always correct," touching on a common experience of many universities that seek to better engage with their neighbors. Therefore, the community engagement process is a "dynamic cycle" in which the university asks for community feedback, incorporates and interprets it and then refines and develops new strategies.

De la Oliva also stressed the challenges of the formal and informal processes for developing community partnerships. In Venezuelan culture "informal relationships are as important as formal ones. Relationships must be developed first before establishing formal partnerships."

Dr de la Oliva summarized the purpose of these policies "The difficulty of working in a developing country is to respond to social needs, but keep the quality of work high. The needs of some communities are very basic and universities must be both innovators of new, high-level knowledge and responsive to the real needs of society. I hope our students can make important changes to strengthen the country."

Apart from the social responsibility coordinating committee directed by Dr de la Oliva, there are two other offices that have responsibilities related to civic engagement. Student community service projects are coordinated by the "Community Service Coordination" directed by Professor Gloria Lopez. The Office of Social Formation, directed by Professor Rosalind Greaves de Pulido, ensures that students receive instruction related to ethics, social and civic values throughout their university experience.

The university has two schemes for evaluation of faculty. The first is academic and the other focuses on social responsibility. Research is still the most important piece in evaluation for promotion, but extension is also important and has historical significance in Latin America, where extension work has always been valued as a central part of higher education institutions.

University–Community Partnerships for Development

Many of the most successful community engagement programs UNIMET has instituted engage both faculty and students with communities to address a specific area of need. The university is in the process of bringing the curriculum more closely in line with its community engagement work in order to strengthen the learning experience of students and to make their community service more relevant. Though these community engagement programs are not the norm across the entire curriculum, they serve as a successful model for future development.

The university has at least 20 community engagement projects with the participation of between 500 and 700 students each semester and 23 faculty members. These projects are grouped into four main areas: (1) Education; (2) Community building and citizenship; (3) Housing and utilities; and (4) Personal development and family support.

For example, students and faculty in administration and business can engage directly with community entrepreneurs through the *Centro de Initiatives Emprendedoras* (CIE), directed by Professor Xavier Figarella. This center aids small enterprises in building business plans, accessing credit and promoting policy that supports small business. The university's model is to work in a collaborative, mutually beneficial way. Students are encouraged to examine the assets of the business and the community it serves to help inform the business development strategies they will develop. Business owners are viewed as the experts, and students gain as much in the exchange of knowledge as business owners. In comparison to other Latin American universities, it is much more common to see these kinds of programs fall under the office of university extension, rather than being directly integrated into the curriculum. This type of community-based service work has come about because of the increasing influence of service-learning as teaching pedagogy in Latin America.

Another community-based project at UNIMET is the Tacarigua de la Laguna community development project "Building Bridges." Tacarigua de la Laguna is a coastal community to the north of UNIMET with African origins. The university was specifically interested in reaching out beyond the metropolitan area of Caracas to a more rural community. This community was eager to preserve their unique cultural traditions, including dance, music and cuisine. Students in partnership with faculty researchers helped to record, using video, audio and written records, the local traditions and practices, with a particular emphasis on preserving the historical memory of community elders.

In speaking with the faculty, students and community members who engaged in this community development project, it was clear that culture played an extremely important role in the project design. All partners emphasized the importance of an "organic process" as personal relationships developed alongside project goals and strategies. The project expanded beyond its initial focus on cultural preservation to include the development of affordable housing designs based on Indigenous knowledge, tutoring and mentoring programs for community children and water-quality assessment of the lake, which is an important source of income from fishing and tourism. All the partners emphasized that the "knowledge of the community is equal to the knowledge of the university." The mutual respect and co-creation of program objectives have helped the university to build real bridges with the community that have resulted in lasting partnership that benefits student learning, faculty research and community development.

A key goal that was emphasized by both university and community members for all the projects discussed during this research was the importance of students seeing the social and economic realities of their country. Given the strong structural inequalities in Venezuela, students are very often exposed to living conditions they have never personally experienced and may never have even been able to observe before. This process of sensitization through outreach is an essential part of the personal and professional formation of students.

Students as Community Bridges

A large and enthusiastic group of students led me through the myriad projects that make up student social service activity at UNIMET. Ana M. Schloeter, Irene Irazábal, Adolfo Yanes, Eleazar Mora, Eduardo Marchán, Federico Black, Marco Purroy, Victoria Mora and Lindaluz Salazar all shared their unique perspectives on university community engagement.

In addition to curriculum or research based community service, students engage independently in service projects. They design and lead a wide variety of programs in which they serve specific needs of the community and expose their peers to difficult conditions in many neighborhoods of Caracas. The university supports this work through faculty and staff mentoring and allowing the use of university facilities. An important aim for students is to build bridges and spaces for exchange between the university and its surrounding communities.

The project "Social Week" is organized by the Student Social Project Foundation and the University Student Center and it was designed to bring together students and community members in activities on campus or outside campus in the nearby communities An important aim of the event is to break down the divide between campus and community and to expose both students and community members to the wide array of projects and services available to them.

Students themselves acknowledge the difficulty in breaking down barriers between the university and the community. They have begun to consider what program elements are most important in order to break down those barriers and change negative perceptions of the community by students and vice versa. One approach is simply to be more present in the community. Students have taken on a number of projects where they go into community neighborhoods with laptops, projectors and screens to show movies to children or to meet with community leaders about their needs so they can go back to the university armed with new information and relationships that will aid in the creation of new projects.

Students are working not only to bridge differences with the community, but also to connect social action with public policy. The student group *Este–Oeste* (East–West, which signifies the direction of the valley in which Caracas is situated) wants to challenge students to see the realities of their country and to be able to actively work to alleviate poverty and build community capacity. According to student Marco Purroy, *Este–Oeste* wants to "unite people in Caracas who are living in two worlds." Once students become aware of and more knowledgeable about community conditions, they can propose and lead projects. The final aim is to create scalable models and covert those into recommendations for public policy.

Conclusion

Though UNIMET has promoted social responsibility and community engagement, as a part of its mission, it has only recently, since 2000, begun to formalize and give structure to these activities. It is seeking to have a greater impact on student formation in citizenship and ethics and to do this in conjunction with increased demands by external groups (both government and community) to respond to local needs. Its reputation as an elite private institution sometimes complicates these efforts, but there is genuine understanding of the need for outreach and engagement.

It is a challenge for UNIMET to remain independent and selective in the current political climate. It must compete for community space and trust with much larger, more established and more trusted public institutions like the Universidad Central de Venezuela. The current government is increasing control and oversight of all higher education institutions and seeking to massify them at an alarming rate. The result is a conflict over academic and institutional freedom, and this conflict extends in to the realm of community engagement work. Indeed, while I was visiting the university, President Chávez spoke out against news networks and other institutions, like universities, who would seek to challenge his social agenda. And in March of 2010, Chávez nationalized a private university for the first time.

Ironically, new requirements for social service under Venezuelan law have caused the university to think more intentionally about how to engage students in the community and to connect their learning to their service hours. Not all government intervention in this area has had a negative impact.

Finally, UNIMET could benefit from engagement with other universities who attempt similar work in the region. They have begun to engage and share with other universities in Colombia, Argentina, and Mexico in order to track community engagement structures and policies, evaluate learning outcomes and build capacity among faculty to do engaged research and teach using experiential methods.

6

FINDINGS

Common Patterns and Influences

This chapter summarizes key findings from the 20 institutional profiles.

Vision, Mission, and Goals

Common Vision that Transcends Major Differences in Context

Though there are distinctive aspects of each of our profiled universities and the contexts in which they operate vary dramatically, there is also a common vision that transcends context. These profiled universities are pursuing similar strategies and programmatic approaches. Their social, political, and economic contexts do indeed shape significant aspects of their civic engagement and social responsibility activities. At the same time, the commonalities transcend these differences in context. Virtually all of the participating institutions are committed to mobilizing their human and intellectual resources to address pressing needs of the societies in which they are located, and in the process to educate their students to be leaders for change. For the vast majority, civic engagement and social responsibility are at the very core of their mission—they are more than an area of emphasis. They support programs that are quite similar in their very nature and in the strategies that guide their conduct—programs of volunteer service, community service, applied research, community development projects, and conscious attention to the social impacts of institutional policies and practices. They maintain staffed offices that are charged with organizing and supporting their civic and social responsibility programs. Many invest significantly in building and supporting the capabilities of their faculty to do this work.

A Central Dimension of Institutional Mission

Almost all of the participating institutions have a universal and explicit commitment to civic engagement and social responsibility. These commitments are expressed in formal mission statements, strategic plans, and annual reports. And most importantly, they are expressed in the policies and programs that they sustain. Their conceptual vocabulary varies, but on close examination shows major similarities. The banner of some reads "social responsibility" (University of Haifa in Israel; Al-Quds University in The Occupied Territories, and Universidad Metropolitana de Caracas in Venezuela); "civic engagement," "service learning," "community-based learning" (Portland State University); "social justice" (Georgetown University, USA); "social development," "human and economic development" (Aga Khan University in Pakistan; Universidad Señor de Sipàn in Peru); "volunteer service" (Notre Dame of Marbel University, Philippines); and "a public-spirited university" (University of Melbourne, Australia).

The founding missions and priorities of many institutions appear to have lasting impacts. For institutions with strong religious ties, their religious principles and affiliations deeply influence how they define and act on their civic missions. For example, the University of Winchester's (UK) Anglican roots have a continuing impact today on that school's strong emphasis on faith and spirituality as core values that influence its civic agenda. In the same vein, as a Marist institution, Notre Dame of Marbel University's (Philippines) religious identity and traditions put service to the poor at the center of the University's civic work.

The cases illustrate the emergence of a new stage in the development of institutional mission—civic and community engagement as a new paradigm, as it has been conceptualized in Part I. This paradigm builds upon and also moves beyond the historic models that emphasize liberal education, and professional formation, and in some instances, the university as research engine. It posits community engagement not as a separate kind of activity, but as a focus of the institution's teaching and research, and as a strategy for achieving greater quality and impacts in the institution's teaching and research.

Institutions of higher education can be categorized in terms of the kinds of capital that they seek to form—human, social, and creative capital. Many of the cases show a focus on the development of social capital, in particular to contribute to the development of civil society (witness the experience of the University of Western Sydney, Australia). In addition, several evidence a concentration on human capital development.

Primary Goals: Community Impacts and Education of Leaders for Change

For all of the participating institutions, addressing community and societal challenges is a major goal of their civic engagement and social responsibility work.

The primary objective is to address urgent unmet needs in their communities and societies. This emphasis is greatest where the community needs are most acute, and also where they affect the functioning of universities most directly. The severity and extent of poverty in Mumbai has to be a central focus of the civic endeavors of SNDT Women's University of Mumbai (India), just as the desperate health conditions in Karachi stimulated the Aga Khan University's (Pakistan) Urban Health Program and related healthcare interventions.

Our cross-section of universities shows both consistency and variation in the goals that are the focus of their civic work. The majority of institutions emphasize the goal of addressing pressing community and societal needs, with considerable concentration on combating poverty, improving public health, and enhancing pre-university education. While some emphasize educational goals, aiming to develop students' leadership values and skills, for many of the participating schools, this is an important, but a lesser goal. It is notable that only a few—one example is Tecnológico de Monterrey (Mexico)—are specific about the student learning outcomes that they seek to achieve through their civic work. Elevating the employability of their students is a priority goal of several institutions, including Universiti Kebangsaan of Malaysia (Malaysia) and Open University (UK). For some of these, civic engagement programs are seen as a promising strategy for enhancing employability of their graduates, which of course is a major concern in areas of high unemployment, including comparatively high unemployment rates for university graduates.

Many institutions aim through their civic work to improve their community relations and to strengthen public support for their institutions. In comparison with community impact and educational goals, community relations and public support are more of a positive by-product than a priority goal.

Programs and Policies

Applied Research and Service-Learning

For many institutions, curricular integration is a major dimension of their civic engagement efforts. The extent of implementation of service learning varies considerably among universities, and in many, it is concentrated in particular fields of study (often including the helping professions). A significant number of participating institutions rely primarily on volunteer service (examples include Notre Dame of Marbel University, Philippines); some have a marked preference for volunteer service as opposed to service-learning. For many, university civic engagement is not equated with the pedagogy service-learning; service-learning is a more marked trend in the Americas, both North and South.

The research enterprises of participating institutions vary dramatically in their scale and stage of development. For those with significant research programs, research is a major form of civic engagement. Examples include Universiti

Kebangsaan of Malaysia (Malaysia), Portland State University (USA), and University of Melbourne (Australia). These schools show a strong commitment to applying their research activities and results to address societal and community problems. At one institution in the study group, the University of Dar es Salaam (Tanzania), civic engagement consists almost exclusively of research projects.

Many of the community service-oriented research programs of the universities studied have a significant interest in community-based research, in scholarship that is co-designed and co-conducted by university personnel and their community partners. This approach is evident in parts of Georgetown University (USA) and Portland State University (USA). At the other end of the spectrum is the University of Melbourne (Australia), where research applied to societal needs is exclusively a story of knowledge transfer.

Institutional Policies and Practices

Several of these universities have developed and implemented institutional policies and practices that aim to contribute to their overall civic and social responsibility missions. The University of Western Sydney (Australia), for example, seeks to model best practices in the development of its physical infrastructure and in the greening of its campuses and work environment.

Variations in Program Mix

The basic dimensions of institutions' civic engagement and social responsibility include volunteer service, service-learning in the curriculum, applied research, community development projects, and institutional policies that have a social responsibility intention. The levels of emphasis or balance among these components vary considerably among our institutions. At some universities, civic engagement is all about volunteer service (Notre Dame of Marbel University, Philippines); at others, community service learning or community-based learning is the focus (Portland State University, USA).

Extensive Investment in Community Partnerships

A hallmark of many of the institutions in this study is their substantial support for community partnerships. Developing and maintaining long-term working relationships with partner organizations—NGOs, government agencies and private businesses—is an essential component of their civic and social responsibility functions. Many universities support employees whose primary responsibility is to build and to maintain their ties, and to broker effective interactions between university students and students and their community partners (for instance, the Institute for Sustainable Social Development at Tecnológico de Monterrey, Mexico, the Office of University–Community Partnerships at Portland State

University, USA, and the Office of Industry and Community Partnerships at Universiti Kebangsaan of Malaysia, Malaysia). The community partnerships of Aga Khan University (Pakistan) include not only relationships with organizations in Karachi, but also with the set of private development institutions that comprise the Aga Khan Development Network with which AKU is affiliated.

At the majority of participating institutions, community partners express high satisfaction with, and support for, their connections with the university. Community representatives at Charles Darwin University in Australia express a deep sense of ownership of that institution. At some—Universidad Metropolitana de Caracas, Venezuela, for example—the community–university interface includes tensions as well as positive elements.

Access to Higher Education is an Important Form of Civic and Social Responsibility

For several of the institutions in this study, providing access to higher education to disadvantaged and underrepresented groups is both a priority and also one that they define as a key part of their civic and social mission. This is abundantly the case, for example, in Charles Darwin University (Australia), and the Open University (UK).

Empowering Women Through Education

At a number of institutions, an important focus of their civic and social responsibility work is to empower women through education—both through classroom teaching and also students' participation in community service projects. At Al-Quds University (The Occupied Territories) community outreach programs focus on women's empowerment. This goal is a defining focus also at SNDT Women University of Mumbai (India) and at Aga Khan University (Pakistan). The vision of Ahfad University for Women (Sudan) is "to create proactive women change agents and leaders . . . who can participate in the development of their families of communities."

Leadership and Organization

The Leadership Dimension

It is not surprising that many of the institutions are led by ardent proponents of civic engagement—Brenda Gourley, Former Vice-Chancellor of the Open University (UK); Janice Reid, University of Western Sydney (Australia); Jack DeGioia, Georgetown University (USA); Vuyisa Tanga, Cape Peninsula University of Technology (South Africa); Humberto LLempen Coronel, Universidad Señor de Sipán (Peru); José Ignacio Moreno León, Universidad Metropolitana

(Venezuela), and Sharifah Hapsah Shahabudin, Universiti Kebangsaan of Malaysia (Malaysia). The presidents, vice-chancellors and rectors are forceful advocates within their institutions for the civic agenda. Several of them are influential leaders in the broader field of higher education civic engagement as well. In many cases, these individuals have had a major impact on the nature and scope of their institution's civic engagement and social responsibility. In these circumstances, the institutions face particular issues of succession (growing the next generation of leaders) and sustainability (is the strategic priority of community engagement fully embedded, or too closely tied to a former, charismatic leader?).

Organizational Strategies

There is considerable variation with respect to the approaches that the institutions follow in organizing their civic engagement and social responsibility activities. In some cases, primary responsibility is located within an academic unit, in others, with student affairs. Some institutions follow a highly centralized model; in others, the responsibilities are entirely decentralized.

The majority of institutions support a designated leadership position or positions that are assigned to develop and to coordinate their civic engagement and social responsibility activities. At Cape Peninsula University of Technology (South Africa), the Center for Community Engagement and Work Integrated Learning houses these functions.

Results and the Future

Outcomes

The civic work of each of the participating institutions appears to be achieving substantial results. These are perceived and valued by a mix of constituencies— students, faculty, administrators, and community partners. It is noteworthy that very few institutions systematically measure these impacts. One that is systematically measuring student civic learning outcomes is Tecnológico de Monterrey (Mexico).

In a number of institutions where rote learning and one-way presentation of information are predominant forms of pedagogy, students' participation in service activities represents a unique opportunity for them to do more experiential learning.

The Future—Expansion and Collaboration

Almost all of the institutions aspire to not only sustain, but also to expand and deepen their civic engagement and social responsibility programs. Many seek to involve additional academic units in this work. They aspire to achieving greater impact on both their students and on their communities. Many aim to develop stronger, more extensive community partnerships. Many express a high interest in greater collaboration with other institutions of higher education in their region and/or internationally.

The civic engagement and social responsibility programs of many institutions are still at a relatively early stage of development; they are not entirely embedded in or are a permanent part of the organization. Therefore, these activities are vulnerable to changes in finances and policy. In some instances, such as the University of Haifa (Israel), financial cutbacks have reduced the institution's civic work.

Influences on University Civic Engagement

This study indicates that several factors are especially influential in shaping the nature and scale of university civic engagement and social responsibility. These variables include institutional leadership, financial constraints, government policies, political context, relative institutional prestige, community needs, academic reward system, support from international agencies, and student expectations and leadership.

Institutional Leadership

As noted above, many of the vice-chancellors, rectors and presidents are dynamic leaders who are deeply committed to elevating the civic engagement and social responsibility of higher education. Their strength of advocacy has had, and continues to have, profound effects on this dimension of the institutions that they lead.

Financial Constraints

Limited funding is cited almost universally as a constraint, even as some universities operate in settings of abundance and others in contexts of real scarcity. Yet several of the institutions have developed and sustained impressive programs in very challenging financial circumstances.

Explicit Government Policies Matter

A few of the institutions have experienced significant positive impacts of government policies that promote or require student service, and that encourage and fund university engagement programs. Countries that stand out in this regard include South Africa, Australia, Mexico, Venezuela, and Israel. There is significant variation in the degree of institutional autonomy from national policies, and similarly variation in extent of governmental guidance and regulation. During the current presidential administration in Venezuela, the national government has stepped up its regulation and control of both public and private institutions of higher education.

Politically Diverse Contexts

Local and national political realities usually are a major influence. In several institutions, national political conflicts constrain what are acceptable or feasible forms of civic engagement. The political transition of the Ukraine, for example, has pronounced constraining effects on the civic work of Petro Mohyla Black Sea State University. Political conflicts and unrest in some places also create obstacles with respect to physical movement and personal safety (witness Al-Quds in The Occupied Territories).

Less Prestigious Institutions Lead in Innovation

The participating institutions enjoy different levels of prestige and reputation. Schools with lower prestige are less constrained, often more ambitious and creative, in their civic engagement and social responsibility work. Much of the more pioneering work is done by colleges and universities that are not overly concerned about where they fit in the academic pecking order.

The Power of Community Needs and Expectations

The nature and extent of unmet needs frequently is a powerful driver. Where there are massive urgent needs, civic engagement is seen by the institution as an absolute necessity; it is not a choice, but rather an imperative of their situation. In Australia, the civic work of Charles Darwin University is guided substantially by regional priorities. And in another part of Australia, the University of Western Sydney was created with an explicit regional mandate. It has been said of Universidad Señor de Sipán (Peru) "this university is wholly of the region and exists to educate people from the region."

A Major Obstacle: The Academic Rewards System

Almost all participating institutions see the traditional academic rewards system as an obstacle. Several of the case study schools have developed additional rewards and incentives for faculty members' participation (Cape Peninsula University of Technology, South Africa, Universidad Metropolitana de Caracas, Venezuela, Universiti Kebangsaan Malaysia, and Notre Dame of Marbel University, Philippines). But even in these instances, the incentives are modest in comparison with those that are provided for performance in research and teaching.

International Agencies are a Major Ally

In many institutions, funding provided by international agencies plays a major role in supporting civic engagement and social responsibility programs. In several instances—such as Petro Mohyla Black Sea State University (Ukraine) and Al-Quds University (The Occupied Territories)—the institutions' participation in networks of universities is an important source of guidance and support.

Student Expectations and Leadership

Who the students are, their expectations and their employment prospects are influential factors. Many institutions report growth in students' interest and participation in civic engagement programs. For some students, these programs are an especially important part of their university experience. At the same time, many students see civic engagement programs as being less important than, and competing with, their academic studies.

The global contemporary drivers that are pushing higher education toward further engagement with communities and society interact with and run up against local drivers and obstacles. As we have seen, universities in extremely diverse contexts have taken up the civic engagement mission as a core function of their institution, despite a multitude of challenges. It is certainly true that higher education today is more globalized than ever, and therefore, even institutions whose core purpose is to serve discreet regions within a country can be influenced positively or negatively by global changes in the sector. While context is crucial, a global picture of higher education community engagement is emerging.

In Part III, our final section of this book, we shall attempt to set these conclusions—based as they are on 20 self-selecting "stories" of members of the Talloires Network—in the wider context of global developments in higher education.

PART III

An Engaged University Movement

7

NETWORKS

A Unifying Force

As the 20 profiles featured in Part II have demonstrated, local context matters immensely when creating institutional policy and practice to support civic engagement. While many challenges and opportunities relate directly to the circumstances, history and purpose of individual universities, national, regional, and global influences have common effects across institutions.

Clearly, there is growing global momentum around university community engagement. A distinct factor in this momentum is networking. Many of the institutions profiled described a sense of isolation as they began their work, particularly those pioneers who have been working in geographically remote areas (for example, Charles Darwin University or Universidad Señor de Sipán) or in politically, economically or socially difficult circumstances (for example, Ahfad University for Women or Al-Quds University).

In response to this sense of isolation, institutions have banded together, including across regional, cultural, economic, and language barriers, to express support for this priority in general and to undertake mutual or collective learning and action. Universities thus join various clubs and interest groups to augment the effectiveness and influence of their civic work. These may operate at one or more of a number of levels:

- Local (neighborhood): for example, collaboration over amenities or community security
- Sub-regional (e.g. a city): for example, the promotion of tourism or inward investment
- Regional: for example, the contribution to regional economic strategies
- National: for example, membership of higher education associations based on perceived mission affinity (like the UK's Russell Group or Australia's

Group of Eight (Newman, 2009) or sector-wide interests such as collective bargaining

• International regional (e.g. Europe, South-east Asia, North Africa): for example, European collaboration under the Bologna agreements on mutual recognition of qualifications and student mobility

• International/global: for example, membership of the Association of Commonwealth Universities (ACU) (Glazer-Raymo, 2002).

In examining how universities have begun to organize themselves around the topic of civic engagement, we have studied regional, national and international networks of higher education institutions. The tables that follow provide summary information about many of the most active higher education networks that focus on civic engagement. Table 7.1 identifies regional, national and international networks that focus entirely on civic engagement. Table 7.2 identifies regional, national and international networks that include civic engagement as one aim within their mission, or who have a special project devoted to the topic.

TABLE 7.1 Higher Education Networks with a Primary Focus on Civic Engagement

Name	Website	Mission	Year founded	Membership
Association of Commonwealth Universities (ACU) Extension Network	www.acu.ac.uk	The ACU University Extension Network is a Commonwealth-wide grouping bringing together practitioners in community engagement, outreach, knowledge mobilization, and extension activity. Established by the Association of Commonwealth Universities, which was founded in 1913.	2008	500 members
Australian Universities' Community Engagement Alliance (AUCEA)	www.aucea.net.au	Committed to promoting social, environmental, economic and cultural development of communities; promotes direct interaction between universities and communities essential for development and application of knowledge and shaping of future citizens.	2002	35 Australian universities

Campus Compact	campus compact.org	Campus Compact advances the public purposes of colleges and universities by deepening their ability to improve community life and to educate students for civic and social responsibility.	1985	1,200 university presidents
Campus Engage: Network for the promotion of civic engagement in Irish higher education	campusengage.ie	The network aims to strengthen relationship between higher education and wider society, through promoting civic engagement activities in higher education in Ireland and facilitating the sharing of knowledge and resources between academic and civic communities.	2008	5 universities
Canadian Alliance for Community Service-Learning (CACSL)	www.community servicelearning.ca	CACSL supports, educates and networks to ensure the effective growth of community service-learning in Canada.	2005	19 universities and 16 individuals from various affiliations
Community Based Research Canada (CBRC)	community researchcanada.ca	A network of people and organizations engaged in Community-Based Research to meet the needs of people and communities.	2008	
El Centro Latinoamericano de Aprendizaje y Servicio Solidario (Latin American Center for Service-Learning)	www.clayss.org.ar	To contribute to the growth of culture through service-learning projects; To promote the development of the service-learning methodology in Latin America; To contribute to the development of service-learning projects in schools, higher educational institutions, universities and youth organizations.	2005	Over 35 higher education organizations, non-profits and schools

TABLE 7.1 *Continued*

Name	Website	Mission	Year founded	Membership
Global Alliance on Community-Engaged Research (GACER)	community researchcanada.ca/ ?action=news& entry=2809	To build capacity for community-centered solutions, to collaborate on the creation, dissemination and use of knowledge, to uncover the root causes of complex issues facing communities, to improve the lives of individuals · and their communities, to challenge our institutions to recognize and reward the value of community based research.	2008	31 individuals and organizations
Higher Education Network for Community Engagement	www.henceonline. org	"To deepen, consolidate, and advance the literature, research, practice, policy, and advocacy for community engagement as a core element of higher education's role in society."	2006	33 institutions and organizations
International Association for Research on Service-learning and Community Engagement	www.researchslce. org	To promote the development and dissemination of research on service-learning and community engagement internationally and across all levels of the education system.	2005	individuals
International Consortium for Higher Education, Civic Responsibility, and Democracy	www.international consortium.org	Established to bring together national institutions of higher education to promote education for democracy as a central mission of higher education around the world.	1999	47 member countries
Living Knowledge:	www.scienceshops. org	Science shops seek to: provide civil society with	1999	

The International Science Shop Network		knowledge and skills through research and education; provide their services on an affordable basis; promote and support public access to and influence on science and technology; create equitable and supportive partnerships with civil society organizations; enhance understanding among policymakers and education and research institutions of the research and education needs of civil society; enhance the transferable skills and knowledge to students, community representatives and researchers.		
Ma'an Arab University Alliance for Civic Engagement	www1.aucegypt. edu/maan	The Ma'an Arab University Alliance for Civic Engagement aims to bring together Arab universities with the collective goal of encouraging and enhancing civic engagement implementation in higher education.	2008	13 universities
The National Co-ordinating Centre for Public Engagement in Higher Education (NCCPE)	www.public engagement.ac.uk	To support universities and to increase the quantity and quality of their public engagement activity.	2008	6 universities
New Eurasia Foundation Community-University Network	http://www. neweurasia.ru/ index.php?option= com_content&task= blogcategory&id= 39&Itemid=112	Supports and promotes community engagement in Russian higher education, with a focus on regional universities.	2004	14 universities

TABLE 7.1 *Continued*

Name	Website	Mission	Year founded	Membership
Rede Unitrabalho (connected to UNISOL)	www.unitrabalho.org.br	Seeks to lessen the social debt that Brazilian universities have to workers; develops projects that help fight for better living standards and merge the knowledge of the academy with the knowledge of the worker.	1996	92 universities and higher education institutions
REDIVU (Ibero-American Volunteer Network for Social Inclusion)	http://www.redivu.org	Help overcome the causes of poverty and social exclusion by promoting higher education with a deep sense of social responsibility that links the training and research with community service, working on a joint integration and sustainable regional development through identification, management and implementation of joint projects of relevant national and regional programs and volunteer outreach university.	2008	59 universities and non-profit organizations
South African Higher Education Community Engagement Forum	sahecef.ning.com	Advocate for community engagement in South African Higher Education with relevant stakeholders . . . share experiences and best practice in terms of community engagement amongst South African Higher Education Institutions	2010	16 university staff

The Talloires Network	www.tufts.edu/ talloiresnetwork	Committed to strengthening civic roles and social responsibilities of higher education.	2005	185 universities from 59 countries
The Research University Civic Engagement Network (TRUCEN)	www.compact. org/initiatives/ civic-engagement- at-research- universities	Works to advance civic engagement and engaged scholarship among research universities and to create resources and models for use across higher education.	2005	No formal membership
Universidad Construye País	www.constru yepais.cl	To disseminate and implement a set of principles and values, through four processes: management, teaching, research and extension.	2001	13 university members

TABLE 7.2 Higher Education Networks with a Secondary Focus on Civic Engagement

Name	Website	Mission	Year founded	Membership
Association of American Colleges and Universities (AACU)	www.aacu.org	To make the aims of liberal learning a vigorous and constant influence on the institutional purpose and educational practice in higher education.	1915	over 1,200 universities
National Association of Universities and Higher Education Institutions (ANUIES)	www.anuies.mx	To contribute to the integration of higher education system and the overall improvement and permanent affiliates in the areas of teaching, research and dissemination of culture in the context of democratic principles of pluralism, equality and freedom . . .	1950	144 universities

TABLE 7.2 *Continued*

Name	Website	Mission	Year founded	Membership
Association of Colombian Universities (ASCUN)	www.ascun.org.co	To promote principles of academic quality and social responsibility.	1957	16 universities
Association of African Universities (AAU)	www.aau.org	To raise the quality of higher education in Africa and strengthen its contribution to African development by fostering collaboration among its member institutions; by providing support to their core functions of teaching, learning, research and community engagement; and by facilitating critical reflection on, and consensus building around, issues affecting higher education and the development of Africa.	1967	212 institutions from 45 African countries
Global University Network for Innovation (GUNI)	www.guni-rmies.net	To contribute to the strengthening of higher education's role in society through the renewal and innovation of higher education main issues across the world under a vision of public service, relevance and social responsibility.	1999	179 institutions from 68 countries

International Association of Universities (IAU)	www.iau-aiu.net	Upholds and contributes to the development of a long-term vision of universities' role and responsibilities in society.	1950	623 institutions from 150 countries
PASCAL International Observatory	pascalobservatory. org/	Aims to connect the communities of policymakers, practitioners and researchers through an innovative approach to the sharing and exchange of cutting-edge best practice research, ideas and policies. One key research theme is the "third mission" of higher education.	2002	38 governments including universities and local and regional governments

These organizations vary along a number of dimensions. Membership in some instances is affected by institutional type, as is the case for the New Eurasia Foundation's Community-University Network in Russia. This network was set up to respond specifically to the changing needs of regional universities who were losing federal financial support under a national restructuring of higher education.

Some are exclusively orientated towards civic and community engagement; for others this activity sits alongside other focal points. It is particularly promising to note that several higher education networks that were established in the early twentieth century have recently adopted a new focus on civic engagement. For example, in 2008, the Association of Commonwealth Universities set up an Extension Network to serve all professionals working in extension, broadly defined to include public dissemination of knowledge, engaged teaching and research, service programs, and much more.

Universities also seem to draw benefit from a variety of network types. For example, regional and local networks can offer context-driven assistance and make globally produced knowledge more accessible to larger numbers of institutions through translation and dissemination. They unite universities which operate under similar circumstances to promote increased communication and cooperative learning.

Global networks provide a gateway to diverse experiences and knowledge that cross cultural, political and economic boundaries. They also provide a higher profile, global platform for the promotion of civic engagement.

National networks also seem to be key, as they are likely to develop in response to national higher education policy. Their evolution can help influence the development of policy, as in the example of *Construye País*. This network, formed in Chile in 2001, was instrumental in promoting university social responsibility at the national level.

Beyond the importance of creating locally relevant, context-driven assistance, building affiliated regional networks could also encourage partnership with local and regional funders, thereby building local traditions of philanthropy—important and worthwhile goals in parts of the world such as the Middle East where, until recently, most funding streams have come from outside the region.

Opportunities and Constraints

The leaders of several of the networks listed above were interviewed about the driving factors for starting the network they were associated with; the effects of the policy environment and the larger political climate on their work; challenges related to sustainability; the impacts they perceive their networks have had, and their perceptions about momentum around civic engagement in the higher education sector globally. The individuals interviewed included:

- Lorraine McIlrath, Director of the Community Knowledge Initiative and Academic Staff Developer (Service Learning), Centre for Excellence in Learning and Teaching, National University Ireland Galway and founder and Principal Investigator of Campus Engage;
- Jerome Slamat, Senior Director of Community Interaction, Stellenbosch University and founding chair of South African Higher Education Community Engagement Forum (SAHECEF);
- Barbara Ibrahim, Director, Gerhart Center for Philanthropy and Civic Engagement, American University in Cairo and founding director of the Ma'an Arab University Alliance for Civic Engagement;
- Mónica Jiménez de la Jara, former Rector of the Catholic University of Temuco, former Minister of Education in Chile and founder of *Construye País*;
- Maria Nieves Tapia, Director of *El Centro Latinoamericano del Aprendizaje y Servicio Solidario* (CLAYSS) in Argentina and founder of the Ibero-American Network for Service-Learning;
- Janice Reid, Vice Chancellor, University of Western Sydney (UWS) and founder of Australian Universities Community Engagement Alliance (AUCEA); and Barbara Holland, University of Sydney;

- Andrey Kortunov, President, New Eurasia Foundation and founder of the Community University Network in Russia;
- Saran Kaur Gill, Deputy Vice-Chancellor for Industry and Community Partnerships, Universiti Kebangsaan Malaysia (UKM) and a founding member of the Committee of Deputy Vice Chancellors for Industry and Community Partnerships in Malaysia;
- Paul Manners, Director, National Co-ordinating Centre for Public Engagement (NCCPE), which coordinates the Beacons for Public Engagement initiative.

Two of the networks (Malaysia and Russia) are only in the early planning stages; all of the other networks mentioned above have been formed in the past 1–10 years. There are other older networks, such as the Campus Compact in the United States, which is celebrating its 25th year, but we chose to focus on several of the more recent networks that have formed around civic engagement in universities. Paul Manners asserts that the Beacons projects funded at UK universities under the auspices of the NCCPE do not constitute a formal network, but rather a project amongst the Beacon projects staff. Nevertheless, Paul offered some interesting observations about networks and whether there is growing momentum for civic engagement in higher education globally.

Driving Factors in Network Development

In many cases, the main driving factors in starting up a network were related to specific changes in the higher education policy environment and, in some cases, to changes in the political situation generally. In Ireland, Lorraine McIlrath cites the reference to the Universities Act for Ireland 1997, as having laid a foundation of the expansion of civic engagement in higher education. As a response to concerns raised by Robert Putnam's *Bowling Alone*, in 2006 the Taoiseach convened a Task Force on Active Citizenship that developed a set of recommendations about the civic life of Ireland, including two recommendations for higher education—students' civic activities should be recognized, and a network of universities should be formed to encourage greater levels of civic engagement. The government made funding available specifically for the purposes of forming and supporting a network, which was named "Campus Engage."

In South Africa, higher education policy and political changes have been major factors in the development of SAHECEF. Jerome Slamat explains that the 1997 "White Paper on Higher Education" policy mandates that universities must be more responsive to society's needs and calls for a new relationship between higher education institutions and communities. This policy is situated within the macro-government policy of development and reconstruction of South Africa in the post-apartheid era. To jumpstart civic engagement in universities after the adoption of the White Paper, the Ford Foundation invested in the development of the Community Higher Education Service Partnerships (CHESP) project that created a network initially of seven universities and eventually became a broader forum with government and other HEIs. When the funding for CHESP ended, staff at many universities decided there was a need for a forum for institutional managers for community engagement. In 2008, Slamat and Kiepe Jaftha at the University of the Free State began a conversation with staff at other universities about the need for a network to sustain their work, which led to the launch of SAHECEF in 2009. All 23 of the public universities currently are members.

Janice Reid sets the context for the development of AUCEA in the framework of higher education policy changes reaching back to the 1980s, during which the Australian government decreed that all colleges of advanced education would be merged with existing institutions or become new universities. Many of these new universities were situated in rural and disadvantaged communities, unlike the traditional universities which are located in major urban areas. According to Professor Reid,

> Communities were very proud of the new universities in their midst, as were the local professionals who were used to working in the community—in schools, hospitals and other community organizations. For us community collaboration and engagement was a no brainer.

In the 1990s and early 2000s efforts were made by the new universities to extend their missions as "universities without walls." As Professor Reid explains, "Community engagement was inherent in our location and our missions. I could name at least a dozen universities that are highly responsive and community-oriented because of where they are and who they serve." In 2002, UWS organized a forum on community engagement in Australian universities, which was repeated in 2003, after which a group of individuals from different Australian universities voiced interest in forming a membership organization around community engagement research and practice issues. UWS funded the start-up of AUCEA, which in 2005 became an independent legal entity and is now located at Victoria University.

Barbara Ibrahim provides context for the founding of the Ma'an Arab University Alliance for Civic Engagement. Higher education in the Arab region has a long history with universities like al-Azhar that are 1,400 years old. The universities that were begun in the twentieth century were opened as part of the optimistic, state-building efforts after independence as part of important equity programs to dismantle old patriarchal societies. Promises for free higher education access to qualified young people (enshrined in the Egyptian constitution) have been impossible to honor as population increases and increased demand for higher education outstripped the resources of these countries. As a result, huge, underfunded, bureaucratized universities are not delivering higher education of a quality necessary for contemporary employment or societal needs. Meanwhile, fears of student politics lead governments to heavily restrict civic and political activity on the part of faculty or students. Most countries are slipping backwards with regards to freedom of expression and university autonomy. But there is also momentum in other directions.

There is broad acknowledgement that higher education is in crisis, and the public policy debate is about the need for major reform. Dr Ibrahim explains that,

> . . . national universities in many Arab countries are like land-grant universities in the US in the sense that there is an assumption about public service built into their mandates. This traditionally has meant that faculty would be available to policymakers for research and policy counsel. This kind of work has rarely been collaborative and almost never included students except for occasionally engaging individual graduate students. This kind of engagement has not infused university curricula or its teaching practices.

However, within the region there are nodes of innovation and more room for optimism. Cairo University and other pioneers are thinking about how this can change, have created senior positions for community outreach linked to NGOs, conduct development research projects and have established experiential/service-learning courses. "This is nascent—but it's there."

In 2008, the Gerhart Center at the American University in Cairo, with the support of the Talloires Network, invited senior staff, faculty and students from universities in the Arab world to a conference in Cairo to test the waters about interest in civic engagement in higher education institutions. Although the organizers' expectations were modest, there was a high level of interest from people at universities across the diverse contexts of the region. The participants expressed a belief that civic engagement might be a way to substantially reform higher education from within instead of waiting for major public policy changes. The Gerhart Center staff were encouraged by the participants to think about how networks can speed up this process of internal reforms.

In 2001, Mónica Jiménez de la Jara, former Rector of the Catholic University of Temuco, founded a network of 13 Chilean universities called *Construye País* [Build the Country]. The need for the network, as Professor Jiménez explains, was rooted in the history of higher education since the 1960s. The reforms that were initiated in the 1960s were violently cut short by the political coup of 1973. During the next 25 years, the imposition of authoritarian rule severely limited the critical role and the creative contributions universities could make to the development of the country. According to Professor Jiménez, since the restoration of democratic government 10 years ago, the dominant view of the role of universities has been limited to their contribution to economic growth, consumed by pragmatism and the immediacy of needs imposed by a university financing system. With support from a private foundation, *Construye País* was launched as a counter-balance to that pragmatism and a wish to restore higher education's leadership in contributing knowledge for the development of Chile.

Interest in civic engagement began seriously in Argentina in 1995, when Maria Nieves Tapia was hired by the Ministry of Education to build a national network of schools that employed service-learning as a teaching and learning pedagogy. Universities in Argentina were at the same time beginning to rethink the extension function that has been a part of higher education in Latin America for nearly a century. Extension services are part of almost every university and encompass a complex and diverse range of activities, including cultural and artistic programs, development projects by faculty and students, and outreach to marginalized groups. But, Professor Tapia explains, the extension function has always been a separate and parallel system to the academic function of the university. In the last 15 years, efforts have been made to move towards a more integrated model of teaching, research, and outreach. The alternative, according to Professor Tapia, is to "risk the marginalization of the civic engagement movement that had gathered strength in universities in Argentina since the return to democracy in 1983."

Elsewhere in Latin America—specifically Mexico and Costa Rica—civic engagement is required of all university students. In Mexico, the *Servicio Social* was enacted in higher education law in the 1930s to apply the skills and knowledge of university students to issues of poverty. In Peru and Columbia, the civic engagement movement is strong in higher education institutions. Professor Tapia recognizes the depth of interest in many parts of Latin America and organized the first conference on service-learning. Through repeated conferences and informal exchanges, momentum grew until, in 2005, the decision was taken by CLAYSS, other NGOs, government representatives and the Inter-American Development Bank to institutionalize the network as the Ibero-American Network for Service-Learning. In addition to people from Latin America, the network bridges to organizations in the United States, Spain, and other countries with a shared interest in service-learning and civic engagement.

Globally, the Talloires Network was formed to unite individuals and institutions working on civic engagement in every region of the world. In the past five years, it has grown from 29 university leaders in 23 countries to 185 universities in 59 countries. The network Steering Committee has adopted a strategy to support the growth of the global network, which focuses on supporting or catalyzing regional networks. The Talloires Network has provided modest financial support to CLAYSS and Ma'an and they have developed MOUs with several existing networks, such as AUCEA, GUNI, Campus Engage, and Campus Compact. Shamsh Kassim-Lakha, founding President of Aga Khan University and a member of the Talloires Network Steering Committee, has this to say about the role of a global network:

> The remarkable diversity of institutions in the Talloires Network has enabled its members to learn from each other about the value, importance

and methodology of engaging with the communities in which they function. Such direct engagement in the community is an important means of universities discharging their obligations to societies that have nurtured and sustained them.

For the two new networks being planned with universities in Russia and Malaysia, recent changes in higher education policy and the political climate have been driving forces. In Russia, Andrey Kortunov explains that the social function of higher education in Russia has always been important. Unlike US universities that emerged after the development of a democratic political system, in Russia and other countries in the region, universities were created before political democracies matured and before civil society organizations were plentiful or strong, so universities have played an important role in harboring independent thinking and social activism. Kortunov sees a danger now in Russia and other post-Soviet countries that have undergone volcanic political transformations, as universities are forced to become "leaner and meaner," the social function could be lost. A key impetus for the New Eurasia Foundation's interest in forming a network of universities to focus on civic engagement is to try to promote and protect the social function so it won't be lost in the transformation. "We started to realize that in order to do that we have to demonstrate to universities that civic engagement is not an add-on, but a way to produce better graduates." The initial research conducted by the Foundation indicated that there are many universities with social engagement activities that have never been inventoried. Staff and faculty at universities had expressed an interest in being connected "so that universities don't feel they are lonely wires, but connected to others doing similar work and to get recognition."

In Malaysia, Saran Gill situates the interest in forming a university network in the context of both Malaysian and ASEAN policy developments. The government's New Economic Model, adopted in 2010, has as its principal goal "to enhance the quality of life for the 'rakyat' (people of the nation)." The success of this strategy will depend to a large extent on the role of universities to create a knowledge economy, development of a skilled workforce and innovative research and development. Also in 2010, the Ministry of Higher Education launched the Strategic Plan for University, Industry and Community Collaboration to support the New Economic Model. As was noted in the profile about Universiti Kebangsaan Malaysia in Part II, one of the infrastructural changes this has brought about in higher education institutions is the creation of a new position of Deputy Vice-Chancellor for Industry and Community Partnerships at five national universities. As the Chair of the new Committee of DVCs, Professor Gill plans to raise the possibility of forming an ASEAN university network for civic engagement. The ASEAN community's macro-policy framework emphasizes the need for collaboration to address challenges in social, economic, and environmental development, and provides an opening for working with the existing ASEAN

University Network and other regional bodies to develop a regional network of universities focused on civic engagement.

Independent or Not?

Each of the network leaders had to make a strategic decision about whether to start an independent network or be part of a larger organization. In the case of Campus Engage in Ireland, the decision was determined by the availability of government funding specifically for the creation of a network of universities to focus on civic engagement through an innovation fund. But now, beyond the initial funding period and with the very serious economic downturn in Ireland, they need to find new sources of funding. Eventually, this may mean the possibility of coming under the umbrella of the Irish Universities Association. But, according to McIlrath, to have been part of IUA from the beginning might have risked having civic engagement lost among a set of the Association's other agenda items. Similarly, in South Africa, the SAHECEF began as an independent forum for staff managing civic engagement portfolios, but the network has no independent funding. Slamat explains that they will seek to become a forum of Higher Education South Africa, comparable with the Registrars' Forum and the Researchers' Forum. The hope is that this will provide SAHECEF with a sustained institutional base and financial support. In Russia, Kortunov describes the need for "horizontal" networks of professionals to balance what is otherwise a vertically structured system that points upwards towards the Ministry of Education. Very few professional associations exist, and this might be a "compelling reason to create a Community-University network." Ma'an has continued to operate independently from other organizations, but has faced serious financial constraints. AUCEA in Australia has taken the route of becoming an independently incorporated organization and will have to generate financial support for its operating costs. The concern about becoming part of a larger organization is the fear of civic engagement being overshadowed by other issues on the organization's agenda. Both Slamat and McIlrath believe that an independent start was important, and once civic engagement becomes better established within universities, the risk associated with becoming part of a larger organization would be diminished.

For most of the networks described in this chapter, the decision to operate as an independent entity or as part of another organization—usually national or regional higher education associations—is linked with concerns about financial sustainability. It is clear that developing and managing a network of universities requires financial resources for, at a minimum: dedicated staff time, as well as other costs associated with communications, identification and development of resources and materials, and activities such as faculty trainings. There does not appear to be a "one size fits all" model for financing the various networks. The recently formed networks mentioned above have received funding from a variety of sources—private foundations, government, investments by the initial host university, and international organizations. AUCEA has recently adopted a membership fee structure, much like Campus Compact, after an initial substantial investment by the University of Western Sydney. Ma'an has relied on contributions of staff time from the host university, AUC, and has sought outside funding primarily from private foundations and corporations in the region. A private foundation supports *Construye País*. Campus Engage has relied heavily to date on government funding and the support of NUI Galway. GUNI is largely supported by UNESCO. The Talloires Network has received significant support from Tufts University and Innovations in Civic Participation as well as private and corporate foundations.

In the initial start-up phase, universities such as the Catholic University of Temuco, NUI Galway, American University in Cairo, Tufts University, and University of Western Sydney, and NGOs, such as Innovations in Civic Participation and CLAYSS, made substantial investments in staff time and other resources to launch the networks. Identifying and capturing ongoing resources will be more difficult. Prospects for government funding in an era of severe government cutbacks look dim, except perhaps in Malaysia. In other countries such as Egypt, government funding is not only unlikely, but perhaps unwelcome. The three most likely options for offering a degree of financial sustainability appear to be associating with a larger higher education organization, moving to a membership structure, or identifying a foundation that is willing to make multiple year contributions to running costs.

Challenges

In addition to the several factors discussed above that are facilitating higher education networks promoting civic engagement, there are significant challenges beyond the obvious issue of financial sustainability. Among the most important is the role of leadership and the challenge of surviving the inevitable change in the leadership of the individual or individuals who were responsible for initiating many of the networks described above. Many of the networks covered in the interviews were begun by charismatic individuals with a deep personal commitment to civic engagement and who either controlled resources themselves, e.g., Janice Reid at UWS, Larry Bacow at Tufts, and Mónica Jiménez at Temuco, or had a close working relationship with the head of the university to be able to marshal the support of the university head and institutional resources, e.g., Lorraine McIlrath at NUIG and Barbara Ibrahim at AUC. Changes in leadership, especially early in the life of a network, can create vulnerability about both leadership and access to resources. Inevitably, leadership, financial sustainability, and developing an institutional base for the stability of the network are inextricably linked and create a set of challenges for which there is no single or easy solution, but rather must be developed, based on idiosyncratic and contextualized circumstances.

Other challenges identified by interviewees may be prompted by their immediate circumstances, but their observations also identify common challenges to establishing civic engagement as an important and integral mission of universities in a wide variety of contexts. Beyond the immediate concern about financial sustainability, the dominant theme in the challenges described are philosophical and strategic, about how to locate civic engagement at the center of universities' missions and the ways in which civic engagement contributes to the transformation of higher education.

Jerome Slamat (SAHECEF) expresses a need to change the perception among faculty and community partners about the nature of civic engagement from thinking of it as a philanthropic activity to a one of reciprocity that respects that knowledge exists both in the university and in the community. Slamat is also concerned about building a body of knowledge about civic engagement "with a South African flavor and that stands up academically." SAHECEF is exploring establishing an independent journal to publish academic work based on university–community interactions. (AUCEA started publishing a refereed Journal in 2007 and publishes two issues per year.)

Nieves Tapia (CLAYSS) echoes Slamat's comments about where knowledge resides:

> The greatest challenge is the perception that knowledge only belongs to academics, universities and libraries. We have to change the way we hire, promote and reward faculty. We have to find ways to evaluate research and publication based on its value to society.

Tapia expresses an interest in having CLAYSS facilitate a discussion among representatives from government, universities and NGOs in the region to build a stronger base for civic engagement work in the Latin American region.

In Australia, according to Janice Reid (UWS), the main challenge is to keep the momentum for civic engagement as an engine for institutional change going:

> The rise of interest in Australia is based on the realization that the 20th century model for building new universities is now passé. We could have tried to imitate the old universities who are largely focused on research, but we wouldn't have succeeded. In the 21st century, young universities can best realize their founding missions through research and teaching strategies that, in part, are shaped by the questions, opportunities and challenges of the communities around them. Community engagement and attention to 'place' has proven to be a powerful tool for building research and teaching quality.

Membership in AUCEA hovers around 30 universities, and in 2010, AUCEA voted to accept members from New Zealand and other countries and to create an

Associate Member category for business, government, community organizations and individuals. "The legitimacy, profile and appreciation of civic engagement have lifted a lot in Australia, and AUCEA has fostered a shared community of understanding about what it is and a collective commitment."

In Russia, Andrey Kortunov (New Eurasia Foundation) sees the main challenge as responding to the changes brought about by government in the higher education sector. Like Janice Reed, he views civic engagement as a possible vehicle for transformation, but also believes that without much experience with civic engagement, more pressing issues such as economic conditions, could overwhelm the interest in civic engagement:

> The need to interact with the local community has become more pressing in the past five years. This is not a matter of good will, but survival. The government is investing heavily only in the federal universities and others will have to figure out how to survive on much more limited funding. Some universities might take a narrowly defined business approach or offer less expensive services to students, but generally speaking the outside environment is pushing them away from the ivory tower model towards more involvement.

Since there is relatively little experience with civic engagement in Russian universities, the highest priority will be sharing best practices from within Russia and other regions. "It is very important for Russian universities not to re-invent the wheel, but get involved in this global trend to increase the speed of our transformation."

Paul Manners (NCCPE) offers a very sobering view of the challenges facing universities promoting civic engagement and networks that support their collective and individual efforts:

> The most exciting revelation to me is that there is a real commitment to engagement within universities. The problem is that it is not necessarily recognized as having strategic importance to the university. There are powerful drivers around producing research income and economic value. The challenge at the moment is the policy pressures on universities to drive economic growth—these are emerging again because of the economic situation—which could sideline the engagement agenda. It doesn't have enough of a foothold to secure its future and could be abandoned when the chips are down. Universities are facing draconian cuts, and it will take confidence and vision from university leaders to continue to keep civic engagement at the center of the university's purposes.

These challenges can be viewed both as constraints, but also as an agenda for continuing action. Indeed, it is striking that several regional and global networks are addressing issues relating to community–university collaboration, the relative priority provided for civic engagement within universities, and governmental policy. These challenges and opportunities are getting attention by individual networks and also in efforts to foster collaboration among networks, as is discussed in the following section.

Growing Global Momentum

Does the fact that several regional or national networks of universities have formed in different parts of the world in the past 5–10 years provide evidence that the civic engagement agenda in higher education is gathering momentum?

Among the individuals interviewed, there is general agreement that civic engagement is finding a stronger foothold in universities around the world. The founders of the specific networks described in this chapter are all aware of developments in other countries and regions of the world, and despite the distances between the network hubs, there has been significant interaction among the principals involved with many of the networks. According to Janice Reid, "Engagement has created a new kind of dialogue among tertiary institutions." Certainly, communications technology has helped to facilitate this dialogue. It is possible to communicate easily and quickly with colleagues in most parts of the world. It has increased the speed with which we can get information and spread news. Information is not only shared among members of a network, but also across multiple networks, reinforcing the perception that civic engagement has gained in importance and visibility among higher education institutions globally.

The question about global momentum also elicited some reflections on the value of networks in facilitating change. Jerome Slamat reflects that "networks are characteristic of our time. We alone can't affect change, so we partner with others to meet various challenges." Barbara Ibrahim offers a similar observation, "The way in which social change now happens is increasingly through networks of many individuals who share interests and may never have face-to-face interaction with each other. Networks are completely well-suited to this way of engaging and making change happen."

Nieves Tapia believes there is growing global interest in higher education to be more socially engaged, but it may be for different reasons in different parts of the world. "In Africa as well as in Latin America the process of democratization and the development of more just societies is pushing universities to become more engaged in their communities. Both in Africa and Latin America, it is almost impossible to have a university that can ignore the issues that are facing communities where you live and work every day." Slamat concurs that the local context is crucial. "We see ourselves as part of a global effort, but we need to develop a body of knowledge about civic engagement with a South African flavor."

Paul Manners expressed some skepticism about whether there will ever be significant momentum for civic engagement because the incentive structures in universities is such that "there is only ever going to be a small subset of faculty who will devote the time and energy needed to do this work, especially if there is no recognition for it within the disciplines."

One of the acid tests may be the extent to which networks are ready, willing and able to work together. That, in turn, will have something to do with the "jurisdiction": the cultural and economic framework in which they work, and towards which most of their advocacy and lobbying is directed.

In September 2010, an attempt was made at the Institute of Education, London, to test out the "common cause" question by organizing a "global conversation" between seven networks: Talloires; the Pascal International Observatory; the Global Alliance on Community Engaged Research; the Living Knowledge Network; GUNI; CEBEM International; the NCCPE; Universiti Sains Malaysia; and the ACU Extension Network. After two hours of debate, the participants were able to agree the following draft communiqué, now under discussion on a worldwide scale.

> We [the participants], being *deeply concerned* with local, national and global challenges in the form of complex issues of an economic, social justice, health, cultural and sustainability nature; *taking account* of the growing interest in global higher education circles of the importance in the expansion of a support for structures, practices and policies to support community-university engagement; *respecting* previous statements of principle by each of our networks; *aware* that while there are some extremely innovative examples of community-university partnerships in the majority world, nevertheless there remains a significant imbalance for the support of community-engagement resources and structures for strengthening strategic knowledge partnerships especially in vulnerable populations and small nation-states of the global South; *supporting evidence* that the co-creation of knowledge through the engagement of our students and scholars jointly by our higher education institutions and our community partners is a critical contribution to meeting the challenges of our times; *recognizing that* knowledge is created in multiple sites including universities, communities, the private sector, civil society organizations, and social movements; *in respect* of Indigenous knowledge systems and ways of knowing and being; *understanding community-engagement to mean* respectful collaboration between institutions of higher education and their larger communities (local, regional. State, national, global) for the mutually beneficial exchange of knowledge and resources in a context of democratic partnership and reciprocity; issue the following principles as a *Call to Action*:
>
> 1. All Higher Education Institutions express a strategic commitment to public engagement as a core principle.

2. Scholars, researchers, students and communities are enabled to participate in public engagement activities through appropriate training support and opportunities.
3. Scholars, researchers, students and community are recognized and valued for their involvement with public engagement.
4. Public engagement activities are guided by the values of inclusion, mutual respect, integrity, freedom and democratic decision-making.
5. Recognition is given to and support provided for the role of non-university community-university research structures in the creation and co-creation of knowledge.
6. In the interest of achieving such global targets and world equity challenges as are expressed by the Millennium Development Goals and other such statements, that investment be strengthened to build Community–University engagement capacities especially in the global South with attention to vulnerable populations and small nation-states.
7. Rather than world ranking systems for higher education institution systems that are not effective in advancing engagement practices, we support appraisal systems such as the Alternative University Appraisal system (in collaboration with the United Nations) as development tools.

We believe that the transformative potential of our community sector organizations and our higher education institutions is enhanced when we combine our collective knowledge, global connections, skills and resources to address the myriad of social, cultural, economic, health and environmental challenges in our places and regions.

Several things are going on here, weaving in and out of the quasi-diplomatic language. One is that universities have to be part of the solution, not another part of the problem sets facing the contemporary world. Another is that the community itself—and its cultural, economic, and political setting—is going to be highly determinative of what can and should be done. Yet another is the recognition (perhaps late in the day) of a serious asymmetry in the power, influence and resulting priorities of the North and South. We turn next to this question in the light of our analysis.

8

THE WORLD UPSIDE DOWN

University Civic Engagement from the South to the North

One of the barriers we have tried to understand—if not to overcome—in this project has been the differential experience of universities in the developed and the developing world: of the contrast between "North" and "South." The centre of gravity of relevant existing scholarship (in English) in the area is firmly in the former. The dominant discourse is one of higher education as serving the community by "being there" (Watson, 2007: 132–134), of developing character and the instincts of democratic citizenship (including through "volunteering" and service learning), and of receiving in return moral and economic support for the other two legs (besides such "service") of university missions: those of teaching and research.

This may connect with a strong revival in "Northern" systems, of interest in "liberal" higher education (the Newmanesque narrative introduced in Part I above: see also Watson, 2007: 141–146). There are several sources of this:

- A recognition that life and work in the twenty-first century requires *breadth* as well as *depth* of knowledge and skills.
- An "ethical turn" in public discourse, not least in response to prominent ethical short-comings in business, professional and political life.
- A student-led redefinition of mutuality that elevates environmental and international concerns above traditional political allegiances (the now out-moded proxies for "engagement"); look, for example, at the revival of student volunteering, at the fact that a majority of UK HEIs now have students from over 100 countries, and that many have a majority of undergraduates who are bilingual).
- One consequence is that the relationship of higher education to the institutions of civil society is increasingly recognized as more important than its role

as an instrument of state policy—if we can have "soft skills" (as employers demand) we probably also need a concept of "soft citizenship"; and more practically.

• The international growth (as higher education systems become "universal" with many societies with more than 50% APRs) of second-cycle participation, moving professional formation from undergraduate to post-graduate levels.

The profiles of the Universities of Winchester and Melbourne (especially the latter's "Melbourne model" for the curriculum) show these priorities in action.

The contribution of universities to economic development is, of course, acknowledged, and indeed stressed by their advocates as an argument for investment. But the arguments can appear unidirectional, as in the theory of Technology or Knowledge Transfer, or the concept of the "multiplier effect."

A classic statement of the Northern consensus is the powerful argument by Barbara Holland for "engaged scholarship" to be added to the standard American classifications of institutional accreditation and research strategy. Ironically, this call to arms was delivered in the Southern hemisphere (in Sydney, Australia in 2005). Holland's approach is led by a re-assessment of the role of the research-intensive universities at the head of all of the categorical schemes: "some of America's most prestigious universities now see engagement as an important and relevant dimension of their agenda." For them, the competitive advantage will increasingly be about:

• developing the skills of transdisciplinary research;
• community-based research;
• making world-class research more visible locally;
• renewing a sense of 'public purpose' to universities that have lost most of their public funding;
• involving their students, from all around the world, in the local community;
• enhancing town and gown relationships;
• attracting private donor support; and
• attracting and retaining more first generation and diverse students.

Beyond these efforts in the vanguard, Holland's prescription is for a mixture of "trickle-down" effects and disciplined mission focus. For many of these (less prestigious) institutions:

> . . . consideration of the role of engagement has clarified their academic identity and scholarly agenda and dramatically enhanced their quality and performance in both teaching and research. By focusing on the alignment of academic strengths with the critical issues of their surrounding communities, these universities developed a more specific teaching and research

agenda that improved their performance as measured by student learning, retention, research productivity and improved political and financial support from community leaders and public funders. The more specific topical and purposeful focus generated by an engagement and community involvement agenda tends to give these institutions a clear sense of mission, academic values and a vision for excellence that they previously lacked.

(Holland, 2005)

Meanwhile the relationship between the universities of the North and South also appears substantively unidirectional, with, for example, most partnerships emphasizing assistance or aid of various kinds. In other words, it is yet another field which confirms the thesis of Raewyn Connell's powerful work *Southern Theory* that (following the French anthropologist Louis Dumont), "social science can only have one, universal, body of social theory, the one created in the global North" (Connell, 2007: ix). One of the popular items in gift shops in Australia and New Zealand is the globe or map with the axes reversed, and the South Pole at the top of the page.

A similar concern informs the work of the sociocultural anthropologist Arjun Appadurai. He contrasts in particular the discourse about globalization inside and outside the academy. In contrast to the competitive positioning of disciplines against the inexorable erosion of their historical "product differentiation," in the outside world the priorities are quite different:

> In the public spheres of many societies there is concern that policy debates occurring around world trade, copyright, environment, science and technology set the stage for life-and-death decisions for ordinary farmers, vendors, slum-dwellers, merchants and urban populations. And running through these debates is the sense that social exclusion is ever more tied to epistemic exclusion and concern that the discourses of expertise that are setting the rules for global transactions, even in the most progressive parts of the international system have left ordinary people outside and behind.

(Appadurai, 2000: 2)

In the course of our fieldwork, in particular, we have been able to probe what a distinctively "Southern" view of university civic and community engagement consists of. In this sense, we wish to add weight to Connell's drive for the "new configurations of knowledge that result when Southern theory is everywhere respected, and differently formed theories speak together" (Connell, 2007: xiv), as well as Appadurai's call for the understanding of "globalization from below" ("it means stepping back from those obsessions and abstractions that constitute our own professional practice to seriously consider the problems of the global everyday"; Appadurai, 2000: 17–18).

In embarking on this analysis, we acknowledge that none of us (the authorial team) is from, or currently has primary employment in, the South. We also wish to stress the rather specific interdisciplinary lens through which we are approaching the issue. Our primary concern in this book is with university strategies for the three "legs" of teaching, research, and service, and how they are implemented, with special emphasis on engagement with the community and the institutions of civil society. We are not qualified or aiming to contribute to the technical field of how higher education contributes to objective development, or the field of Development Studies in general. Nonetheless, we do regard this rather special lens as valuable and provocative.

From the perspective of the engaged university, the following elements seem important in any understanding of the "global everyday":

- There is apparently an inverse relationship between external national power and internal power of governments over their institutions: "autonomy" may be seen as something of a Northern luxury. As they become more powerful, the BRIC economies (Brazil, Russia, India, and China) may require this thesis to be amended. The last decade saw the BRICs make their mark on the global economic landscape. Over the past 10 years they have contributed over one-third of world GDP growth and grown from one-sixth of the world economy to almost one-quarter (in PPP terms). Looking forward to the coming decade, we expect this trend to continue and become even more pronounced (Goldman Sachs, 2010).
- Social, political and especially economic circumstances loom larger as both priorities and constraints for institutions. There is an immediacy about imperatives such as the alleviation of poverty, the eradication of disease, and the identity of nations and their component parts.
- There are more pressing demands for both professional and vocational training on the one hand and "translational" research on the other.
- The influence of and exposure to international agencies (both "official" and independent, is high). "Aid" is an inescapable, although highly nuanced part of the picture.
- In certain circumstances, academic and institutional freedoms are under threat or pressure from state or establishment power (including instances of straightforward corruption).
- In many respects, the model of a global header tank rules with the North in control of competitive markets and the distribution of opportunities (for example, in terms of the "brain drain" of skilled professionals from the South to the North).

Building on these, can a "Southern" perspective add to or revise creatively the set of "grand narratives" of university histories, or the mix of "capitals" set out in our introductory section?

Of our profiles, only three are unambiguously "of the North": Georgetown, Portland, and Winchester, and these all emphasize solidarity with the developing world. Thirteen are "of the South" both geographically and in terms of strategic priorities. These include: two of the Australian cases (CDU and GWS); the three African universities (CPUT, Dar es Salaam); the three Latin American cases (Monterrey, Sipán and Caracas); the Asia cases of UKM (Malaysia) and Marbel (Philippines); SNDT and Aga Khan from the sub-continent; and Al –Quds in the Middle East. The remaining four sit in a fascinating "transitional zone." Melbourne—our highest rated university in terms of "world-class prestige"—for all its comparators with the European and North American elite, has to play its part in responding to Australian Aboriginal priorities and its government's Asian agenda. It is a Northern university in a Southern skin. Haifa has a similar split personality, seen as an "outlier" within its own system in its concern for social justice for Arabs, nationally and regionally. The Open University is transforming its pioneering status in technology-enabled access into a position on the world stage: it is the UK (and probably Europe's) most genuinely "global" university. It is becoming a Southern university with its headquarters in a Northern garden. (Dar es Salaam also exhibits "transitional" features: in its search for rehabilitation it emphasizes Northern success factors, but the pull of its Southern operational context is irresistible.)

Exploring these profiles has led us to an improved understanding of differing perspectives: from the North; from the South; and in the transitional zone. Here are 11 areas in which our investigation (of 20 cases worldwide) would suggest that the Southern experience of university–community engagement is emphatically different:

- The relative lack of a "comfort zone";
- The drive for "transformation" or "solidarity";
- The priority of "development" (or social returns) over "character" (or individual returns), and of "national cohesion" over personal enrichment;
- A strong focus on human capital, and "employment" over "employability";
- Circumstances where "necessity trumps choice," and investment in HE is seen as more than a consumer good;
- The use of private bodies for public purposes;
- The use of international partnerships for assistance not "positioning";
- Fewer hang-ups about the instrumentality of the "vocational curriculum";
- A higher likelihood of acceptance that religion and science should work in harmony (this is not to say that the dilemmas of the modern Enlightenment university in strongly religious societies are absent);
- A very practical world of "Mode 2" engagement, alongside Mode 2 research and teaching; and above all—
- A sense of societal pull over institutional push.

Each of the elements is worth exploring in more detail on the basis of what we have learned.

Comfort Zones

The crude and obvious point is that it is more dangerous in the South. Our profiles draw attention, for example, to universities dealing with civil war in Sudan, the racial dimensions of political conflict in the new South Africa, the urban spaces in which the universities are trying to work (this is, of course, also true of Washington).

Political Priorities

The dangers can come from those you view as your allies and supporters as well as those representing the problems you are trying to overcome. Hegemonic priorities like "transformation" (in South Africa) or "solidarity" (a Latin American term of art) can loom very large.

Character or Development

In these circumstances, the liberal emancipationist goal of higher education as a form of individual self-realization (albeit it with strong but secondary "social" implications), may appear a luxury. Not that this point escapes some critics in the North and West. As Romand Coles puts the point in a contribution to a discussion of "values" in the modern American University:

> What does teaching 'values' mean, when many of these values are often articulated in ways that are complicit with this system of power/suffering, or relatively silent about it, or incapable of disturbing the production of deafening indifference or lead only to the occasional trip to the soup kitchen on the way to the oblivious high-paying job in the corporate firm?
>
> *(Coles, 2010: 224)*

Human Capital

"Development" priorities also cohere around certain sets of skills. It is no accident that the popularity of scientific and technological subjects remains high here (see below), while students in the North and West have led the system in migrating towards the service and creative economies.

Necessity Over Choice

There is also a sense that more is being done with less. In the North there is a not always attractive connection with arguments about autonomy and special pleading for resources. Urgent priorities (which might include aspects of community engagement) are seen as vital, but also as "extras," support from which is sought through philanthropy or through public or government funding on a project basis (or in the English phrase, a "special initiative"). Meanwhile, as a team, we were constantly struck in our Southern cases, by how much was being done by universities for the community with so little resources (and with relatively little complaint).

Empanelling the Private Sector

We also see (sometimes enforced—as in Venezuela) use of the private sector for public purposes. There is also a highly pragmatic willingness to use the private sector of higher education to play its part within coordinated strategies for development through higher education. The role of the NGO (or "third sector" of "non-governmental organizations") is likely to be more strongly mandated (if rarely funded) through public channels rather than acting as a classical buffer between communities and the state.

International Partnerships

International agencies are used, as far as possible, strategically. So, too, are relationships with other universities. The collection in this series edited by Roberta Malee Bassett and Alma Maldonado-Maldonado includes a wide-ranging analysis of the interlocking roles within higher education in the developing world of global institutions like UNESCO and the World Bank, Foundations (especially US-based) and a variety of other donor organizations (Bassett and Maldonado-Maldonado, 2009: 29–63, 99–112, 229–299).

A fundamental issue is whether or not higher education systems from the richer North and West are serious about reviving their historical role in assisting the development of systems elsewhere in the world, even if that means overcoming some of the features of "colonial" sponsorship. The recent, and current, very heavy emphasis of the global market for students, both travelling to the countries of major providers (historically USA, the UK and Australia) and participating in "transnational" arrangements (such as branch campuses and locally supported distance learning), has been affected not only by the global recession but also by a drive to develop (with assistance if available) indigenous provision.

Religion and Science

Our group of 20 institutions include several with specifically religious foundations, which in most cases they are seeking to enhance (and modernize) rather than to suppress (or apologize for). This in no sense reduces their commitments to play a full part in a global community of academic inquiry (Tec de Monterrey, for example, strives to break loose of religious models of charity in their engagement work). It also reflects the association with communities that define themselves through religious solidarity.

Vocational Courses and Translational Research

All of this influences both the curriculum and research priorities. In the North, there is a general moral panic about the decline of interest in scientific and technological studies (many university departments in these subjects are kept alive by recruitment of students from overseas). A report from the Nuffield Foundation points to a negative correlation between objective "development" and enthusiasm for science and technology (Nuffield Foundation, 2008). In the South "practical subjects" and "applied" research (especially the variety of research-informed practice that the surgeon Atul Gawande calls "the science of performance" (Gawande, 2008: 231–248) are at the very top of the priority tree.

Mode 2

To put it to a use for which it was probably never intended, all of this betokens a "Mode 2" world of civic and community engagement. This powerful formulation of trends in knowledge production (set out in the table below) was originally aimed at improving our understanding of the process of research. Later, its relevance for learning and teaching became apparent. Now and especially in a Southern context it seems directly applicable to the way in which communities and their universities work together.

Pull Over Push

Above all it is clear that the institutions are not in the driving seat, in a way that they claim to be in the North and West. The dialogue between governments (and

TABLE 8.1 Mode 1 and Mode 2

Mode 1	Mode 2
Pure	Applied
Disciplinary	Problem-centered
Homogeneous	Transdisciplinary
Expert-led	Heterogeneous
Supply-driven	Hybrid
Hierarchical	Demand-driven
Peer-reviewed	Entrepreneurial
University-based	Network-embedded

Based on Gibbons et al. (1994).

funders) on the one hand and institutions on the other may be more directive by the former, but it may also represent a stronger sense of alignment of interests.

The contrasts should not be overdrawn. Northern societies have their own crises, of poverty and of social justice, and universities claim to play a role in their exposure and alleviation. Nor should there be any romanticization of a Southern battle for liberation when it creates victims as well as objective progress.

There are other potential challenges to the thesis. Is it more about relative prosperity than anything else (or will the South become inevitably more North-like as it develops)? Are some of the role models inescapable (as in the aping of metropolitan institutions during the colonial era or the current obsession with world-classness)? Are university systems able (finally) to "leap-frog" eras of institutional higher education development as they have waves of technology (as in the "one-step" move to Wi-Fi and mobile telephony)?

Does "Southern"-style engagement represent a narrowing of academic vision, or a lowering of expectations for participants (staff and students)? On balance, and in response to this final challenge, we would say not. We are persuaded that the Southern model of university–community engagement represents a rich and fruitful addition to the available models, mixes of intellectual capital and narratives in the field, and we hope that we have made some useful ground in trying to describe it.

9

IMPLICATIONS FOR POLICY AND PRACTICE

We have reflected on practical lessons that can be drawn from our research. Some of these are directed at policymakers; some relate to internal management of institutions; and a third set defy such classification—they relate to the complex set of relationships that apply on the border between universities, colleges and their communities.

Aspects of Policy

Government Policies

Our research shows that government policies can have a substantial impact on university civic engagement—through mandates, and through incentives and exhortation. The positive experience to date of several countries should encourage other nations to consider adopting such policies as requiring that all university students complete a specified amount of volunteer service and as making civic engagement a positive criterion in decision-making processes with respect to governmental funding for research and other programs.

A dilemma that arises is the disconnection between governments' desires for some or all of "their" universities to be "world-class" and the priorities they set for them in other fields. What counts in the tables (like research citations and self-evaluation by members of academic fields) is the opposite of most of the features that governments say they want from "their" institutions (like high teaching quality, contributions to social justice, and entrepreneurialism).

Funding and Sustainability

Another major governmental influence is the extent and terms of financial support. This is a particularly important factor, since so many institutions of higher education around the world are public institutions, ones that are funded primarily by public monies. Public sector support is a story of painful cross-pressures—on the one hand, of massive pressures to expand enrollment and of growing societal expectations that the higher education sector directly address pressing societal problems, yet on the other hand, these expectations are rarely accompanied by proportionate increases in public investment. The global engaged universities movement has a shared opportunity to build and communicate more persuasively the case for sustained and increased public investment.

Financial resources are a positive, and essential, ingredient for successful university civic engagement and social responsibility programming. All of the institutions that participated in this study have invested in and/or attracted significant funding in order to develop and to maintain their work. While a near-universal refrain is that financial constraints are a serious limiting factor, the level of financial support with which they operate varies dramatically. Several of the participating institutions have built and maintain impressive programs and impacts with comparatively low budgets.

These universities evidence a considerable variety of sources of financial support—including student fees; core institutional budget allocations; grants and contracts from public agencies, private foundations, and individuals; and international agency grants and contracts. It is in the common interest of proponents of the engaged university to affect positively the future levels of support from these various sources. This is a consideration for individual colleges and universities, and also is one that collective action has the special potential to address. A challenge that accompanies the question of source of financial support is "accountability." What do these funders expect in return for their investment? In what ways does their support either reinforce or deflect university policies and programs?

University civic engagement activities can amplify and reinforce the work of other sectors—governmental, philanthropic, non-governmental, and private business. The willingness of these diverse sources to invest indicates that they believe this to be the case. The overall level of financial support for university civic and social responsibility seems modest in relation to its impressive impacts on student learning outcomes, knowledge development, and community conditions. The growing success of university civic engagement programs provides a solid rationale for greater investment.

At many of the institutions, their civic and social responsibility work is well-established and there is every reason to predict that it will be sustained, but this is not always the case. In some instances, budgetary cutbacks have caused institutions to reduce their civic programming. These experiences are a reminder that the civic and social responsibility dimensions are comparatively young and they are vulnerable to changing economic realities. In other words, sustainability is the key challenge—one that cannot be taken for granted.

Aspects of Management

At the same time, there are contending goals at work in relation to the influence and impact of institutions on their environment on the one hand and on the learning and personal development of their students on the other. These can be made to align, but will often require specific interventions to make them do so.

A related problem concerns benchmarking and measurement. The search for truly effective, generalizable metrics for civic and community engagement activity and impact goes on (see, for example, Hart et al., 2009). At present, a lot of effort is going into classifying and counting, but not much into the hardest institutional research (or self-study) question: not "How good are we, compared with the rest? But "How good could, or should we be?"

Leadership

Our profiles document the power of individual and collective leadership. They show how individuals and small groups—of heads of institutions, professors, students, and community partners—can make a decisive difference in university civic engagement. The implication of this finding is that the leaders and potential leaders are out there; they just need concerted support in order to be fully successful. Leadership elements and strategies that are effective in this realm include vision, coalition-building and collaboration. Leaders also have to ensure the continuity and sustainability of their ideas. Our profiles include some good examples of this in practice, particularly through the encouragement and development of successors.

Faculty Incentives

A key conclusion that emerges from this study is that low or non-existent rewards and incentives for faculty to do civic engagement and social responsibility work are a major brake on this area of university activity around the world. This is a problem for several reasons. First, it obviously holds back the civic work of higher education. But second, it is important to come to terms with other implications as well. There is growing evidence that university civic engagement enhances the quality of education, improves community conditions, and elevates public support for higher education. Each of these consequences directly affects the well-being and self-interests of universities. Therefore, faculty rewards and incentives should be a priority for innovation.

On the brighter side, some of the institutions that we studied have begun to assess and provide credit for professors' civic activities, even though the incentives that are provided in those institutions are modest in comparison to those that are related to research and teaching. Therefore, one area of opportunity may be to learn from and build upon the experience of these pioneering institutions. We recommend documenting how these policies operate and what impacts they have in those institutions. In addition, these institutions could be encouraged to exert leadership by elevating the extent to which civic engagement performance is weighted in their reviews of faculty members' performance.

There are potential steps that government agencies and public and private funders of higher education can consider in order to address this challenge. When funders increase their support for professors' community and public service projects, they powerfully reinforce that work and can indirectly advance the prospects for changing institutional rewards systems as well. In addition, funders and regulators could consider requiring or encouraging greater civic engagement activity and results, as a condition for the provision of core operating support and/or scholarship aid to university students.

Another approach that holds promise is to integrate civic engagement work with research and teaching, so that it can be rewarded as part of professors' performance in research and teaching rather than only as a separate category of endeavor. A related strategy can be to grow and to publicize examples of professors whose civic and social responsibility work has been a route to exceptionally strong teaching and to significant advances in the development of knowledge. At each of the institutions in this study, there are faculty members who are recognized leaders in community work and who also are highly respected for their scholarship and teaching. Expanding the number of these teacher–scholar–civic leaders, and supporting and publicizing their leadership, can, over time, change the culture of the academy.

Organizational Structure

An important lesson from the institutions in this study is the powerful positive impact that can be achieved by creating and supporting a high-level position and office to lead and coordinate the institution's civic engagement and social responsibility. The organizational approach to organizing such a role that is most effective for a given institution will be very much the result of its individual circumstances. At the University of Haifa, establishment of the new position of Advisor for Social Responsibility to the President yielded impressive benefits while the position was operational. At Universiti Kebangsaan Malaysia, the national government mandated the creation the office of Deputy Vice-Chancellor for Industry and Community Partnerships, which is dramatically elevating the institution's community service activities. Another strategy that is proving to be successful in several universities—including Tec de Monterrey, Cape Peninsula University of

Technology, Georgetown University and Portland State University—is establishment of a center with responsibility for coordinating civic and social responsibility programs across the university, providing training to students and faculty, administering seed grants, brokering and maintaining community partnerships, and leading the development of new programs and policies.

A universal challenge is to evolve an organizational approach with maximal institution-wide impact and one that avoids the "separate center" syndrome that can concentrate institutional responsibility and capabilities in one place, limiting the role and potential of other parts of the university. A second challenge is to provide adequate financial and other forms of support. Doing excellent civic and social responsibility work does not require vast staff, but it this is complicated work and some of it is reasonably labor-intensive. Because it is important, it needs to be supported adequately.

Operating on the Boundary: The Place of Partnerships

The civic engagement and social responsibility activities of many of the participating institutions have benefited substantially from the extent and quality of their collaborations with other institutions, including development assistance agencies, governmental agencies, NGOs, private businesses, public services, and other universities. The success of these partnering strategies suggests that this approach is an area of significant opportunity for universities that aim to strengthen their civic work, as well as for other actors that wish to influence higher education to move in this direction.

Our 20 institutional profiles document the central importance of community partnerships to university civic engagement. In addition, they demonstrate a range of approaches and principles for the effective development and maintenance of partnerships. Lessons include the importance of: committing to real two-way collaboration, supporting skilled personnel whose primary job is to foster and strengthen partnerships, investing in building the capacity of both university and community representatives to be effective collaborators, and focusing on building and sustaining long-term partnerships. One of our participating universities, Portland State University, is making community partnerships a major focus of research, training, and policy advocacy. The field has a golden opportunity to support this initiative and to encourage several other universities in different parts of the world to do likewise.

The participating institutions have also demonstrated a spectrum of engagement with international agencies, philanthropic bodies and alliances of higher education institutions. This spread of experience is, according to our evidence, highly pragmatic. Some will seek resources, with as few constraining strings as possible. Others will be in search of reputational enhancement (the power of "positive association"); and still others will aim for mutual learning, and contributions to relevant research.

More Research is Needed

While this study adds to the collective knowledge base on the topic, there are many important questions that it has not fully answered. The higher education civic engagement movement has been long on rhetoric, yet short on evidence. In order for the field to advance—to guide the future decision-making of individual institutions, and also to attract the support that is required in order to sustain and expand their civic missions—we need to develop a much stronger factual foundation of information about results and alternative strategies. Among the topics that need further study are:

- *Impacts on learning.* There is an urgent need to know more about the central question: What do college and university students learn as a result of the civic and social responsibility policies and programs of their institutions? How and why? Furthermore, because these activities aim to improve community conditions, it is essential to know more about their actual impacts on those conditions—on poverty, public health, and so forth. The methodological barriers to answering these questions are daunting, but this should not keep us from working harder and more systematically to assess impacts.
- *Effectiveness of alternative civic engagement strategies.* What are the alternative approaches to developing and operating civic and social responsibility programs, and what is their comparative effectiveness?
- *The experience of colleges and universities with low civic engagement and social responsibility.* Why are some institutions less engaged? And what are the consequences of lower engagement? It is not enough to study only high engagement models.

This last injunction can apply in particular to this study, centered as it is on 20 representatives of a self-selecting group of "striving" institutions. However, we hope that their experience—in a wide variety of contexts, and with differing assets and resources—has helped to map the conceptual field, and to encourage others to follow.

APPENDIX 1

Institutional Questionnaire

The questionnaire aims to address the following five issues:

1. clarifying the institution's historical and mission-based commitments to its host society;
2. identifying how engagement informs and influences the institution's range of operations;
3. describing how the institution is organized to meet the challenge of civic engagement and social responsibility;
4. assessing the contribution of staff, students and external partners to the engagement agenda; and
5. monitoring achievements, impacts, constraints and future opportunities for civic engagement and social responsibility.

If any of the questions below do not fit the context or realities of your institution, please skip or modify them to be more appropriate.

1. Mission and History

The following questions ask you to describe how the origins and development of your institution incorporate commitments to address challenges that face your society and community, including the development of the region and locality.

1.1. What relevant objectives are set for the institution in its founding document (charter or equivalent)?
1.2. What relevant expectations are held by those who fund your work and support it (including politically)?

1.3. Which external groups are represented ex officio and de facto on the institution's governance or senior management bodies?

1.4. To whom does the institution regard itself as accountable for its civic mission? For example, is there a "stakeholder group" such as a University Court, and if so, how does this work?

1.5. Are civic engagement and social responsibility objectives (as defined by answers to question 1.1 above) specified in the institution's strategic plan? If so, how, and with what indicators of success?

1.6. How has the institution's engagement agenda changed over time and why?

1.7. How do governmental policies affect the institution's civic engagement and social responsibility work?

2. Balance of Activities

The following questions investigate how your institution's pattern of activities reflects a civic engagement and social responsibility agenda.

2.1. Give a brief assessment of the chief economic and social needs of your society, region and/or locality.

2.2. How does the institution's teaching profile (by subject and level, and including continuous professional development (CPD) and lifelong learning) reflect the needs of the society, local community and region? To what extent does the curriculum incorporate relevant features of the following:

   a. structured and assessed work experience and/or work-based learning;
   b. "service learning"; and/or
   c. prior or concurrent informal work experience?

   2.2.1. How can representatives of the local, regional and national economy and community influence curriculum and other choices?

2.3. What proportion of the institution's research activity is directed towards the needs of the local, regional, and national economy and society?

   2.3.1. How can representatives of the local, regional, and national economy and community influence research priorities?

2.4. How would the institution describe its service objectives (i.e. its commitments to business and the community)?

   2.4.1. How can representatives of the local, regional and national economy and community influence activities in this area?

2.5. Using as a proxy an estimate of staff time (academic and support), how far is engagement in each of the areas outlined in this section (teaching, research, and service) directed towards:

    a. large business and industrial interests (including global and national organizations present in the region);
    b. small and medium-sized enterprises;
    c. other public services (e.g. education, health, social services);
    d. the voluntary sector, community groups and NGOs; and
    e. cultural and artistic organizations?

2.6. Does the institution have any other policies (e.g. on environmental responsibility, equality of opportunity, recruitment, procurement of goods and services), which can act positively or negatively on the society, region and the locality?

3. Organization

The following questions seek to understand how your institution organizes itself and deploys its resources (including human resources) to meet civic objectives.

3.1. Does the institution have specialized services to meet civic and related objectives (e.g. web-based resources, business advisory services, help-desks, formal consultancy and related services)?

3.2. Does the institution have either dedicated or shared services which are community-facing (such as libraries, performance or exhibition spaces, and sports facilities)?

3.3. On what terms and with what frequency and volume of uptake are the institution's campus or campuses accessible to the community?

3.4. What arrangements are made for the security of the members, guests, and property of the institution?

3.5. How much financial support does your institution allocate to its civic and social responsibility activities? What is the source(s) of these funds?

3.6. Does your institution collaborate with other organizations in planning and conducting its civic engagement and social responsibility work (for example, community partner agencies, higher education associations)? With which other organizations and how does it collaborate?

4. People

The following questions will help to describe how policies and practice involve members of the institution including staff at various levels, students and formal partners in achieving goals related to civic engagement and social responsibility.

4.1. Who takes primary responsibility for the institution's work in civic engagement and social responsibility as defined in response to question 1.5 (above)?

4.2. Does the institution's policy for student recruitment have a local or a regional dimension? If so, how is this determined and what impact does it have on the make-up of the institution community?

4.3. To what extent are civic engagement and social responsibility objectives built into contractual terms for, and evaluation of:

    a. senior managers;

    b. academic staff; and

    c. support staff (including the specialized staff referred to in question 3.1 above)?

4.4. Reflecting on the answer to question 2.2 (above), how far is the student body engaged in the economic and cultural life of the community through formal requirements?

4.5. What proportion of the student body (for example, postgraduate or post-experience students) is concurrently in full-time local or regionally-based employment?

4.6. What encouragement is there for members of staff to undertake aspects of community service (e.g. service on boards of other organizations, pro bono advice, elected political office)?

4.7. What is the extent of student volunteering in the community, and how is this organized? Does it attract:

    a. formal support (e.g. timetable concessions, payment of expenses); and/or

    b. academic credit?

5. Monitoring, Evaluation, Impacts, and Communication

The following questions seek to understand how your institution sets objectives and targets for civic engagement and social responsibility, monitors and evaluates achievement, and communicates both their intentions and related activities.

5.1. What steps does the institution take to consult upon and publicize its civic engagement and social responsibility agenda? (It may be helpful to review such publications as Annual Reports, newsletters and alumni communications.)

5.2. What do you regard as the level of public confidence held at the national, regional and local level in the overall performance of your institution? What steps can be taken either to maintain or improve this level?

5.3. How successful is the institution's civic engagement and social responsibility work? What are, or have been, its most effective engagement activities?

5.4. What factors have supported and reinforced the institution's engagement activities and how? What factors have limited or obstructed this work, and how?

5.5. What are the institution's future plans with respect to civic engagement and social responsibility?

APPENDIX 2

Field Research Questions

Administration

1. What do you understand by higher education civic engagement?
2. How high a priority is this work for you compared to other university functions?
3. What are the specific goals that you're trying to achieve through this work?
4. What are the key influences that determine what you do in this area?
5. What is your own evaluation of the progress that you have made?
6. What are the things that have helped and hindered you in these developments?
7. Who are the key stakeholders in this area, and how do you think your work is regarded by them?
8. How do you see this work developing into the future?

Senior Staff Responsible for Relevant Policies and Programs

1. What do you understand by higher education civic engagement?
2. What is your role in relation to civic engagement work and how did you come to take it up?
3. How is the university organized to achieve this work?
4. What are the key civic engagement activities and how do they relate to other university functions, e.g. teaching and research?
5. Who is involved in these activities?
6. What factors have helped and hindered you in these developments?
7. How do you see this work developing into the future?

Academic Staff

1. What do you understand by higher education civic engagement?
2. What is your role within the university and how does this relate to civic engagement?
3. How much do you value this work, and how much do you think it is valued by the institution?
4. What are the specific goals that you're trying to achieve through this work?
5. How do you see this work developing into the future?
6. What factors have helped and hindered you in these developments?

Community Partners

1. What do you understand by higher education civic engagement?
2. Describe your relationship with the university and what it is you're trying to achieve together.
3. What is the value to your objectives of partnering with the university?
4. Who resources the work and how?
5. What factors have helped and hindered you in these developments?

Students

1. What do you understand by higher education civic engagement?
2. Please describe your field of study and your involvement in civic engagement.
3. Why are you involved in civic engagement activities and what are you trying to achieve?
4. How much do you value this work, and how much do you think it is valued by the institution?
5. What factors have helped and hindered you in these developments?

BIBLIOGRAPHY

Accreditation and Quality Assurance Commission (2008) "Description of Organization/ Agency." Available at: www.aqac.mohe.gov.ps/ (Accessed January 27, 2009).

Ahier, J., Beck, J., and Moore, R. (2002) *Graduate Citizens? Issues of Citizenship and Higher Education*, London: Routledge Falmer.

Albornoz, O. (2003) "Venezuelan Higher Education: The Trend toward State Control," *International Higher Education*. No. 31. Spring 2003. Available at: www. bc.edu/bc_org/avp/soe/cihe/newsletter/News31/text009.htm (Accessed December 29, 2008).

Albornoz, O. and Jiménez, E. (2007) "Managing contradictions: the University Under a Radical Political View," paper presented to the 29th Annual EAIR Forum, August 26–29, 2007, Innsbruck. Available at: www.nano.ua.ac.be/download.aspx?c=*TEW HI&n=57322&ct=55843&e=145431 (Accessed December 29, 2008).

Al-Quds University (2007) "Annual Report 2006–2007: Facts and Figures." Available at: www.alquds.edu/factbook/annual_report_0607.pdf (Accessed January 27, 2009).

Al-Quds University (2008) "Overview." Available at: www.alquds.edu/gen_info/index. php?page=overview (Accessed January 27, 2009).

Al-Quds University in Facts and Figures: University Annual Report (2008–2009). Available at: www.alquds.edu/images/stories/annual-reports/annual_report_0809_ draft.pdf (Accessed September 10, 2010).

Al-Quds University Office of Research (2001) "Facts and Figures." Available at: www. alquds.edu/factbook/factbook2001.pdf (January 27, 2009).

Appadurai, A. (2000) "Grassroots Globalization and the Research Imagination," *Public Culture*, 12: 1–19.

Asia One (2010) "What Ails Higher Education in India?" June 16, 2010. Available at: http://news.asiaone.com/News/Education/Story/A1Story20100616-222362.html (Accessed June 16, 2010).

Association of Commonwealth Universities (ACU) (2002) Engagement As a Core Value for the University: A Consultation Document, London: ACU.

Australian Government Department of Education, Employment and Workplace Relations

(2008) "Higher Education Summary." Available at: www.dest.gov.au/sectors/higher_education/ (Accessed December 12, 2008).

Altbach, P. (2002) *Global Perspectives on Higher Education*, Teipei: Sense.

Azam, M. and Blom, A. (2008) "Progress in Participation in Tertiary Education in India from 1983 to 2004." World Bank, December 2008. Available at: www-wds.worldbank. org/external/default/WDSContentServer/WDSP/IB/2008/12/09/000158349_20081209111153/Rendered/PDF/WPS4793.pdf (Accessed January 6, 2009).

Banajai, S. (2008) "The Trouble with Civic: a Snapshot of Young People's Civic and Political Engagements in Twenty-First-Century Democracies," *Journal of Youth Studies*, 11: 543–560.

Baribeau, S. (2006) "Loans To Grants: University Funding Plan for a New Venezuela." Venezuelanalysis. Available at: www.venezuelanalysis.com/analysis/1758 (Accessed December 29, 2008).

Bassett, R. and Maldonado-Maldonado, A. (2009) *International Organization and Higher Education Policy: Thinking Globally, Acting Locally*, New York and London: Routledge.

Batool, Z. and Qureshi, R. H. (2006) "Quality Assurance Manual for Higher Education in Pakistan." Higher Education Commission Pakistan. Available at: http://hec.gov. pk/components/com_bnvcontent/images/resources/2724_2249_qaulity-assurance-manual-for-higher-education-in-pakistan%5B1%5D.pdf (Accessed July 10, 2009).

BBC News (2008) "Country Profile: Indonesia," 7 August, 2008. Available at: http://news.bbc.co.uk/2/hi/asia-pacific/country_profiles/1260544.stm (Accessed January 30, 2009).

BBC News (2008) "Country Profile: Malaysia," 22 October, 2008. Available at: http://news.bbc.co.uk/2/hi/asia-pacific/country_profiles/1304569.stm (Accessed January 30, 2009).

BBC News (2008) "Country Profile: The Philippines," 23 August, 2008. Available at: http://news.bbc.co.uk/2/hi/asia-pacific/country_profiles/1262783.stm (Accessed January 29, 2009).

BBC News (2008) "Tense Karachi Returns to Normal," 2 December 2008. Available at: http://news.bbc.co.uk/2/hi/south_asia/7759980.stm (Accessed July 10, 2009).

Beddington, J., Cooper, C., Field, J., Goswami, U., Huppert, F., Jenkins, R., Jones, H., Kirkwood, T., Sahakian, B., and Thomas, S. (2008) "The Mental Wealth of Nations," *Nature*, 455: 1057–1060.

Ben-Ze'ev, A. and Ben-Artzi, Y. (2008) "Report of the President and the Rector," University of Haifa. Available at: www.haifa.ac.il/html/html_eng/ANNUAL_ENGLISH. pdf (Accessed January 9, 2009).

Bjarnson, S. and Coldstream, P. (2003) *The Idea of Engagement: Universities in Society*, London: Association of Commonwealth Universities.

Blair, T. (2008) "An Alliance of Values," *International Herald Tribune*, December 19: 8.

Bloom, D., Canning, D., and Chan, K. (2006) "Higher Education and Economic Development in Africa." Human Development Sector. Available at: www.arp.harvard.edu/AfricaHigherEducation/Reports/BloomAndCanning.pdf (Accessed September 23, 2010).

Brennan, J., Burton, A., and Lawi, Y. (eds.) (2007) *Dar es Salaam: Histories from an Emerging African Metropolis*, Chapter 1. Available at: http://eprints.soas.ac.uk/3189/1/Brennan_%26_Burton_chapter.pdf. (Accessed September 9, 2010).

Brown, G. (2004) *Britishness*, London: The British Council.

Brown, D. and Gaventa, J. (2009) "Constructing Transnational Action Research Networks: Observations and Reflections from the Case of the Citizenship DRC," Citizenship DRC, Working Paper No. 32. Sussex: Institute of Development Studies.

Butters, L. J., Quiroga, L. B., and Dammert, P. L. (2005) "Internationalization of Higher Education in Argentina." In: Hans de Wit, Isabel Cristina Jaramillo, et al. (eds.) *Higher Education in Latin America: The International Dimension*, The World Bank. Available at: http://siteresources.worldbank.org/EXTLACREGTOPEDUCATION/Resources/Higher_Ed_in_LAC_Intnal_Dimension.pdf (Accessed March 17, 2009).

Campus Compact (2010) "Who We Are." Available at: http://www.compact.org/about/history-mission-vision/ (Accessed July 14, 2010).

Carnegie Foundation for the Advancement of Teaching (2010) "Classifications." Carnegie Foundation for the Advancement of Teaching. 2010. Available at: http://classifications.carnegiefoundation.org/ (Accessed July 14, 2010).

Census 2001. *Statistics South Africa*. Available at: www.statssa.gov.za/census01/html/default.asp (Accessed August 12, 2010).

Census of India. Office of the Registrar General (2001) "Census GIS Household." Available at: www.censusindiamaps.net/page/Religion_WhizMap1/housemap.htm (Accessed July 13, 2010).

Centre of Rural Development (2007) Shreemati Nathibai Damodar Thackersey Women's University. Available at: http://sndt.digitaluniversity.ac/Content.aspx?ID=877 (Accessed July 14, 2010).

Central Bureau of Statistics (2008) "Statistical Abstract of Israel," No. 59. Available at: www1.cbs.gov.il/reader/shnatonenew_site.htm (Accessed January 8, 2009).

Charter of Ukrainian Universities (2009) Mykolayiv. Available at: http://217.77.213.42/

Chiang, L. (2004) "The Relationship between University Autonomy and Funding in England and Taiwan," *Higher Education*, 48:189–212.

CIA (2010) *The World Factbook* Available at: www.cia.gov/library/publications/the-world-factbook/ (Accessed July 14, 2010).

City District Government Karachi (2007) "Geography and Demography." Available at: http://221.132.118.186/cdgk/Home/AboutKarachi/GeographyDemography/tabid/270/Default.aspx (Accessed September 9, 2010).

Clark, T. (2006) "OECD Review of Tertiary Education, Country Report: UK," Organization for Economic Cooperation and Development. Available at: www.oecd.org/dataoecd/22/3/37211152.pdf (Accessed December 11, 2008).

Coles, R. (2010) "Hunger, Ethics and the University: A Radical Democratic Goad in Ten Pieces." In: Kiss, E. and Euben, P. (eds.) *Debating Moral Education: Rethinking the Role of the Modern University*, Durham and London: Duke University Press, 223–246.

Commission on Higher Education, Philippines (2009) "Higher Education Responding to the Challenges of a Dynamic Environment." Available at: www.ched.gov.ph/aboutus/medterm_plan.html (Accessed January 28, 2009).

Community Survey (2007) "Basic Results Municipalities. Statistics South Africa." Available at: www.statssa.gov.za/Publications/P03011/P030112007.pdf (Accessed August 12, 2010).

Connell, R. (2007) *Southern Theory: the Global Dynamics of Knowledge in Social Science*, Cambridge: Polity Press.

Constitution of the Bolivarian Republic of Venezuela. Ratified by the National Constitutional Assembly in 1999. Article 109. Available at: www.analitica.com/bitblioteca/venezuela/constitucion_ingles.pdf (Accessed January 15, 2009).

Cook, S. (2008) "Participation Rates in Higher Education: Academic Years 1999/2000 – 2006/2007 (Provisional)," Department for Innovations, Universities, and Skills. Available at: www.dcsf.gov.uk/rsgateway/DB/SFR/s000780/sfrdius02–2008.pdf (Accessed December 12, 2008).

Côté, J. (2002) "The Role of Identity Capital in the Transition to Adulthood: the individualization thesis examined," *Journal of Youth Studies*, 5:117–134.

Council for Higher Education Law (1958) Article 15. Available at: www.cepes.ro/hed/policy/legislation/pdf/Israel.pdf (Accessed January 9, 2009).

Council on Higher Education (2010) Available at: www.che.ac.za/ (Accessed July 15, 2010).

D'Ancona, M. (2009) *Being British: the Search for the Values That Bind the Nation*, Edinburgh and London: Mainstream.

Daniel, J. (1996) *The Mega-Universities and Knowledge Media*, London: Routledge.

Datta, K., Jones, G. A. (1999) *Housing and Finance in Developing Countries*, Vol. 7. Routledge Studies in Development and Society (illustrated edn.), London: Routledge.

Department of Education, Science and Training (2007) "Thematic Review of Tertiary Education: Country Background Report: Australia," Organisation for Economic Cooperation and Development (OECD). Available at: www.oecd.org/dataoecd/51/60/38759740.pdf (Accessed December 11, 2008).

Department of Education (2010) "Education Statistics in South Africa: 2008." Available at: www.education.gov.za/emis/emisweb/08stats/Education%20Statistics%20in%20South%20Africa%202008.pdf (Accessed July 15, 2010).

Department for International Development (2008) "Country Profiles: Tanzania." Available at: www.dfid.gov.uk/countries/africa/Tanzania.asp (Accessed December 23, 2008).

EdInvest (2005) "Country Snapshot: Philippines." Available at: www.educationforum.org.nz/documents/private_education/EdInvest_Philippines.pdf (Accessed January 29, 2009).

Edwards, M. (2004) *Civil Society*, Cambridge: Polity.

El Ministerio del Poder Popular para la Educación Superior (2008) "Reseña Histórica." Available at: www.mes.gov.ve/mes/resena.php (Accessed December 29, 2008).

El Tom, M. E. (2003) "Country Higher Education Profiles: Sudan." The Boston College Center for International Higher Education. Available at: www.bc.edu/bc_org/avp/soe/cihe/inhea/profiles/Sudan.htm (Accessed January 8, 2009).

European Commission (2005) "The Education Sector in Ukraine." Available at: http://eacea.ec.europa.eu/tempus/participating_countries/higher/ukraine.pdf (Accessed January 5, 2009).

European University Association (EUA)/American Council on Education (ACE) (2004) "Charting the Course between Public Service and Commercialisation: Prices Values and Quality," Conference Proceedings, Turin, June 3–5.

Fergany, N. (2003) "Arab Higher Education and Development, An Overview," World Bank. Available at: www.worldbank.org/mdf/mdf3/papers/education/Fergany.pdf (Accessed February 2, 2009).

Florida, R. (2002) *The Rise of the Creative Class, and How It's Transforming Work Leisure, Community and Creative Life*, New York: Basic Books.

Foong, K. K. (2008) "Funding Higher Education in Malaysia," East Asian Bureau of Economic Research (EABER). Available at: www.eaber.org/intranet/common/folderstree_popup.php?category=100&document_select=&marker_select=&folder_select=&class_select=&edit_select=&view_select= (Accessed March 3, 2009).

Forum, 5 July 2005, Sydney Australia, published in the Forum Proceedings. Available at: www.auqa.edu.au/

Gacel-Ávila, J. (2005) "Internationalization of Higher Education in Mexico." In: Hans de Wit, Isabel Cristina Jaramillo, et al. (eds.) *Higher Education in Latin America: The International Dimension.* The World Bank. Available at: http://siteresources.worldbank. org/EXTLACREGTOPEDUCATION/Resources/Higher_Ed_in_LAC_Intnal_ Dimension.pdf (Accessed December 18, 2008).

Gangemi, J. (2005) "B-Schools Ranked on Social Studies," *Business Week.* Available at: www.businessweek.com/bschools/content/nov2005/bs2005111_4475_PG2.htm (Accessed May 28, 2010).

Garrod, N. and Macfarlane, B. (eds.) (2009) *Challenging Boundaries: Managing the Integration of Post-Secondary Education,* New York: Routledge.

Gawande, A. (2007) *Better: a Surgeon's Notes on Performance,* New York: Picador.

Georgetown University (2010) "Office of the President: University Mission Statement." Available at: http://president.georgetown.edu/sections/governance/missionstatement/ (Accessed July 9, 2010).

Gibbons, M., Limoges, C., Nowotny, H., Schwarzman, S., Scott, P. and Trow, M. (1994) *The New Production of Knowledge: the Dynamics of Science and Research in Contemporary Societies,* London: Sage.

Glazer-Raymo, J. (2002) "Consortia in Higher Education," *Encyclopedia of Education,* The Gale Group Inc. Available at: www.encyclopedia.com/doc/1G2–3403200155.html (Accessed November 23, 2009).

Global University Network for Innovation (GUNI) (2008) *Higher Education in the World 3: New Challenges and Emerging Roles for Human and Social Development,* Houndmills: Palgrave Macmillan.

GMANews (Manila) (2008) "Arroyo Forms Body to Work on Quality Education in Colleges, Universities." Available at: www.gmanews.tv/story/92067/Arroyo-forms-body-to-work-on-quality-education-in-colleges-universities (Accessed September 9, 2010).

Goddard, J. (2009) *Reinventing the Civic University,* London: National Endowment for Science Technology and the Arts (NESTA).

Goldman Sachs (2010) "Is this the BRICs' decade?" Available at: www2.goldmansachs. com/ideas/brics/brics-decade.html (Accessed May, 2010).

Graduate School of Education, SUNY-Buffalo (2007) "Higher Education Finance and Cost-Sharing in Tanzania." Available at: http://gse.buffalo.edu/org/inthigheredfinance/ files/Country_Profiles/Africa/Tanzania.pdf (Accessed September 9, 2010).

Graduate School of Education, SUNY-Buffalo (2006) "Indonesia Country Profile," International Comparative Higher Education Finance and Accessibility Project. Available at: www.gse.buffalo.edu/org/inthigheredfinance/CountryProfiles/Asia/Indonesia_ country_profile.pdf (Accessed January 10, 2009).

Guardian (2009) "World Fact Files." Available at: guardian.co.uk

Hahn, R. (2007) "The Global State of Higher Education and the Rise of Private Finance," Institute for Higher Education Policy. Available at: www.case.org/files/AsiaPacific/ PDF/Global_State_of_Higher_Education.pdf (Accessed December 29, 2008).

Hall, M. et al. (2010) "Community Engagement in South African Higher Education," Council on Higher Education. Available at: www.che.ac.za/documents/d000204/ Kagisano_No_6_January2010.pdf (Accessed July 15, 2010).

Hallberg, P. and Lund, J. (2005) "The Business of Apocalypse: Robert Putnam and Diversity", *Race and Class,* 46:4, 53–67.

Hart, A., Northmore, S., and Gerhardt, C. (2009) "Auditing, Benchmarking and Evaluating Public Engagement," Briefing paper: Bristol: National Coordinating Centre for Public Engagement.

Hasan, A. and Mohib, M. (2002) "The Case of Karachi, Pakistan," University College, London. Available at: www.ucl.ac.uk/dpu-projects/Global_Report/pdfs/Karachi.pdf (Accessed August 19, 2010).

Haskins, C. (2006) "Development Issues in Cape Town," Presented to the IDP Spatial Coordination workshop, August 21, 2006. Available at: www.capetown.gov.za/en/stats/CityReports/Documents/IDP/IDP_Wprkshop_-_Development_Issues_in_Cape_Town_2382006101152_359.pdf (Accessed September 9, 2010).

Hayward, F. (2009) "Higher Education Transformation in Pakistan: Political and Economic Instability," *International Higher Education*, No. 54 (Winter 2009). Boston College Center for International Higher Education. Available at: www.bc.edu/bc_org/avp/soe/cihe/newsletter/Number54/p19_Hayward.htm (Accessed July 10, 2009).

Higher Education Authority (2008) "National Plan for Equity of Access to Higher Education: 2008–2013." Available at: www.hea.ie/files/files/file/New_pdf/National_Access_Plan_2008–2013 (English).pdf (Accessed March 19, 2009).

Higher Education Commission Pakistan (2008a) "About HEC." Available at: http://hec.gov.pk/abouthec.html (Accessed July 2, 2009).

Higher Education Commission Pakistan (2008b) "Enrollment by Area & Sector," Statistics. Available at: http://hec.gov.pk/stats.html (Accessed July 10, 2009).

Higher Education Commission Pakistan (2008c) "Student Enrollment at University, 2001–08," Statistics. Available at: http://hec.gov.pk/stats.html (Accessed July 10, 2009).

Higher Education Funding Council for England (2006a) "Financial Memorandum between DfES and HEFCE." Available at: www.hefce.ac.uk/aboutus/history/finmem.pdf (Accessed December 10, 2008).

Higher Education Funding Council for England (2006b) "Mission," About Us. Available at: www.hefce.ac.uk/aboutus/mission.htm (Accessed December 10, 2008).

Higher Education Funding Council for England (2006c) "Revised Management Statement for HEFCE." Available at: www.hefce.ac.uk/aboutus/history/manage.pdf (Accessed December 10, 2008).

Higher Education Funding Council for England (2008a) "What HEFCE Does," About Us. Available at: www.hefce.ac.uk/aboutus/history/ (Accessed December 10, 2008).

Higher Education Funding Council for England (2008b) "Quality Assurance Agency." Available at: www.hefce.ac.uk/Learning/qual/qaa.asp (Accessed December 10, 2008).

Higher Education Research Institute, UCLA (2009) "U.S. faculty: Civic engagement, diversity important goals for undergraduate education." Higher Education Research Institute, UCLA. 5 March 2009. http://www.heri.ucla.edu/pr-display.php?prQry=40

Higher Education Statistics Agency (2008) "Press Release 121, HESA 2006/2007 Finance Report." Available at: www.hesa.ac.uk/index.php/content/view/1162/161/ (Accessed December 10, 2008).

Holland, B. (2005) "Scholarship and Mission in the 21st Century University: The Role of Engagement," Keynote address to the Australian Universities Quality Agency.

Hollister, R. M., Mead, M., and Wilson, N. (2006) "Infusing Active Citizenship: The Tisch College of Citizenship and Public Service at Tufts University," *Metropolitan Universities Journal*, 17:38–54.

Holm-Nielsen, L. B., Thorn, K., et al. (2005) "Regional and International Challenges to Higher Education in Latin America." In: Hans de Wit, Isabel Cristina Jaramillo, et al. (eds.) *Higher Education in Latin America: The International Dimension*, The World Bank. Available at: http://siteresources.worldbank.org/EXTLACREGTOPEDUCA-TION/Resources/Higher_Ed_in_LAC_Intnal_Dimension.pdf (Accessed December 18, 2008).

Hoodhboy, P. (2008) "Pakistan's Universities – Problems and Solutions." Available at: www.chowk.com/articles/13507 (Accessed July 2, 2009).

Independent Online (South Africa) (2008) "University Drop-Out Rate Alarming," 24 June 2008. Available at: www.iol.co.za/index.php?set_id=1&click_id=105&art_id=nw200 80624130212759C966201 (Accessed March 20, 2009).

India Education Network (2009) "Higher Education Spending: India at the Bottom of BRIC." Available at: http://news.education4india.com/2507/higher-education-spending-india-at-the-bottom-of-bric/ (Accessed January 6, 2009).

Institution of Education Sciences, US Department of Education (2010) "Fast Facts." National Center for Education Statistics, Institution of Education Sciences. Available at: http://nces.ed.gov/ fastfacts/# (Accessed July 14, 2010).

International Affairs Office, U.S. Department of Education (2007) "Accreditation and Quality Assurance: Postsecondary Accreditation." Available at: www.ed.gov/ international/usnei/us/accred-postsec.doc (Accessed February 5, 2009).

International Affairs Office, U.S. Department of Education (2008) "Organization of U.S. Education: Tertiary Institutions." Available at: www.ed.gov/about/offices/list/ous/ international/usnei/edlite-index.html (Accessed February 5, 2009).

International Association of Universities (2001) "Peru Higher Education System," IAU, World Higher Education Database. Available at: www.unesco.org/iau/onlinedata-bases/systems_data/pe.rtf (Accessed March 17, 2009).

International Household Survey Network (IHSN) (2007–2008) *Pakistan Social and Living Measurement Survey 2007–2008* (PSLM). Islamabad, Pakistan: Federal Bureau of Statistics.

IAU World Higher Education Database (2006) "Sudan Education System." Available at: www.unesco.org/iau/onlinedatabases/systems_data/sd.rtf (Accessed January 9, 2009).

Ireland Higher Education Authority (2009) "2007–2008 Student Statistics." Available at: www.hea.ie/en/node/1216 (Accessed March 19, 2009).

James Coffman (2009) "Private Higher Education in Pakistan: The Need for Order." International Higher Education, Fall 1997. 2 July 2009. http://www.bc.edu/bc_org/ avp/soe/cihe/newsletter/News09/text2.html

Jardine, D. (2008) "Indonesia: Concern Grows Over Religious Conservatism," *University World News*, December 14, 2008. Available at: www.universityworldnews.com/article. php?story=20081212095716894 (Accessed January 30, 2009).

Jardine, D. (2008) "Indonesia: Deregulation of Higher Education," *University World News*, October 12, 2008. Available at: www.universityworldnews.com/article.php?story=20 081010092601112 (Accessed January 30, 2009).

Kanter, R. A. (1997) *World Class: Thriving Locally in the Global Economy*, New York: Free Press.

Kapur, D. and Mehta, P. B. (2004) "Indian Higher Education Reform: From Half-Baked Socialism to Half-Baked Capitalism," CID Working Paper No. 108 (September 2004). CID, Harvard University. Available at: www.cid.harvard.edu/cidwp/pdf/108.pdf (Accessed January 7, 2009).

Kenyon Jones, C. (2008) *The People's University: 150 Years of the University of London and Its External Students*, London: University of London.

Khan, A. (2009) "Officials: Shootouts Leave 20 Dead in Pakistan," *The Guardian*. 29 April 2009. Available at: www.guardian.co.uk/world/feedarticle/8480878 (Accessed July 10, 2009).

Kiss, E. and Euben, P. (2010) *Debating Moral Education: Rethinking the Role of the Modern University*, Durham and London: Duke University Press.

Koh, C. et al. (2008) "Indian Higher Education: Broadening the Horizon," *Updates on Global Higher Education*, No. 44, 30 November 2008. Available at: www.usm.my/ipptn/v2/documents/Globalupdates/Indian%20Higher%20Education-Broadening%20the%20horizon-No.44.pdf (Accessed January 7, 2009).

Kremen, V. and Nikolajenko, S. (eds.) (2006) "Higher Education in Ukraine," *Monographs on Higher Education*, UNESCO. Available at: http://unesdoc.unesco.org/images/0014/001465/146552e.pdf (Accessed December 31, 2008).

Kubler, J. and Sayers, N. (2010) *Higher Education Futures: Key Themes and Implications for Leadership and Management*, London: Leadership Foundation for Higher Education.

Lay, S. (2004) *The Interpretation of the Magna Charta Universitatum and its Principles*, Bologna: Bononia University Press.

Learn and Serve America (2010) "President's Higher Education Community Service Honor Roll." Available at: http://www.learnandserve.gov/about/programs/higher_ed_honorroll.asp (Accessed July 14, 2010).

Library of Congress (2004) "Country Profile: Sudan." Available at: http://lcweb2.loc.gov/frd/cs/profiles/Sudan.pdf (Accessed February 9, 2009).

MacGregor, K. (2009) "South Africa: Debate Moves on from Access to Success," *University World News*, March 15, 2009. Available at: www.universityworldnews.com/article.php?story=20090313111607177 (Accessed March 20, 2009).

MacLeod, D. (2008) "South Africa 'Needs at Least Six More Universities,'" *The Guardian* (UK). July 14, 2008. Available at: www.guardian.co.uk/education/2008/jul/14/internationaleducationnews.highereducation (Accessed March 20, 2009).

Maharashtra Universities Act (1994) Available at: www.mu.ac.in/act1994.pdf (Accessed January 7, 2009).

Malaysian Qualifications Agency (2008) "MQA at a Glance." Available at: www.lan.gov.my/eng/introduction.cfm (Accessed January 29, 2009).

Media Freedom Index (2009) "Reporters Without Borders." Available at: http://en.rsf.org/press-freedom-index-2009,1001.html (Accessed July 14, 2010).

Menahem, G. (2008) "The Transformation of Higher Education in Israel since the 1990s: The Role of Ideas and Policy Paradigms," *Governance: An International Journal of Policy, Administration, and Institutions*, 21: 499–526.

Mény, Y. (2008) "Higher Education in Europe: National Systems, European Programmes, Global Issues. Can they be reconciled?" Higher Education Policy Institute Annual Lecture, January 15.

Mexican Secretariat of Public Education (2006) "OECD Thematic Review of Tertiary Education: Country Background Report for Mexico." Available at: www.oecd.org/dataoecd/22/45/37746065.pdf (Accessed December 30, 2008).

Ministry of Education, South Africa (1997) "Education White Paper 3—A Programme for Higher Education Transformation." Available at: http://chet.org.za/manual/media/files/chet_hernana_docs/South%20Africa/National/White%20Paper%20on%20Higher%20Education%203%201997.pdf (Accessed September 9, 2010).

Ministry of Higher Education and Scientific Research and World Bank (2002) "Palestinian Higher Education Financing Strategy." Available at: http://siteresources.worldbank.org/EDUCATION/Resources/278200–1099079877269/547664–1099079956815/Palestinian_higher_Ed_financing_strategyEN03.pdf (Accessed January 27, 2009).

Ministry of Higher Education, Malaysia (2009) "Education System of Malaysia." Available at: www.educationmalaysia.gov.my/education.php?article=system (Accessed January 30, 2009).

Ministry of Higher Education, Palestine (2006) "Higher Education Financing Strategy." Available at: www.moe.gov.ps/ENG/strategies/f-h-stra.html (Accessed January 27, 2009).

Ministry of Higher Education, Palestine (2005) "Palestinian Higher Education Statistics." Available at: www.mohe.gov.ps/downloads/pdffiles/statisticsHE.pdf (Accessed January 15, 2009).

Ministry of Higher Education, Peru (2006) "Higher Education Financing Strategy." Available at: www.moe.gov.ps/ENG/strategies/f-h-stra.html (Accessed January 27, 2009).

Ministry of Science and Technology and Higher Education (2005) "Summary 2: Students Enrollment in Higher Learning Institutions 2004/2005," The United Republic of Tanzania. Available at: www.msthe.go.tz/statistics/summary2.pdf (Accessed December 22, 2008).

Mkude, D. and Cooksey, B. (2003) "Country Higher Education Profiles: Tanzania," The Boston College Center for International Higher Education. Available at: www.bc.edu/bc_org/avp/soe/cihe/inhea/profiles/Tanzania.htm (Accessed December 22, 2008).

Mkude, D., Cooksey, B., and Levey, L. (2003) "Higher Education in Tanzania: A Case Study," *Partnership for Higher Education in Africa*, New York University. Oxford: James Currey Ltd.; Dar es Salaam: Mkuki na Nyota. Available at: www.foundation-partnership.org/pubs/tanzania/tanzania_2003.pdf (Accessed March 20, 2009).

Muhr, T. and Verger, A. (2006) "Venezuela: Higher Education for All," *Journal for Critical Education Policy Studies*, 4.1:March. Available at: www.jceps.com/?pageID=article&articleID=63 (Accessed December 29, 2008).

Mumbai Metropolitan Region Development Authority (MMRDA) (2008) "Mumbai Urban Infrastructure Project." Available at: http://mmrdamumbai.org/projects_muip.htm (Accessed July 13, 2010).

Murakami, Y. and Blom, A. (2008) "Accessibility and Affordability of Tertiary Education in Brazil, Colombia, Mexico and Peru within a Global Context," The World Bank, Latin America and Caribbean Region, Human Development Sector. Available at: wwwwds.worldbank.org/external/default/WDSContentServer/IW3P/IB/2008/02/14/000158349_20080214082424/Rendered/PDF/wps4517.pdf (Accessed March 17, 2009).

National Assessment and Accreditation Council, India (2007) "Assessment Report of Institutional Accreditation, SNDT Women's University, Mumbai." Available at: naacindia.org/Reports/SNDT%20Womens%20university.doc (Accessed July 13, 2010).

Newcastle University (2009) "Characterising Modes of University Engagement with Wider Society: A Literature Review and Survey of Best Practice," Office of the Pro-Vice-Chancellor (Engagement), Newcastle University, June 10.

Newman, M. (2009) "Do you want to be in my gang?" *Times Higher Education*, November 19: 33–35.

Ngor, Mading (2010) "Southern Sudan Faces Uncertainty As it Modifies Decree Ahead of Goss Formation," *New Sudan Vision*, May 25, 2010. Available at: www. newsudanvision.com/index.php?option=com_content&view=article&id=214 3:southern-sudan-faces-uncertainty-ahead-of-goss-formation-modifies-decree-relieving-caretaker-government-&catid=1:sudan-news-stories&Itemid=6 (Accessed May 27, 2010).

Nuffield Foundation (2008) *Science Education in Europe: Critical Reflections*, London: The Nuffield Foundation.

O'Day, R. (2009) "Universities and Professions in the Early Modern Period," In: Cunningham, P., Oosthuizen, S., and Taylor, R. (eds.) *Beyond the Lecture Hall: Universities and Community Engagement from the Middle Ages to the Present Day*, Cambridge: Faculty of Education and Institute of Continuing Education, 79–102.

OECD (2008a) "Indicator B1: How much Money is Spent Per Student?" *Education at a Glance* 2008: OECD Indicators. Available at: www.oecd.org/document/9/0,3343,en_2649_39263238_4126676–1_1_1_1_1,00.html (Accessed January 9, 2009).

OECD (2008b) "Indicator B3: How Much Public and Private Investment is there in Education?" *Education at a Glance* 2008: OECD Indicators. Available at: www.oecd. org/document/9/0,3343,en_2649_39263238_-41266761_1_1_1_1,00.html(Accessed January 9, 2009).

OECD (2008c) "Table B5.1a: Estimated Annual Average Tuition Fees Charged by Tertiary-Type A Educational Institutions for National Students (Academic Year 2004/05)" *Education at a Glance* 2008: OECD Indicators. Available at: http://dx.doi. org/10.1787/402038326553 (Accessed March 26, 2009).

OECD (2008d) "Review of Higher Education Institutions in Regional Development 2008–10: The Galilee, Israel." Available at: www.oecd.org/document/27/0,3343,en_2649_35961291_41814235_1_1_1_1,00.html (Accessed January 9, 2009).

OECD IMHE-HEFCE (2004) "Financial Management and Governance in HEIs: Ireland." Project on International Comparative Higher Education Financial Management and Governance. Available at: www.oecd.org/dataoecd/21/2/33643745.PDF (Accessed March 19, 2009).

OECD/IMHE-HEFCE, (2007) "On the Edge: Securing a Sustainable Future for Higher Education," Report of the Project on Financial Management and Governance of Higher Education Institutions. Education Working Paper No. 7. Available at: www. oecd.org/dataoecd/20/24/38309943.pdf (Accessed March 19, 2009).

OECD/UNESCO WEI (2005) "Table 2.13: Annual Expenditure on Educational Institutions Per Student." Available at: www.uis.unesco.org/template/html/Exceltables/WEI2005/Table2.13.xls (Accessed March 23, 2009).

Palestinian Human Rights Monitor (2000) "Academic Freedom in the Palestinian Universities." Available at: www.phrmg.org/monitor2000/mar2000-academic.htm (Accessed January 27, 2009).

Palestinian Law No. 11 for Higher Education (1998). Available at: www.peace-programme.org/content/view/64/6/ (Accessed January 27, 2009).

Petro Mohyla State University for the Humanities (PMBSU) (2007) "Talloires Network Institutional Assessment." Available at: www.tufts.edu/talloiresnetwork/downloads/PetroMohylaAssessment.pdf (Accessed January 5, 2009).

Planning and Budgeting Committee of the Council for Higher Education (2008) "Higher Education in Israel." Available at: http://ec.europa.eu/education/programmes/tempus/countries/higher/israel.pdf (Accessed January 9, 2009).

Privy Council Office (2008) "Higher Education." Work of the Privy Council. Available at: www.privy-council.org.uk/output/Page27.asp (Accessed December 10, 2008).

Quality Assurance Agency (2008) "About Us," Higher Education Commission, Pakistan. Available at: www.hec.gov.pk/InsideHEC/Divisions/QALI/Pages/QualityAssurance. aspx (Accessed July 10, 2009).

Quality Assurance Agency for Higher Education (2008) "The QAA Board." Available at: www.qaa.ac.uk/aboutus/qaaBoard/board.asp (Accessed December 10, 2008).

RNCOS Industry Research Solutions (2008) "By 2011–12 the Private Spending on Education to Top Rs 100,000 Cr in India." Available at: www.rncos.com/Press_Releases/By-2011-12-the-Private-Spending-on-Education-to-Top-Rs-100000-Cr-in-India.htm (Accessed January 6, 2009).

Reuben, J. (2010) "The Changing Contours of Moral Education in American Colleges and Universities." In: Kiss, E. and Euben, P. (eds.) *Debating Moral Education: Rethinking the Role of the Modern University*, Durham and London: Duke University Press, 27–54.

Rice, Xan (2010) "Sudan President Omar al-Bashir Sworn in Amid Outcry," *The Guardian* (World News Sudan). May 27, 2010. Available at: www.guardian.co.uk/world/2010/may/27/sudan-president-omar-al-bashir-sworn-in (Accessed May 27, 2010).

Samoilovich, D. (2008) "Pathways to Innovations: Re-thinking the Government of Public Universities in Latin America," Chapter 9, Trends in Higher Education in Latin America and the Caribbean. Available at: www.cres2008.org/upload/documentosPublicos/docs_base_en/Chapter%209.pdf (Accessed March 17, 2009).

Schuller, T. (1998) "Social Capital and Community-Building." In K. Hurley (ed.) University Continuing Education in Partnership for Development, UACE Annual Conference 1997, Proceedings. Leeds: UACE.

Shaw-Miller, L. (ed.) (2001) *Clare Through the Twentieth Century*, Lingfield, Surrey: Third Millennium.

Slackman, Michael (2010) "Invoking Ancient Voices of Islam to Promote Tolerance," *International Herald Tribune*, July 5.

Smith, C. (2005) "Understanding Trust and Confidence: Two Paradigms and Their Significance for Health and Social Care," *Journal of Applied Philosophy*, 22: 299–316.

South African Government Information (2008) "Education." Available at: www.info.gov.za/aboutsa/education.htm (Accessed: 20 March 2009).

South African Higher Education Community Engagement Forum (SAHECEF) (2010) "Constitution." June 10, 2010. Available at: http://sahecef.ning.com/notes/Constitution (Accessed July 15, 2010).

State Bank of Pakistan (2009) Annual Report 2008–2009. Volume 1, Chapter 8: Social Sector Developments. 2009. http://www.sbp.org.pk/reports/annual/arFY09/Chp-8.pdf

State University.com (2008) "Mexico: Higher Education." Available at: http://education.stateuniversity.com/pages/984/Mexico-HIGHER-EDUCATION.html (Accessed December 30, 2008).

Stella, A. (2002) "Institutional Accreditation in India," *International Higher Education* (Spring 2002). Available at: www.bc.edu/bc_org/avp/soe/cihe/newsletter/News27/text010.htm (Accessed January 7, 2009).

Stetar, J. and Berezkina, E. (2002) "Evolution of Private Higher Education in Ukraine," *International Higher Education* No. 29. Boston College. Available at: www.bc.edu/bc_org/avp/soe/cihe/newsletter/News29/text010.htm (Accessed December 31, 2008).

Strehl, F. (2007) "Funding Systems and their Effects on Higher Education Systems – International Report (Education Working Paper No. 6)," OECD. March 20, 2007. Available at: www.oecd.org/dataoecd/36/23/38279332.pdf (Accessed March 19, 2009).

Subotzky, G. (2003) "Country Higher Education Profiles: South Africa," The Boston College Center for International Higher Education. Available at: www.bc.edu/bc_org/avp/soe/cihe/inhea/profiles/South_Africa.htm (Accessed March 19, 2009).

Talloires Network (2009) "UNIMET Institutional Assessment." Available at: www.tufts.edu/talloiresnetwork/downloads/UniversidadMetropolitanadeCaracas.pdf (Accessed July 9, 2010).

Talloires Network (2010) "Bellagio Meeting Report." Available at: www.tufts.edu/talloiresnetwork/downloads/Bellagiomeetingreport.pdf (Accessed September 23, 2010).

Task Force on Improvement of Higher Education in Pakistan (2002) "Pakistan," *Higher Education in Developing Countries: Peril and Promise*. Available at: www.tfhe.net/resources/pakistan.htm (Accessed July 2, 2009).

Transparency International (2008). Available at: www.transparency.org/news_room/in_focus/2008/cpi2008/cpi_2008_table. (Accessed September 10, 2010).

UN Data (2007) "Gross Enrolment Ratio in Tertiary Education." Available at: http://data.un.org/Data.aspx?d=GenderStat&f=inID%3A68 (Accessed January 15, 2010).

UNESCO (2009) "Trends in Global Higher Education: Tracking an Academic Revolution," UNESCO.

UNESCO Institute for Statistics (2010) "Education in the United States." UNESCO Institute for Statistics. 2010. Accessed 12 July 2010. http://stats.uis.unesco.org/unesco/TableViewer/document.aspx?ReportId=121&IF_Language=eng&BR_Country=8400

UNESCO Institute for Statistics (1999) "Custom Table: Tanzania." Available at: http://stats.uis.unesco.org/unesco/Tableviewer/document.aspx?ReportId=136&!F_Language=eng&BR_Topic=0 (Accessed March 23, 2009).

UNESCO Institute for Statistics (2006a) "Education in the Philippines: UIS Statistics in Brief." Available at: http://stats.uis.unesco.org/unesco/TableViewer/document.aspx?ReportId=121&IF_Language=eng&BR_Country=6080 (Accessed January 28, 2009).

UNESCO Institute for Statistics (2006b) "Global Rankings: Public expenditure on education as % of GDP – 2006." Available at: http://stats.uis.unesco.org/unesco/TableViewer/document.aspx?ReportId=125&IF-_Language=eng&BR_Fact=EEGDP&BR_Region=40535 (Accessed March 23, 2009).

UNESCO Institute for Statistics (2006c) "UIS Statistics in Brief." Available at: http://stats.uis.unesco.org/unesco/TableViewer/document.aspx?ReportId=121&IF_Language=eng&BR_Country=4580&BR_Region=40515 (Accessed January 29, 2009).

UNESCO Institute for Statistics (2006d) "Table 2.a.i: Expenditure on Educational Institutions As a Percentage of GDP by Source of Funds," Education Counts: Benchmarking Progress in 19 WEI Countries. Available at: www.uis.unesco.org/template/publications/wei2006/Chap2_Tables.xls. (Accessed March 27, 2009).

UNESCO Institute for Statistics (2008) Education in Pakistan. "Table 14: Tertiary Indicators." Available at: http://stats.uis.unesco.org/unesco/TableViewer/tableView.aspx?ReportId=167 (Accessed March 23, 2009).

UNESCO International Bureau of Education (2006a) "Profile of the Education System, Malaysia." Available at: www.ibe.unesco.org/en/access-by-country/asia-and-the-pacific/malaysia/profile-of-education.html (Accessed January 29, 2009).

UNESCO International Bureau of Education (2006b) "Profile of Education, Philippines." Available at: www.ibe.unesco.org/en/access-by-country/asia-and-the-pacific/philippines/profile-of-education.html (Accessed January 28, 2009).

UNESCO International Bureau of Education (2006c) "Profile of the Education

System, South Africa." Available at: www.ibe.unesco.org/en/access-by-country/africa/south-africa/profile-of-education.html (Accessed March 19, 2009).

UNESCO International Bureau of Education (2006d) "Profile of the Education System, Sudan." Available at: www.ibe.unesco.org/en/access-by-country/africa/sudan/profile-of-education.html (Accessed January 13, 2009).

UNESCO International Bureau of Education (2006e) "Profile of the Education System, Tanzania." Available at: www.ibe.unesco.org/en/access-by-country/africa/united-republic-of-tanzania/profile-of-education.html (Accessed July 9, 2010).

UNESCO International Bureau of Education (2006f) "Profile of the Education System, United States." Available at: www.ibe.unesco.org/en/access-by-country/europe-and-north-america/united-states/profile-of-education.html (Accessed February 2, 2009).

United Nations Press Release (2000) Available at: www.unis.unvienna.org/unis/press-rels/2000/sg2625.html (Accessed September 23, 2010).

United Republic of Tanzania (1995) "An Act to Amend the Education Act, 1978, To Establish the Higher Education Accreditation Council, to Provide the Procedure for Accreditation and Other Related Matters." Available at: www.parliament.go.tz/Polis/PAMS/Docs/10–1995.pdf (Accessed December 23, 2008).

United Republic of Tanzania, Ministry of Science, Technology and Higher Education (1999) "National Higher Education Policy." Available at: www.tanzania.go.tz/pdf/nationalhighereducationpolicy.pdf (Accessed December 23, 2008).

United Republic of Tanzania. Ministry of Science and Technology and Higher Education (2008) "Teacher/Students Ratio." Available at: www.msthe.go.tz/statistics/Table108–111.pdf (Accessed December 22, 2008).

United States, Department of Education (2008) "Summary of Discretionary Funds, FY 2009 Request," Washington. Available at: www.ed.gov/about/overview/budget/budget09/summary/appendix1.pdf (Accessed January 5, 2009).

Universidad Metropolitana (2006) "UNIMET Institutional Assessment." Talloires Network. Available at: www.tufts.edu/talloiresnetwork/downloads/UniversidadMetropolitanadeCaracas.pdf (Accessed December 30, 2008).

Universities UK (2008) "Briefing: House of Lords Debate on the Future Direction of Higher Education." Available at: www.universitiesuk.ac.uk/ParliamentaryActivities/Briefings/Pages/House-of-Lords-Debate-on-the-future-direction-of-Higher-Education.aspx (Accessed December 11, 2008).

Universities UK (2009) "Higher Education in Facts and Figures." Available at: www.universitiesuk.ac.uk/Newsroom/Facts-and-Figures/Pages/Higher-Education-in-Facts-and-Figures (Accessed November 15, 2010).

Universities UK (UUK) (2010) *The Growth of Private and for-Profit Higher Education Providers in the UK*, London: UUK.

University Grants Commission (2006–2007) "Adult Continuing Education, Extension, and Field Outreach." Available at: www.ugc.ac.in/financialsupport/adultedu.html (Accessed July 13, 2010).

University Grants Commission (2006–2007) "Pay Order Regulations." Available at: www.ugc.ac.in/policy/payorder.html#appointetc (Accessed July 13, 2010).

University Grants Commission (2007) "Guidelines on Lifelong Learning and Extension during the XI Plan Period, 2007–2012." Available at: www.ugc.ac.in/financialsupport/xiplan/lifelong2.pdf (Accessed July 14, 2010).

University Grants Commission (2008) "National Eligibility Test." Available at: www.ugc.ac.in/inside/net.html#intro (Accessed January 7, 2009).

University of Ballarat (2010) "Dual-Sector University Cohesion," A discussion paper, June. Available at www.ballarat.edu.au/projects/dscp/docs/discuss.pdf

Van Harte, M. et al. (2006) "Higher Education Finance and Cost-Sharing in South Africa," Graduate School of Education, SUNY-Buffalo. International Comparative Higher Education Finance and Accessibility Project. Available at: http://gse.buffalo.edu/org/inthigheredfinance/files/Country_Profiles/Africa/South_Africa.pdf. (Accessed September 9, 2010).

Vorotnikov, E. (2010) "Ukraine: Radical Reforms Will Not Follow Elections," *University World News* (11 April). Available at: www.universityworldnews.com/article.php?story=20100409202520381 (Accessed April 12, 2010).

Watson, D. (2007) *Managing Civic and Community Engagement*, Maidenhead: Open University Press.

Watson, D. (2010) "Universities' Engagement with Society." In: Peterson, P., Baker, E., and McGaw, B. (eds.) *International Encyclopedia of Education*, Vol 4, 398–403. Oxford: Elsevier.

Watson, D. (2008) "The University in the Modern World: Ten Lessons of Civic and Community Engagement," *Education, Citizenship and Social Justice*, 3: 46–57.

West Virginia University Extension Service (2010) "About the Land-Grant System." Available at: http://www.ext.wvu.edu/about_extension/land_grant_system (Accessed July 14, 2010).

Wiley, D. (2007) "Open Source, Openness, and Higher Education," *Innovation: The Journal of Online Education*. Available at: http://innovateonline.info/pdf/vol3_issue1/Open_Source,_Openness,_and_Higher_Education.pdf (Accessed September 23, 2010).

Willetts, D. (2010) "University Challenge," a speech at Oxford Brookes University, June 10.

Wolff, R. A. (2006) "An Overview of American Accreditation and Quality Assurance." Presented at IUCEA November 16, 2006. Available at: www.uneca.org (Accessed January 20, 2009).

World Bank (2003) "A Policy Note on The Grant-in-Aid System in Indian Education." Available at: www-wds.worldbank.org/external/default/WDSContentServer/WDSP/IB/2006/10/27/000310607_20061027150313/Rendered/PDF/378340PAPER0SA10Aid0System01PUBLIC1.pdf (Accessed January 6, 2009).

World Bank (2006a) "Indonesia: Country Summary of Higher Education." Available at: http://siteresources.worldbank.org/EDUCATION/Resources/278200–1121703274255/1439264–1193249163062/Indonesia_CountrySummary.pdf (Accessed January 29, 2009).

World Bank (2006b) "Malaysia: Country Summary of Higher Education." Available at: http://siteresources.worldbank.org/EDUCATION/Resources/278200–1121703274255/1439264–1193249163062/Malaysia_CountrySummary.pdf(Accessed January 29, 2009).

World Bank (2006c) "Pakistan: Country Summary of Higher Education." Available at: http://siteresources.worldbank.org/EDUCATION/Resources/278200–1121703274255/1439264–1193249163062/Pakistan_countrySummary.pdf (Accessed July 1, 2009).

World Bank (2007) "Country Profile: Ukraine." Available at: http://siteresources.worldbank.org/EXTECAREGTOPEDUCATION/Resources/444607–1192663551820/4293995–1193243530233/CP_Ukraine_revised_2.pdf (Accessed January 5, 2009).

World Bank (2008a) "Country Brief: Sudan." Available at: http://web.worldbank. org/WBSITE/EXTERNAL/COUNTRIES/AFRICAEXT/SUDANEXTN/ 0,,menuPK:375432~pagePK:141132~piPK:141107~theSitePK:375422,00.html (Accessed January 9, 2009).

World Bank (2008b) "Tanzania," Competitiveness Profiles. Available at: http:// siteresources.worldbank.org/EXTAFRSUMAFTPS/Resources/Tanzania.pdf (Accessed July 14, 2010).

World Bank (2008c) "The World Bank's Operations in West Bank and Gaza." Available at:http://siteresources.worldbank.org/INTWESTBANKGAZA/Resources/ PorfolioJune08.pdf (Accessed January 27, 2009).

Wynne, Rhonda (2010) "The Civic Role of Universities: General Concepts and Irish Practices," unpublished EdD Thesis, University of Sheffield.

Xinhua (2010) "China Welcomes Darfur Peace Talks Resumption in Doha." Available at: http://news.xinhuanet.com/english2010/china/2010–05/27/c_13319579. htm (Accessed May 28, 2010).

Younge, G. (2009) "Where Will We Find the Perfect Muslim for Monocultural Britain?" *The Guardian*, March 30, 27.

INDEX